はじめに

　本書は、三省堂発行の高等学校の教科書『CROWN English Communication I』で英語を学習するみなさんの予習と演習のために書かれました。

　教科書の学習は、教室でみなさんに直接英語を教えられる先生方のご指導によらなくてはなりませんが、英語の勉強は事前に自ら調べたり、また、授業のあとで復習し演習することで、学習した内容を確かなものにすることができます。本書はこうした予習・演習をより効果的に進めることを目的に作られた案内書であり、問題の解答をそのまま与えるものではありません。

　本書では、教科書の内容を正しく理解するだけでなく、教科書で扱われる表現を文法の体系からわかりやすく解説し、さらに多くの例題を解くことにより応用力をつけることを目指しました。本書を教科書学習の理解に役立たせるばかりでなく、積極的に英語でコミュニケーションをはかる手がかりとして利用していただければ幸いです。

2022年2月

編集部

本書の構成と学習の進め方

本書では、教科書本文の1セクションを1つの単位として取り上げ、重要項目ごとに解説をつけました。

次のような流れで学習できるように、構成されています。

■教科書本文

教科書本文の1セクションを1単位として転載しています。

セクション分けされていない課は、便宜的にいくつかのまとまりに区切り、それぞれを1単位として転載しています。

■このセクションの内容

そのセクションの概要がつかめているか、空所補充問題で確認できるようになっています。

解答は、次ページのいちばん下に掲載されています。

■解説

教科書本文を理解する上で重要な箇所を取り上げ、文型、文法、および語句や表現の観点からわかりやすく解説しています。

解説が理解できたかどうかをチェックするために、解説のあとに、適宜基本的な演習問題を入れています。解説が理解できているかを確認しましょう。

■Grammar for Communication

各課で新たに学習する文法事項を詳しく解説しています。

文法の決まりや文構造をより深く理解し、定着を図るために、基本的な例文を多く示しています。

■確認問題

次のような項目ごとに、段階を踏んで英語の理解を総合的に確認しましょう。

語彙・表現

教科書で学んだ語彙・発音・表現などについて、さまざまな形式の問題を解くことで確認します。

文のパターン・文法

教科書本文で学んだ文法・語法・表現を演習します。

総合

教科書本文を掲載し、英文和訳・和文英訳・整序問題など、さまざまな形式の問題を付しました。文法や内容の理解を総合的に確認します。

教科書ガイド

ガイド

三省堂 版

クラウン
English
Communication I

TEXT

BOOK

GUIDE

文研出版

CONTENTS

Lesson 1　The Blue White Shirt

- ☐ Steve [stíːv]
- ☐ confusing [kənfjúːzɪŋ]
- ☐ since [síns]
- ☐ recognize [rékəgnàɪz]
- ☐ a piece of cake
- ☐ complicated [kámpləkèɪtɪd]
- ☐ go (out) for a walk
- ☐ step into ~
- ☐ caffè latte [kæ̀feɪ láːteɪ]
- ☐ Would you like ~?
- ☐ mug [mʌ́g]
- ☐ That is not the case.
- ☐ cider [sáɪdər]
- ☐ confused [kənfjúːzd]
- ☐ waiter [wéɪtər]
- ☐ soda pop [sóʊdə pàp]

①Steve is a 16-year-old high school student from America. He lives with a host family. ②He came to Japan to study Japanese. ③It hasn't been easy. ④Here he talks about a few of his confusing experiences.

1

⑤I was really surprised when I discovered that many Japanese words come from English. For example, "spoon" is スプーン and "table" is テーブル. ⑥Since these words are written in *katakana*, it is easy for me to recognize them. ⑦"Learning Japanese is a piece of cake," I thought.

⑧But I soon discovered that the situation was much more complicated.

Last Sunday, I went out for a walk. ⑨I stepped into a coffee shop and ordered a caffè latte. ⑩I was asked, "Would you like a マグカップ?" ⑪I thought it was a choice, since a cup and a mug are quite different. ⑫But that was not the case. I learned a little later that a マグカップ simply means a mug.

Another time, I ordered a glass of サイダー. In America, cider means apple juice. ⑬I really got confused when the waiter brought me soda pop.

このセクションの内容

スティーブは（A.　　　　　　）出身の16歳の高校生で、今は日本語を学ぶために、日本のホストファミリーの家に住んでいる。彼が日本語を勉強していて戸惑うことは、英語に由来する（B.　　　　　）で書かれた日本語だ。例えば、英語のcider は（C.　　　　　）のことだが、その cider に由来する「サイダー」は、実際にはソーダ水（soda pop）だったのだ。

6

① **Steve is a 16-year-old high school student from America.**

▶ 16-year-old「16歳の」。〜-year-old は名詞の前に置いて、「〜歳の」という意味を表す。year は×16-years-old としないように注意。

【✐ 次の各英文を下線部に注意して日本語に直しなさい。】

Kana is <u>8 years old</u>.

――――――――――――――――――――――――――――

Kana is an <u>8-year-old</u> girl.

――――――――――――――――――――――――――――

② **He came to Japan to study Japanese.**

▶ to study Japanese は「日本語を勉強するために」という意味。この不定詞は〈目的〉を表す副詞的用法。

③ **It hasn't been easy.**

▶ 主語の It は Studying Japanese を指す。

▶ hasn't been easy は〈継続〉を表す現在完了形。過去の始点を表す since he came to Japan が文末に省略されていると考える。

④ **Here he talks about a few of his confusing experiences.**

▶ Here は「ここで、今」という意味の副詞。

⑤ **I was really surprised when I discovered that many Japanese words come from English.**

▶ 主節 I was really surprised「私は本当に驚いた」のあとに、副詞節の when 〜「〜したとき」が続く構造。

▶ discovered that 〜は「〜ということを発見した」という意味。that 節の動詞が過去形（came）になっていないのは、その内容が「日本語には英語起源のものが多い」という〈一般的な事実〉を表し、時制の一致が適用されないため。

⑥ **Since these words are written in *katakana*, it is easy for me to recognize them.**

▶ 文前半の Since 〜は「〜なので」（≒ because）という〈理由〉を表す副詞節。

▶ it is easy for me to recognize them は「私にとってそれらを見分けるのは簡単だ」という意味。〈It is ... for − to 〜〉の形式主語構文。この不定詞は名詞的用法で、「〜すること」という意味。　　　　　　　⇒p.16 G-❶

【✐ 英文を完成させなさい。】

私にとってフランス語を学ぶことは難しい。

(　　　) (　　　　) difficult (　　　　) me to learn French.

⑦ **"Learning Japanese is a piece of cake," I thought.**

▶ Learning Japanese は「日本語を学ぶこと」という意味を表す。動名詞

(V-ing) が主語のとき、このあとに続く動詞は単数で受ける。　⇒p.17 G-❷

✐ (　)内の語を1語の適切な形に変えなさい。

毎日運動をすることは健康によいです。

(do) exercises every day (be) good for your health.

▶ a piece of cake は「とても簡単なこと」(≒ something that is very easy to do) という意味を表す慣用句。

⑧ **But I soon discovered that the situation was much more complicated.**

▶ discovered that ～は「～ということを発見した」という意味。

▶ that 節は「状況ははるかに複雑だ」という意味。the situation とは、具体的には教科書 p.10 の 11 行目以降でスティーブが述べている「日本語における和製英語の使われ方」のことを指している。主節の動詞 discovered に合わせて、that 節の中の be 動詞は過去形の was を用いる (時制の一致)。

▶ much more complicated は〈much + 形容詞の比較級〉で、この much は「はるかに～、ずっと～」という〈強調〉を表す。

⑨ **I stepped into a coffee shop and ordered a caffè latte.**

▶ step into ～は「～に入る」(≒ enter) という意味。

⑩ **I was asked, "Would you like a マグカップ?"**

▶〈Would you like ～?〉は「～になさいますか」とていねいにたずねる文。

⑪ **I thought it was a choice, since a cup and a mug are quite different.**

▶ it は前文で喫茶店の店員が "Would you like a マグカップ?" とたずねた、その意図を指す。

▶ choice は、動詞 choose「選ぶ」の名詞形で、「選択」という意味。スティーブは、日本の喫茶店でカフェラテを注文したとき、日本語の「マグカップ」が英語の mug に相当する和製英語だと知らなかった。そのため、"Would you like a マグカップ?" ときかれたとき、カフェラテを入れる容器として mug「マグ」か cup「カップ」を選ぶように求められたと勘違いした。

⑫ **But that was not the case.**

▶ that was not the case は「事実はそうではなかった」(≒ that was not true) という意味。具体的には、前文でスティーブが it was a choice と考えたのが間違っていたことを表す。

⑬ **I really got confused when the waiter brought me soda pop.**

▶ confused「混乱した」は、動詞 confuse「混乱させる」の過去分詞が形容詞として使われるようになったもの。get confused で「混乱する」という意味。

2

□ a friend of mine
□ mansion [mǽnʃən]
□ palace [pǽləs]
□ dress up
□ clerk [klɔ́ːrk]
□ over here
□ ordinary [ɔ́ːrdənèri]
□ condominium [kàndəmíniəm]

①Ryo, a friend of mine, invited me to visit. ②He told me he lived in a mansion. ③To me, a mansion is a very large house, almost like a palace, so I knew that Ryo was rich. ④I thought I should dress up.

⑤I asked my host mother, "Where should I go to buy a dress shirt?" She said I should go to a デパート. ⑥I found a department store and went to the men's fashion floor. ⑦I said to the clerk, "I'm looking for a dress shirt." She said, "Oh, you are looking for a ワイシャツ." "⑧No, I don't want a white shirt. I want a *blue* shirt." "Oh yes. ⑨Right over here." Finally, I bought a blue ワイシャツ.

⑩I met Ryo at the station and we walked to an ordinary condominium. "Where is the mansion, Ryo?" I asked. ⑪"This is it," he said. I learned that a マンション means a condominium.

このセクションの内容

友人のリョウから自宅に招待されたスティーブは、彼が「マンション」に住んでいると聞いて、きちんとした（A.　　　）で行かなくてはいけないと思った。彼は日本語の「マンション」が「（B.　　　　）」を意味する英語のcondominiumに当たることを知らなかった。スティーブは、リョウが（C.　　　）のような大邸宅に住んでいると思ってしまったのだ。

① **Ryo, a friend of mine, invited me to visit.**

▶〈invite + O（人）+ to *do*〉は「（人）に〜するように誘う」という意味の構文。この構文では、O（人）と to *do* の間には〈主語＋動詞〉の関係が成り立つ。

⇒p.16 G-❶

🖉（　）内の語を適切な形に変えなさい。ただし、1語とは限りません。

サラは私にいっしょにサイクリングに行こうと誘ってくれた。

Sarah invited me (go) cycling with her.

▶a friend of mine は「私の友人」という意味。of のあとに、目的格の me ではなく所有代名詞の mine を続ける点に注意。

▶Ryo, a friend of mine, ... のように、名詞（句）とそれを補足的に説明する名詞（句）がコンマ（,）をはさんで並列される場合、両者は〈同格〉の関係にあると言う。同格の詳細については、p.81 G-❸参照。

② **He told me he lived in a mansion.**

▶〈tell + O（人）+ that 節〉「（人）に〜と言う」の構文。that 節の that は省略されることがある。

③ **To me, a mansion is a very large house, almost like a palace, so I knew that Ryo was rich.**

▶日本語の「マンション」をそのまま mansion と英語にしているが、英語本来の意味は、スティーブの説明にあるとおり、「大邸宅」（large house）である。

▶almost like 〜は「ほとんど〜のような、〜といってもいいような」という意味。この like は前置詞。

④ **I thought I should dress up.**

▶dress up は「（パーティーなどのために）正装する」が本来の意味。ここでは、「きちんとした身なりをする」（≒ wear nice clothes）という意味。

⑤ **I asked my host mother, "Where should I go to buy a dress shirt?"**

▶Where should I 〜? は「どこに［で］〜したらいいでしょうか」と相手に助言を求める言い方。

▶dress shirt は「正装用のワイシャツ」を指すが、アメリカでは「（仕事着としての）ワイシャツ」も指す。

▶to buy a dress shirt は〈目的〉を表す不定詞の副詞的用法。　　⇒p.16 G-❶

🖉 次の英文を日本語に直しなさい。

I went to the supermarket to buy some food for dinner.

⑥ **I found a department store and went to the men's fashion floor.**

　　▶「デパート」は和製英語で、正しい英語は department store である。departmentは個々の「売り場」のことで、例えば「おもちゃ売り場」は toy department という。

　　▶ floor は「階、フロア」のこと。the men's fashion floor は「紳士服を売っているフロア」のこと。

⑦ **I said to the clerk, "I'm looking for a dress shirt."**

　　▶ clerk はここでは「店員」のこと。salesclerk ともいう。

　　▶ look for 〜は「〜を探す」という意味。

　　　　例 May I help you? — I'm looking for some candles for Christmas.
　　　　「いらっしゃいませ。— クリスマスに使ううろうそくを探しているのです。」

⑧ **No, I don't want a white shirt. I want a _blue_ shirt.**

　　▶ スティーブには店員の"you are looking for a ワイシャツ"が"you are looking for a white shirt"に聞こえたため、自分が探しているのは「青いシャツ」であって、「白いシャツ」ではないと訂正している。

　　▶ 英語の書き言葉では、特定の単語や語句を強調する場合、I want a _blue_ shirt.のようにイタリック体（斜体）を用いる。強調部分の_blue_は強く発音する。

　　▶ 日本語の「シャツ」は「ワイシャツ」のほかに「肌着のシャツ」のことも表すが、英語では単にshirtと言えば、「ワイシャツ」を指す。「肌着のシャツ」は英語ではundershirt、「Ｔシャツ」はT-shirtと言う。

⑨ **Right over here.**

　　▶ right は「まさに」という強調の意味。

　　▶ over here は「こちらへ、こちらに」という意味で、話し手のいる場所を指す表現。ここでは女性店員がスティーブを売り場に案内しながら、「（ブルーのシャツは）ここにあります」と指し示しているので、over there「あちらに」ではなく over here「こちらに」を使っている。

⑩ **I met Ryo at the station and we walked to an ordinary condominium.**

　　▶ meetは「（待ち合わせ場所で）会う」の意味。meet − met − metと変化する。

　　▶ an ordinary condominium「ふつうのコンドミニアム」。リョウが住んでいるような「分譲マンション（の１部屋）」を英語ではcondominiumと呼ぶ。口語では略してcondoと言うこともある。

⑪ **"This is it," he said.**

　　▶ リョウは自分が住んでいる「マンション」を指さしながら、スティーブに「これがそうだよ」と答えている。itは前文のthe mansionを指す。

Lesson 1

□ once again
□ the same
□ French fries [frẽntʃ fráɪz]
□ menu [ménjuː]
□ one of these days
□ Viking [váɪkɪŋ]
□ curious [kjuəriəs]
□ so far
□ deceptive [dɪséptɪv]
□ and yet
□ confusion [kənfjúːʒən]
□ in V-ing
□ advice [ədváɪs]
□ native [néɪtɪv]
□ puzzled [pʌzld]

3

①My host family always has a Japanese-style breakfast — *nori, natto, miso* soup, and rice. ②That's fine with me. ③But yesterday they took me to a ファミレス. ④They wanted to give me a chance to enjoy some Western food. ⑤They ordered ホットケーキ, フライドポテト, and ブレンド. ⑥Once again, I was confused, but I ordered the same. The waiter brought pancakes, French fries, and coffee. I noticed some strange and interesting desserts on the menu: チョコバナナパフェ, ソフトクリーム, シュークリーム.

⑦After breakfast, my host father suggested that one of these days he would invite me to a *Viking* dinner. I didn't understand *Viking*, but I'm curious.

⑧So far, I have learned lots of these words. ⑨My teacher calls them *wasei-eigo*. ⑩These words can be deceptive; they look like real English, and yet they are not. ⑪I find them confusing. However, confusion is not a bad thing. ⑫It's a first step in learning something new.

Finally, my advice to you: ⑬Don't be surprised if native speakers look puzzled when you use *wasei-eigo*.

このセクションの内容

スティーブは日本に来てから、(A.　　　　) と呼ばれるカタカナ語に出合うたびに戸惑いを覚えてきた。これらの言葉は、(B.　　　) のように見えて、実はそうではない。だが、彼は困惑することは悪いことではないと話す。それは何か (C.　　　) を学ぶうえでの第一歩だと彼は話している。

① **My host family always has a Japanese-style breakfast — *nori*, *natto*, *miso* soup, and rice.**

▶ family は人の集合体を表す集合名詞の１つ。この文のように「家族全体」を表す場合は単数扱いとなり、動詞は三人称単数で has となる。一方、「家族の構成員」それぞれに注目するときは、複数扱いとなる場合がある。

✍ 次の各英文を下線部に注意して日本語に直しなさい。

My *family* has lived in Osaka for ten years.

My *family* are all soccer fans.

② **That's fine with me.**

▶ That は前文の内容、つまり「ホストファミリーの朝食がいつも和食のスタイル［和風］であること」を指す。

▶ be fine with ~ は「~にとって都合がよい［問題はない］」という意味。

③ **But yesterday they took me to a ファミレス.**

▶ take ~ to ... で「~を…に連れて行く」という意味。

④ **They wanted to give me a chance to enjoy some Western food.**

▶ 〈give +（人）+ a chance to *do*〉で「（人）に~する機会を与える」という意味。

▶ to enjoy は直前の a chance を修飾する不定詞の形容詞的用法。　⇒p.16 G-❶

⑤ **They ordered ホットケーキ, フライドポテト, and ブレンド.**

▶ 「ホットケーキ」に相当する英語は pancake。

▶ 「フライドポテト」はアメリカでは French fries、イギリスでは chips と呼ばれる。

▶ 「ブレンド（コーヒー）」は blended coffee（「混ぜ合わさったコーヒー」の意）だが、一般的な「ブラックコーヒー」は単に coffee と言うのがふつう。

⑥ **Once again, I was confused, but I ordered the same.**

▶ once again は「またしても、またもや」（≒ one more time）という意味。ここでは、前文でホストファミリーが注文時に使った和製英語に、スティーブがまたまた戸惑ったことを述べている。

▶ the same は「同じもの、同じこと」（≒ the same things）という意味。

✍ 英文を完成させなさい。

タケシがみそ汁に七味唐辛子を入れたので、私も同じようにした。

Takeshi put some *shichimi-togarashi* into his *miso* soup, so I
(　　　)(　　　)(　　　).

このセクションの内容 の答え→　A. 和製英語　B. 本当の英語　C. 新しいこと

⑦ **After breakfast, my host father suggested that one of these days he would invite me to a *Viking* dinner.**

▶ one of these days は「近いうちに、いずれそのうち」(≒ in the (near) future) という意味。

▶〈suggest + that 節〉で「〜と提案する」という意味。suggested に合わせて、that 節の中の助動詞も will→過去形 would となっている（時制の一致）。

▶ invite 〜 to ... で「〜を…に招待する」という意味。

⑧ **So far, I have learned lots of these words.**

▶ so far は「今までのところ」(≒ until now) という意味。〈継続〉や〈経験〉などを表す現在完了といっしょに使われることも多い。

✍ 次の英文を日本語に直しなさい。

More than fifty thousand people have visited the museum so far.

_____

▶ lots of 〜は「〜の多く」という意味。these words「こうした言葉」は、スティーブが本文中で挙げてきた和製英語を指す。

⑨ **My teacher calls them *wasei-eigo*.**

▶〈call + O + C〉の構文。them は前文の these words を指す。

⑩ **These words can be deceptive; they look like real English, and yet they are not.**

▶ look like 〜は「〜のように見える」という意味。like は前置詞なので、このあとには名詞（句）が続く。

▶ and yet は「それでも、しかし」(≒ but) という意味。they are not のあとには real English が省略されている。

⑪ **I find them confusing.**

▶〈find + O + C〉「Oが〜だとわかる」の構文。confusing は「(人・ものが) 困惑させる」という意味の形容詞。

⑫ **It's a first step in learning something new.**

▶ 前置詞 in のあとに動名詞が続く形で、「〜における」という意味。a first step in learning 〜で「〜を学ぶことにおける第一歩」となる。⇒p.17 G-❷

✍ ( )内の語を適切な形に変えなさい。

スパイスはカレー作りにおいてとても重要です。

Spice is very important in (make) curry.

⑬ **Don't be surprised if native speakers look puzzled when you use *wasei-eigo*.**

▶ Don't be surprised は「驚いてはいけません」という否定の命令文。

▶ look puzzled は〈look ＋形容詞〉で、「戸惑っているように見える」という意味。

動詞の種類と文の基本パターン

英文は基本的にS（主語）、V（動詞）、O（目的語）、C（補語）から構成されている。英文の基本パターンは、文の中心となる動詞の性質によって、以下の5つに分類できる。

1. 〈S＋V〉「～は…する」　主語と動詞のみで成り立っている文。動詞は補語、目的語を必要とせず、自動詞と呼ばれる。修飾語句を伴うことが多い。
<u>Fish</u> <u>swim</u> <u>in water</u>.（魚は水の中を泳ぐ）
　　S　　　V　　　修飾語句

2. 〈S＋V＋C〉「～は…である」など　このパターンの文を作るのは、be、look、become、seemなど、補語を必要とする自動詞である。補語になるのは名詞、形容詞、不定詞、動名詞など。S＝Cの関係が成り立つ。
<u>They</u> <u>are</u> <u>kind</u> <u>to us</u>.（彼らは私たちに親切だ）
　　S　　V　　C　　修飾語句

3. 〈S＋V＋O〉「～を…する」　このパターンの文を作るのは、目的語を必要とする他動詞である。目的語は動作の対象などを表し、名詞（節）、代名詞、不定詞、動名詞などが目的語の働きをする。
<u>We</u> <u>like</u> <u>soccer</u> <u>very much</u>.（私たちはサッカーがとても好きである）
　　S　　V　　O　　　修飾語句

4. 〈S＋V＋O1＋O2〉「～に…を与える」など　このパターンの文を作る動詞は、目的語を2つとる。
<u>She</u> <u>gave</u> <u>me</u> <u>this CD</u>.（彼女は私にこのCDをくれた）
　　S　　V　　O1　　O2

5. 〈S＋V＋O＋C〉「～を…と呼ぶ」など　このパターンの文を作る動詞は、目的語と（目的語の）補語の両方をとる。O＝Cの関係が成り立つ。補語になるものは名詞、形容詞などである。
<u>People</u> <u>called</u> <u>the dog</u> <u>Hachiko</u>.（人々はその犬をハチ公と呼んだ）
　　S　　　V　　　O　　　C
（＊the dogとHachikoはイコールの関係）
<u>The news</u> <u>made</u> <u>us</u> <u>happy</u>.（その知らせは私たちを幸せにした）
　　S　　　V　　O　　C
（＊happyはusの状態を表す）

≷ **Grammar for Communication** ≷

1　不定詞

1. 名詞的用法：「〜すること」という意味。主語、目的語、補語になる。

主語：**To study** English is interesting.（英語を勉強することは興味深い）
形式主語Itを用いて次のように表すことが多い。

◆ **It** is interesting **to study** English.
　　└─ to以下の内容を形式的に受ける ─┘

目的語：I want **to travel** abroad.（私は海外旅行をしたい）
補語：Her dream is **to be** a singer.（彼女の夢は歌手になることだ）

2. 形容詞的用法：「〜するための、〜するべき、〜することができる」という意味。前の(代)名詞を修飾する。

He has a lot of things **to do** today.（彼は今日はすることがたくさんある）

3. 副詞的用法：目的や原因・理由などを表し、「〜するために」、「〜して」などの意味を表す。

目的：She went to Italy **to study** music.
　　　（彼女は音楽を勉強するためにイタリアに行った）
原因・理由：I was glad **to see** him again.（私は彼にまた会えてうれしかった）

4. 不定詞の否定形：否定語（notやnever）はtoの直前に置く。

We decided **not to go** there.（私たちはそこに行かないことにした）

5. 〈S＋V＋O＋to do〉

O（目的語）は不定詞の意味上の主語となるため、「Oが〜する」という関係が成り立つ。このパターンの構文を作る動詞には、以下のようなものがある。
want「〜してほしい」、ask「頼む」、tell「言う、命じる」、order「命令する」
advise「助言する」、force「強制する」、encourage「勧める」

◆ We **asked** Nami **to sing** a song for us.（＊歌うのはNami）
　（私たちはナミに私たちのために1曲歌ってくれるように頼んだ）

◆ Jack **told** his son **not to eat** too much chocolate.（＊食べるのはhis son）
　（ジャックは息子にチョコレートをあまり食べすぎないように言った）

2 動名詞

1. **基本用法：動詞のあとに -ing を付けた V-ing は、「～すること」という意味を表す。動詞としての性質を保ったままで名詞のような働きをし、主語、補語、動詞・前置詞の目的語になる。**

主語：**Playing** soccer is fun. （サッカーをするのは楽しい）

補語：His hobby is **playing** the guitar. （彼の趣味はギターを弾くことだ）

目的語：She likes **listening** to music. （彼女は音楽を聞くことが好きである）

Alan left the room without **saying** anything.

（アランは何も言わずに部屋を出て行った）

名詞的用法の不定詞も動名詞も「～すること」の意味を表すが、不定詞は〈未来志向〉が強く、動名詞は〈現実（過去）志向〉が強い。

◆ My hobby is **watching** movies. （私の趣味は映画を見ることである）

　［過去にも、今も映画を見ること］

◆ My dream is **to be** a musician. （私の夢は音楽家になることである）

　［未来に音楽家になること］

2. **動名詞と不定詞の使い分け**

①目的語に動名詞だけをとる動詞

◆ Paul has just finished **cooking** dinner.

　（ポールはちょうど夕食を作り終えたところだ）

　It'll stop **raining** soon. （もうすぐ雨はやむでしょう）

②目的語に不定詞だけをとる動詞

◆ Mike decided **to join** the art club.

　（マイクは美術部に入ることに決めた）

◆ I'm planning **to spend** my summer vacation in Italy.

　（私は夏休みをイタリアで過ごす予定です）

③目的語が不定詞か動名詞で意味が異なる動詞

◆ I'll never **forget visiting** Canada this winter. （＊すでに起きたこと）

　（私はこの冬にカナダを訪れたことを決して忘れないでしょう）

◆ Don't **forget to** take medicine after lunch. （＊これから起きること）

　（昼食後に薬を飲むのを忘れないようにね）

確認問題

語彙・表現

1 次の語を ( ) 内の指示にしたがって書きかえなさい。

(1) confuse（名詞に）　　　　　(2) meet（過去形に）

(3) wait（人を表す名詞に）　　　(4) bring（過去形に）

2 次の各組で下線部の発音がほかと異なる語を 1 つずつ選び、記号で答えなさい。

(1) ア　palace　　　　イ　chance　　　ウ　native　　　エ　mansion

(2) ア　advice　　　　イ　Viking　　　ウ　cider　　　エ　condominium

3　日本語に合うように、( ) 内に適切な語を入れなさい。

(1) クッキーをもう少しいかがですか。

(　　　) you (　　　　) some more cookies?

(2) こっちにおいでよ、ローズ。いっしょにサンドイッチを食べよう。

Come (　　　) (　　　　), Rose. Let's eat some sandwiches together.

(3) 朝食のあとでポールは散歩に出かけた。

Paul (　　　) (　　　) a walk after breakfast.

(4) 英語を勉強する際にはよい辞書を選ぶことが大切です。

Choosing a good dictionary is important (　　　) (　　　) English.

文のパターン・文法

1 次の英文と同じパターンを持つ文を、下のア〜オより選びなさい。

(1) David showed us his new car.　　　　　　　　　　　(　　)

(2) They arrived at the village around noon.　　　　　　(　　)

(3) She looks very young for her age.　　　　　　　　　(　　)

(4) We will never forget your kindness.　　　　　　　　(　　)

(5) I found the book very interesting.　　　　　　　　　(　　)

　　ア　Lisa told an interesting story to the children.

　　イ　They got angry to hear the news.

　　ウ　Birds are flying in the sky.

　　エ　Please tell me the best way to do it.

　　オ　She always keeps her room very clean.

2 次の各組の文がほぼ同じ意味になるように、（　）内に適切な語を入れなさい。

(1) I collect stamps as a hobby.

My hobby is (　　　) (　　　).

(2) To be kind to others is important.

(　　　) (　　　) important (　　　) (　　　) kind to others.

(3) Please close all the windows before you leave the room.

Please close all the windows before (　　　) the room.

3 （　）内の語句を並べかえて、英文を完成させなさい。

(1) (always / to / me / listening / makes / music) happy.

_____ happy.

(2) You (to / special glasses / wear/ need / watch / to) this movie.

You _____ this movie.

総合

次のスティーブの文を読んで、あとの問いに答えなさい。

> My host family always has a Japanese-style breakfast — *nori*, *natto*, *miso* soup, and rice. ①That's fine with me. But yesterday they took me to a ファミレス. ②They wanted to give me a chance to enjoy some Western food. They ordered ホットケーキ, フライドポテト, and ブレンド. ③(　　　) (　　　), I was confused, but I ordered ④the same. The waiter brought pancakes, French fries, and coffee. I noticed some strange and interesting desserts on the menu: チョコバナナパフェ, ソフトクリーム, シュークリーム.

問1　下線部①が指す内容を日本語で説明しなさい。

問2　下線部②を日本語に直しなさい。

問3　③の（　）内に入る最も適切な語を選びなさい。

ア　These days　　　イ　Once again

ウ　So far　　　　　エ　And yet

問4　下線部④が指すものを本文中の英語で3つ答えなさい。

問5　スティーブはメニューに並んでいる何を見て戸惑ったのですか。漢字4字で答えなさい。

Does It Spark Joy?

☐ spark [spá:rk]
☐ tidy [táidi]
☐ consultant [kənsʌ́ltənt]
☐ tidy up
☐ insist [ɪnsíst]
☐ only if ~
☐ fashionable [fǽʃənəbl]
☐ put ~ into ...
☐ be filled with ~
☐ source [sɔ́:rs]
☐ frustration [frʌstréɪʃən]
☐ belonging [bɪlɔ́:ŋɪŋ]
☐ turn out (to be) ~
☐ for short
☐ solution [səlú:ʃən]
☐ neat [ní:t]
☐ fascinated [fǽsɪnèɪtɪd]
☐ be fascinated with ~
☐ article [á:rtɪkl]
☐ not only ~ but also ...
☐ put ~ in order

①Marie Kondo, a tidying consultant, tells you to tidy up your personal space. ②She insists that you should keep things only if they "spark joy."

1

③It is human nature to collect things: a lot of colorful pens, a new pair of pants, a fashionable T-shirt, a pair of cool sneakers. We love these things when we buy them. ④However, we put them into a drawer or a closet and forget about them.

⑤Soon our living space is filled with too many things: too many pairs of socks in our drawers, too many shoes in our closet. Books. Books. Books. ⑥That can be a source of frustration. ⑦Our belongings have turned out to be a real headache for us. ⑧What should we do?

Marie Kondo (KonMari, for short) has a solution. ⑨From an early age she liked keeping her room neat and tidy. ⑩She was fascinated with magazine articles about how to organize your space. ⑪She not only put her own space in order, but she also cleaned and tidied up her sister's room.

このセクションの内容

　(A.　　　　) ことは人間が本来的に持つ性質である。しかし、買ったまま使わずにいるものが増えると、それらは私たちの (B.　　　　) を圧迫し、いらいらの原因となってしまう。(C.　　　　) のコンサルタントである近藤麻理恵さん (略称：こんまり) は、そうした問題に1つの解決策を提供してくれる。

① **Marie Kondo, a tidying consultant, tells you to tidy up your personal space.**

▶〈tell＋O（人）＋to ～〉は「（人）に～するように言う」という意味の不定詞構文。目的語youが不定詞to tidy upの意味上の主語になっている。

> ✍ 次の英文を日本語に直しなさい。

Mr. Tanaka told his students to write a short story in English.

▶tidy upは「～をきれいに片づける」という意味。動詞に副詞のupを付け加えると、「完全に、きれいに」などの強調の意味を表す。*cf.* eat up「～（料理）を残さず食べる、たいらげる」、use up「～を使い果たす」

② **She insists that you should keep things only if they "spark joy."**

▶insist that ～は「～と主張する」という意味。目的語となるthat節の中に助動詞shouldが使われることがある。

▶only if ～は「～の場合だけ」という意味。theyはthingsを指す。

③ **It is human nature to collect things: a lot of colorful pens, a new pair of pants, a fashionable T-shirt, a pair of cool sneakers.**

▶〈It is＋名詞＋to ～〉「～することは…だ」という意味。Itはto以下の内容を形式的に受けるだけで、真の主語はto collect thingsである。

▶pants「ズボン」、sneakers「スニーカー」のように、2つの部分から成るものを数えるときは、習慣的にa pair of ～を用いる。

④ **However, we put them into a drawer or a closet and forget about them.**

▶put ～ into ...は「～を…に入れる、しまう」という意味。

⑤ **Soon our living space is filled with too many things**

▶be filled with ～は「～でいっぱいである」という意味。〈状態〉を表すbe filled with ～は、be full of ～で言いかえ可能な場合もある。

> 例 The box is filled with fresh fruit.（≒The box is full of fresh fruit.）
> 「その箱は新鮮な果物でいっぱいだ」

⑥ **That can be a source of frustration.**

▶Thatは前文の内容、つまり「生活空間があまりにも多くの物でいっぱいになっている」状態を指す。

▶助動詞のcanは、「（時として）～ことがある」という〈一般的な可能性・推量〉を表す。

⇒p.33 G-❸

このセクションの内容 の答え→　A. ものを集める　B. 生活空間　C. 片づけ

✍ 次の英文を日本語に直しなさい。

Too much exercise can be bad to your health.

⑦ **Our belongings have turned out to be a real headache for us.**

▶ belongings は「持ち物、所持品」という意味。

cf. one's personal belongings「私物、身の回りの物」

▶ have turned out to be a real headache for us は〈結果〉を表す現在完了形で、「(あれこれ買い込んだ)品物が結局私たちにとっての頭痛の種となってしまっているのだ」という意味。　　　　　　　　　　⇒p.32 G-❶

✍ ( )内の語を適切な形に変えなさい。ただし、1 語とは限りません。

ジョンはパスポートをなくしてしまったので、非常に困っている。

John is in great trouble because he (lose) his passport.

▶ turn out to be 〜で「(結局) 〜であるとわかる」という意味。

例 The brand-name bag I bought has turned out to be a fake.
「私が買ったブランドもののバッグは偽物だとわかった」

⑧ **What should we do?**

▶ What should we do? で「私たちはどうすべきなのだろうか」という意味。この should は「〜すべきである」という〈義務・当然〉を表す助動詞。

⇒p.33 G-❸

✍ 次の英文を日本語に直しなさい。

Which climbing route should we take?

⑨ **From an early age she liked keeping her room neat and tidy.**

▶〈keep + O + C〉「O を C の状態に保つ」。この tidy は形容詞。

⑩ **She was fascinated with magazine articles about how to organize your space.**

▶ be fascinated with 〜は「〜に魅了される」という意味。

▶ how to organize 〜は「〜を整理整頓する方法」という意味。

⑪ **She not only put her own space in order, but she also cleaned and tidied up her sister's room.**

▶ not only 〜 but also ... は「〜だけでなく…もまた」という意味。「〜」と「...」には、文法的に同じ働きをする語句が置かれるのがふつう。

例 The painter is popular not only in Japan but (also) overseas.
「その画家は日本だけでなく海外でも人気がある」(＊場所を表す語句)

例 He not only plays the piano, but he also writes music for piano.
「彼はピアノを弾くだけでなく、ピアノのための音楽の作曲もする」
(＊動詞句)

- □ principle [prínsəpl]
- □ client [kláɪənt]
- □ unread [ʌnréd]
- □ which to 〜
- □ discard [dɪskáːrd]
- □ sometime [sʌ́mtàɪm]
- □ if not
- □ throw 〜 away
- □ apply [əpláɪ]
- □ apply to 〜
- □ That's how 〜
- □ process [práses]

2

①While in college, KonMari started working as a tidying consultant in Japan. ②In 2014, she went to the U.S. to introduce the "KonMari Method." ③She has been working hard, and her method is a great success all over the world.

④One of KonMari's most important principles is this: "Keep things only if they 'spark joy.'"

⑤Some of her clients have lots of unread books. ⑥But they don't know which to keep and which to discard. ⑦Perhaps they will read them sometime. ⑧But "sometime" never comes. ⑨KonMari's advice is to take each book in your hands, and if it sparks joy, keep it. ⑩If not, throw it away. ⑪But don't forget to say, "Thank you for your good service."

She adds: "⑫You never read the book, but you still learned something from it. ⑬You learned that you didn't need that book."

⑭The same applies to all of your belongings. ⑮That's how the process of tidying starts.

このセクションの内容

近藤さんが生み出した（A.　　）は「こんまり®メソッド」と呼ばれ、世界中で成功を収めている。「こんまり®メソッド」で最も重要な原則の１つは、「手にしたときに（B.　　）を感じさせるものだけを手元に残す」、そして「ものを処分するときには、ものへの（C.　　）を忘れずに」というものである。

23

① **While in college, KonMari started working as a tidying consultant in Japan.**

▶ While in college は While she was in college の she was が省略された形。she は主節の KonMari のことで、主節と主語が同じときは while の節の主語と be 動詞を省略することができる。

▶ start V-ing は「〜し始める」という意味。

② **In 2014, she went to the U.S. to introduce the "KonMari Method."**

▶ to introduce「〜を紹介するために」は、〈目的〉を表す不定詞の副詞的用法。

③ **She has been working hard, and her method is a great success all over the world.**

▶ has been working「ずっと働いている」は、現在完了進行形 (have [has] been V-ing)。過去のある時点から現在までの動作の継続を表す。⇒p.33 G-❷

▶ 現在完了進行形は、since「〜以来」(動作の開始時点) や for「〜の間」(継続期間) などを伴うことが多いが、この文のように明示されないこともある。

✐ 英文を完成させなさい。

アランは 2 時間ずっとギターを弾いています。

Alan (　　　) (　　　) (　　　) the guitar for two hours.

④ **One of KonMari's most important principles is this: "Keep things only if they 'spark joy.'"**

▶ コロン (:) 以下は、直前の this、つまり「こんまり」が最も重視している原則の内容を具体的に述べている。

▶ only if は「ただ〜の場合だけ」という意味。they は things を指す。

▶ spark はもともとは「火花を出す」という意味。spark joy は「喜びを感じさせる」という意味。「こんまり®メソッド」では、このフレーズを「心がときめく」、「心をときめかせる」という意味で用いている。

⑤ **Some of her clients have lots of unread books.**

▶ lots of 〜は「たくさんの〜」という意味。a lot of 〜よりも口語的。

⑥ **But they don't know which to keep and which to discard.**

▶ which to 〜で「どちらを〜すべきか」という意味。「読んでいない本のどれを手元に残しどれを処分するか」ということ。

⑦ **Perhaps they will read them sometime.**

▶ 助動詞の will は「〜することになるだろう」という〈単純未来〉を表す。〈意志未来〉の用法との違いに注意。　　　　　　　　　　　⇒p.33 G-❸

例 My brother will be 8 years old next month.

「弟は来月 8 歳になります」(*単純未来：未来に必ず起こると予想されること)

このセクションの内容 の答え→ A. 片づけ法　B. 喜び　C. 感謝 (の気持ち)

例 We will get back our normal days.
「私たちはきっと正常な日々を取り戻します」（＊意志未来：話者の意志）

▶ read them の them は、文⑤の unread books を指す。

⑧ But "sometime" never comes.

▶ never は「決して～ない」という強い否定を表す。

⑨ KonMari's advice is to take each book in your hands, and if it sparks joy, keep it.

▶ KonMari's advice is to ～で「こんまりのアドバイスは～することである」という意味。〈S＋V＋C〉のCに名詞的用法の不定詞がきた形。

▶ if以下の2つのit は、どちらも「手に取った（未読の）本」を指す。

⑩ If not, throw it away.

▶ if not は直前のif節の内容を受けて、「もしそうでないなら」という意味を表す。この文では、If not = If it does not spark joy。

⑪ But don't forget to say, "Thank you for your good service."

▶ don't forget to ～で「～することを忘れないように」という意味。

⑫ You never read the book, but you still learned something from it.

▶ never read は、〈never＋動詞の過去形〉で「（結局）～することなく終わった」という意味。〈経験〉を表す現在完了形（⇒p.32 G-❶）との違いに注意。

✐ 次の各英文を下線部に注意して日本語に直しなさい。

I never visited the theater during my stay in New York.

_____

I have never visited the theater in New York.

_____

⑬ You learned that you didn't need that book.

▶ learn that ～は「～ということを学ぶ」という意味。

⑭ The same applies to all of your belongings.

▶ The same「同じこと」は、前文までで述べている「こんまり」式の処分方法、つまり「手に取った物が喜びを感じさせるかどうかを目安にして、それを処分するか手元に残すかを決める」ことを指す。

▶ apply to ～は「～に当てはまる」という意味。

⑮ That's how the process of tidying starts.

▶ That's how ～「そのようにして～する」は〈S＋V＋C（疑問詞節）〉の構文。

✐ 英文を完成させなさい。

事故はそのようにして起きたのです。

(   ) (   ) the accident happened.

Lesson 2

☐ throw out
☐ ruthlessly [rúːθləsli]
☐ treat [tríːt]
☐ immediately [ɪmíːdiətli]
☐ text [tékst]
☐ be surprised to ～
☐ blank [blǽŋk]
☐ screen [skríːn]
☐ go dead
☐ after V-ing
☐ admit [ədmít]
☐ coincidence [kouínsɪdəns]
☐ illustrate [íləstrèɪt]
☐ respect [rɪspékt]
☐ relationship [rɪléɪʃənʃip]

3

①KonMari is not telling us to throw out stuff ruthlessly. ②She treats her belongings like living things. ③One day, while she was in high school, she bought a new cell phone. Then she sent a message to her old phone: "④You have been helping me for many years. Thank you." ⑤Her old phone rang immediately, and she checked the text. ⑥Of course, it was her message. She said to her old phone, "Great. ⑦My message reached you." Then, she closed it.

⑧When she opened her old phone a little later, she was surprised to find a blank screen. ⑨Her old cell phone went dead after receiving her message. ⑩Its job was done.

⑪KonMari admits that this was probably just a coincidence. ⑫But it illustrates her idea: we should show respect to our belongings, even when we are throwing them away. ⑬We have a very close relationship with our belongings.

このセクションの内容

「こんまり®メソッド」では、ものを無慈悲に処分するのではなく、(A.　　　)
として扱う。このような考え方の根底にあるのは、近藤さんが高校時代に
(B.　　　) を買い換えたときに経験した、ある出来事である。近藤さんは、
私たちはものを処分するときにも (C.　　　) を示すべきだと言う。

① **KonMari is not telling us to throw out stuff ruthlessly.**
> ▶〈tell + O（人）+ to ～〉で「（人）に～するように言う」という意味。目的語 us は不定詞 to throw out の意味上の主語。
> ▶ throw out stuff ruthlessly は「ものを無慈悲に処分する」という意味。

② **She treats her belongings like living things.**
> ▶ treat ～ like ...「～を…のように扱う」。この like は前置詞。
> ▶ living things は「命あるもの、生き物」という意味。

③ **One day, while she was in high school, she bought a new cell phone.**
> ▶ while は接続詞で、「～している間」という意味。
> ▶ be in high school は「高校に在学している」という意味。

④ **You have been helping me for many years.**
> ▶ have been helping「ずっと助けてきた」は現在完了進行形で、過去のある時点から継続する動作を表す。for many years は継続する期間を表す。

⇒p.33 G-❷

⑤ **Her old phone rang immediately, and she checked the text.**
> ▶「（電話が）鳴る」ことを、英語では動詞 ring で表す。ring – rang – rung と不規則に変化する。
> ▶ text は、ここでは携帯電話でやりとりされる text message「テキストメッセージ」のこと。なお、text は動詞としても用いられ、携帯電話やスマートフォンでテキストメッセージをやりとりする行為は、texting と呼ばれる。

⑥ **Of course, it was her message.**
> ▶ of course「もちろん」は談話標識の１つで、当然予想されることを述べる際に用いる。談話標識の働きについては、教科書 p.108 を参照のこと。
>> 例 Of course, AI is very useful for us, but it must be controlled by humans.「もちろん AI（人工知能）は私たちにとって非常に役に立つが、それは人間によって制御されなければならない」
> ▶ it は前文の the text、つまり「こんまり」が古い携帯電話に向けて送った最後のメッセージの文面を指す。

⑦ **My message reached you.**
> ▶ reach は「～に届く、達する」という意味。you は「こんまり」がそれまでずっと使っていた古い携帯電話のこと。

⑧ **When she opened her old phone a little later, she was surprised to find a blank screen.**
> ▶ a little later は「少しあとで」という意味。この later は副詞で、しばしば具体的な時間を表す語句とともに用いられる。

このセクションの内容 の答え→　A. 命あるもの　B. 携帯電話　C. 敬意

例 About ten minutes later, Daiki called me back.
「10分ほどして、大輝から折り返し電話がかかってきた」

▶ be surprised to ～は「～して驚く」という意味。感情を表す形容詞のあとに不定詞を続けると、その理由・原因を表すことができる。

<u>✍ 英文を完成させなさい。</u>

ロンはその知らせを聞いて悲しかった。

Ron was (　　　) (　　　) (　　　) the news.

⑨ **Her old cell phone went dead after receiving her message.**

▶ go dead は「(機械などが)動かなくなる」という意味。このgoは「(好ましくない状態)になる」という意味。*cf.* go bad「(食べ物・飲み物が)腐る」

▶ after receiving her message「彼女のメッセージを受け取ったあとで」。前置詞afterのあとに動名詞(V-ing)が続いた形。

⑩ **Its job was done.**

▶ Its job = Her old cell phone's job。

▶ be動詞のあとのdoneは「終わった、完了した」という意味。

例 Dad, can you pass me the newspaper when you're done with it?
「パパ、新聞を読み終わったら、私に回してくれる？」

⑪ **KonMari admits that this was probably just a coincidence.**

▶ admit that ～は「～ということを認める」という意味。

▶ coincidenceは「偶然(の出来事)」という意味。

例 What a coincidence to see you here!
「ここであなたと会うなんて、何という偶然でしょう！」

⑫ **But it illustrates her idea: we should show respect to our belongings, even when we are throwing them away.**

▶ コロン(:)のあとのwe should ～ them awayは、直前のher ideaの具体的内容。

▶ show respect to ～「～に敬意を払う」という意味。

▶ even when ～「～するときでさえ」のevenは強調を表す。

▶ we are throwing them awayは、現在進行形によって近い未来に起こる出来事を表す。

<u>✍ 次の英文を日本語に直しなさい。</u>

Jane is leaving for London tomorrow.

⑬ **We have a very close relationship with our belongings.**

▶ have a close relationship with ～で「～と密接な[深い]関係を持っている」という意味。このcloseは形容詞で、発音は[klóus]。

☐ No wonder ～
☐ rid [ríd]
☐ get rid of ～
☐ have trouble V-ing
☐ because of ～
☐ attachment [ətǽtʃmənt]
☐ fear [fíər]
☐ value [vǽljuː]
☐ livable [lívəbl]
☐ learn to ～
☐ priority [praɪɔ́ːrəti]
☐ decision [dɪsíʒən]
☐ make a decision
☐ thus [ðʌ́s]
☐ profoundly [prəfáundli]
☐ affect [əfékt]
☐ transform [trænsfɔ́ːrm]
☐ uncertain [ʌnsɔ́ːrtn]
☐ sort [sɔ́ːrt]
☐ sort ～ out
☐ give it a try

4

　　Our belongings are the result of our choices. ①No wonder getting rid of things is so difficult. ②KonMari tells us to ask ourselves: "Am I having trouble throwing this away because of an attachment to the past or because of fear of the future?" ③Asking that question will help us discover our life values.

　　④Tidying up is not just a way to make our space more livable. ⑤It's also a way to set our values and decide our future. ⑥When we organize our rooms, we learn to set priorities. ⑦When we throw away old belongings, we learn to make decisions. ⑧Thus, putting our space in order profoundly affects our lives, even work and family. ⑨Tidying up can transform our lives.

　　⑩If you are uncertain about your future, start sorting things out. ⑪What are you truly interested in? What do you want to do in the future? ⑫Why not give it a try?

このセクションの内容

私たちが身の回りのものを処分できない原因は（A.　　　　）へのこだわりのためなのか、それとも（B.　　　　）への恐れのためなのか？ ― このように自問しながら身の回りのものを片づけることを通して、私たちは空間をより暮らしやすくできるだけでなく、（C.　　　　）を発見し、未来をどう生きるかを見定め、自分の人生を変えることもできるのだと近藤さんは言う。

① No wonder getting rid of things is so difficult.

▶ No wonder 〜で「〜も不思議ではない、〜も無理はない」という意味。It's no wonder that 〜の It is と that が省略された形で、no wonder のあとには〈S + V〉が続く。

> **✍ 次の英文を日本語に直しなさい。**

(It's) no wonder (that) you look tired after practicing soccer for hours.

_____

▶ 動名詞句の getting rid of things 全体が that 節の主語。動名詞が主語の場合、あとに続く動詞は必ず単数で受ける。

▶ get rid of 〜で「〜を処分する、駆除する」という意味。ここでは throw away とほぼ同じ意味で使われている。

② KonMari tells us to ask ourselves: "Am I having trouble throwing this away because of an attachment to the past or because of fear of the future?"

▶ 〈tell + O（人）+ to 〜〉で「（人）に〜するように言う」という意味の構文。目的語 us は不定詞 to ask ourselves の意味上の主語。

▶ ask ourselves は「自問する、自分の胸に聞く」という意味。引用符（" "）内の疑問文は、「こんまり」が私たちに求めている自問の内容。

▶ have trouble (in) V-ing は「〜するのに苦労する」という意味。前置詞の in は、現在では省略されるのがふつう。

> 例 Mina had a lot of trouble writing a history report in English.
> 「美奈は英語で歴史のレポートを書くのにとても苦労した」

▶ because of 〜は「〜のために、〜のせいで」という意味。ここでは as a result of 〜とほぼ同じ意味で使われている。

> **✍ 次の英文を日本語に直しなさい。**

We changed our plans because of the bad weather.

_____

③ Asking that question will help us discover our life values.

▶ 動名詞を主語とする文。that question は前文の引用符（" "）内の疑問文を指す。

▶ help us discover ... は〈help + O（人）+ 動詞の原形〉「（人）が〜するのを助ける」の構文。us は discover の意味上の主語。

④ Tidying up is not just a way to make our space more livable.

⑤ It's also a way to set our values and decide our future.

▶ 文④は、動名詞 Tidying up を主語とする〈S + V + C〉の文。

▶ not just 〜 also ...で「〜だけでなく…もまた」（= not only 〜 also ...）という意味。このように2つの文にまたがって使われることもあり、その場

このセクションの内容 の答え→ A. 過去　B. 未来　C. 人生の価値

合はbutが省略されるのがふつうである。文⑤のalsoを見落とさないように注意する。

📝 **次の英文を日本語に直しなさい。**

Mr. Brown is not just a math teacher.　He's also a top athlete.

───────────────────────

▶文④⑤に出てくる2つのa way to 〜は、どちらも「〜する方法」という意味を表す。a way of V-ingもほぼ同じ意味。

▶文④のmake our space more livableは「私たちの空間をもっと暮らしやすくする」という意味。〈make + O + C（形容詞）〉「Oを〜の状態にする」。

⑥ **When we organize our rooms, we learn to set priorities.**

⑦ **When we throw away old belongings, we learn to make decisions.**

▶⑥⑦のlearn to 〜は、どちらも「〜することを学ぶ、〜の仕方を覚える」という意味。learn how to 〜も同じ意味で用いられる。

📝 **英文を完成させなさい。**

昨年の夏、私の妹は水泳の授業で泳ぎ方を習った。

My sister (　　　) (　　　) swim in swimming class last summer.

▶文⑥のset prioritiesは「優先順位を付ける」という意味。

▶文⑦のmake a decisionは「決心をする、決定を下す」という意味。

⑧ **Thus, putting our space in order profoundly affects our lives, even work and family.**

▶putting our space in order profoundlyは動名詞句で、これ全体が文の主語。動名詞句が主語の場合は単数扱いとなるので、動詞はaffectsとなる。

⑨ **Tidying up can transform our lives.**

▶動名詞句Tidying upを主語とする文。

⑩ **If you are uncertain about your future, start sorting things out.**

▶be uncertain about 〜は「〜がはっきりわからない、〜について自信［確信］がない」という意味。

▶sort 〜 outは「〜を整理する」という意味の熟語。本課で用いられているorganizeやput 〜 in orderとほぼ同じ意味。

⑪ **What are you truly interested in?**

▶興味の対象をたずねる疑問文なので、be interested in 〜「〜に興味［関心］がある」の前置詞inを文末に置く必要がある。

⑫ **Why not give it a try?**

▶Why not 〜?は「〜してはどうですか」と提案・助言を行うときの表現。Why don't you 〜?もほぼ同じ意味で用いられる。

▶give it a tryは「やってみる、試してみる」という意味。

Grammar for Communication

1 現在完了：have [has] ＋過去分詞

現在完了形〈have / has ＋過去分詞〉　過去のある時点に始まったことが現在まで続いていたり、過去の出来事の影響や結果が現在にまで及んでいたりすることを表す。その用法は以下の４つに分類できる。

1. 完了「〜したところだ、もう〜してしまった」

already、just、疑問文・否定文でyetを用いることが多い。

◆ I **have** already **finished** my homework.
（私はすでに宿題をすませてしまっている）

◆ She **hasn't arrived** yet.（彼女はまだ到着していない）

2. 結果「(もう) 〜してしまった (ので、その結果今は…だ)」

動作の結果を表す文では、時を示す副詞（句）はふつう用いない。

◆ He **has lost** his watch. He has to buy a new one.
（彼は時計をなくしてしまった。彼は新しいのを買わなければならない）

◆ Alice **has left** Japan, and we miss her.
（アリスは日本を離れてしまったので、私たちは彼女がいなくてさびしい）

3. 継続「(現在まで) ずっと〜である[〜している]」

since 〜、for 〜、for the past 〜、how longなどが用いられる。

◆ He **has lived** in this city since last year.
（彼は昨年からずっとこの市に住んでいる）

◆ How long **have** you **known** him?（彼とはどれくらいの間お知り合いですか）

4. 経験「(今までに) 〜したことがある」

ever〔疑問文で〕、never〔否定文で〕、before、頻度・回数を表す語句（once、twice、〜 times、oftenなど）を伴う。

◆ **Have** you ever **been** to Canada?（カナダに行ったことがありますか）

◆ I **have visited** the tower twice.
（私はそのタワーを２度訪れたことがあります）

■ 現在完了形といっしょに使えない副詞（句）

現在完了では、「基準となる時」はあくまでも現在なので、明らかに過去のある時点を表す副詞（句）といっしょに用いることはできない。

（例）yesterday、〜 ago、last 〜、just now、in 1945、When 〜？など

2 | 現在完了進行形：have [has] been V-ing 「ずっと～している」

現在完了進行形は、過去のある時点から現在まで継続している動作を表す。現在完了形の継続用法で挙げた語 (句) は、現在完了進行形でも用いることができる。

◆ She **has been watching** TV for more than three hours.
（彼女は3時間以上テレビを見続けている）

◆ It **has been raining** since last night.
（昨晩からずっと雨が降り続いている）

3 | 助動詞のまとめ：助動詞は動詞に主観的な判断を付け加える働きをする。

1. 単純未来の will　主語の意志に関係のない未来の事柄を述べる。
◆ It **will** be cloudy tomorrow. (明日は曇りになるだろう)

2. 意志未来の will　主語の意志に関わる未来の事柄を述べる。
◆ I **will** go to the library to borrow some books this afternoon.
（私は今日の午後何冊かの本を借りるために図書館に行くつもりだ）

3. can 「～できる」　可能や能力を表す。
◆ We **can** ski today because it snowed a lot last night.
（昨夜は雪がたくさん降ったから、私たちは今日はスキーができる）

4. can't 「～のはずがない」　かなりの確信がある推量を表す。
◆ He **can't** be hungry. He has just eaten a big lunch.
（彼が空腹のはずはない。彼はたっぷり昼食を食べたところだ）

5. may 「～してもよい」　丁寧な許可を表す。
◆ **May** I leave? (帰ってもいいですか) — Yes, you may. (ええ、いいですよ)

6. may 「～かもしれない」　可能性が低い、弱い推量を表す。
◆ They **may** be late for the meeting. (彼らは会合に遅れるかもしれない)

7. must 「～しなくてはならない」　義務や必要を表す。否定文では、「～してはいけない」という禁止の意味を表す。
◆ You **must** do it now. (今すぐにそれをしなくてはいけない)
◆ You **must not** use this computer. (このコンピュータを使ってはいけません)

8. must 「～にちがいない」　可能性が高い、断定的な推量を表す。
◆ She looks unhappy. She **must** be in some trouble.
（彼女は悲しげな様子だ。何か困っているにちがいない）

確認問題

語彙・表現

1 次の語を（　）内の指示にしたがって書きかえなさい。

(1) decide（名詞に）　　　　　(2) solve（名詞に）

(3) fashion（形容詞に）　　　　(4) certain（反意語に）

2 第1音節にアクセント（強勢）のある語を2つ選び、記号で答えなさい。

ア　con-sult-ant　　　イ　re-la-tion-ship　　　ウ　fas-ci-nat-ed

エ　in-sist　　　　　　オ　proc-ess 名　　　　　カ　dis-card 動

3 日本語に合うように、（　）内に適切な語を入れなさい。

(1) ミカは古い雑誌を捨てました。

Mika (　　　　) (　　　　) her old magazines.

(2) チェスはやったことがないけど、試してみるよ。

I haven't played chess before, but I'll (　　　) (　　　) a (　　　).

(3) そのキャビネットは音楽CDでいっぱいでした。

The cabinet (　　　) (　　　) with music CDs.

(4) 金田さんは英語だけでなくフランス語も話せます。

Mr. Kaneda can speak (　　　) (　　　) English (　　　) also French.

文のパターン・文法

1 次の現在完了形は、a.完了、b.結果、c.継続、d.経験のうちのどの用法にあたるか、記号で答えなさい。同じ記号を何回選んでもかまいません。

(1) Have you ever visited Himeji Castle?　　　　　　　　　　(　　)

(2) We have known each other since we were children.　　　(　　)

(3) She has just finished practicing the piano.　　　　　　　(　　)

(4) Kaito has been playing video games for two hours.　　　(　　)

(5) My computer has broken down, so I can't use the Internet.　(　　)

2 日本語に合うように、（　）内に適切な助動詞をあとから選んで書きなさい。ただし、各助動詞は1回しか使えません。

(1) このあたりでは野生動物に気をつけなければならない。

You (　　　) be careful about wild animals around here.

(2) 今日の午後遅くに雨になるかもしれない。

It ( ) rain late this afternoon.

(3) バスが来たら、すぐに出発するつもりです。

We ( ) leave as soon as the bus arrives.

(4) 英語を話す機会を逃すべきでない。

We ( ) not miss a chance to speak English.

[should   must   will   may]

3 ( )内の語を並べかえて、英文を完成させなさい。

(1) (to / I / Mina / surprised / see / was) in the theater.

_____ in the theater.

(2) (you / how / studying / have / long / been) Japanese?

_____ Japanese?

(3) I ordered the book two weeks ago, but (has / yet / it / arrived / not).

I ordered the book two weeks ago, but _____ .

総合

次の文を読んで、あとの問いに答えなさい。

One of KonMari's most important (①) is this: "Keep things only if they 'spark joy.'"

Some of her clients have lots of unread books. But they don't know (②) to keep and (③) to discard. Perhaps they will read ④them sometime. But "sometime" never comes. KonMari's advice is to take each book in your hands, and if it sparks joy, keep it. ⑤If not, throw it away. But don't forget to say, "Thank you for your good service."

問1 ①の( )内に入る最も適切な語を選びなさい。

ア drawers   イ values   ウ belongings   エ principles

問2 ②、③の( )内に入る共通の1語を書きなさい。

問3 下線部④が指す内容を本文中のひと続きの英語2語で答えなさい。

問4 下線部⑤を次のように言いかえるとき、( )内に入る適切な語を書きなさい。

If it ( ) ( ) ( ), throw it away.

問5 こんまりはどのような本を手元に残すようにアドバイスしていますか。日本語で説明しなさい。

Hatching the Egg of Hope

教科書p.42　Section 1

- [ ] hatch [hǽtʃ]
- [ ] share ~ with ...
- [ ] journey [dʒə́ːrni]
- [ ] Belgium [béldʒəm]
- [ ] spend ~ V-ing
- [ ] pass by ~
- [ ] even though ~
- [ ] bring ~ together
- [ ] graduate [grǽdʒuèit]
- [ ] part-time [pàːrttáim]
- [ ] work part-time
- [ ] guest [gést]
- [ ] a guest house
- [ ] gallery [gǽləri]
- [ ] anger [ǽŋgər]
- [ ] injustice [indʒʌ́stis]
- [ ] live a ~ life

①For Miyazaki Kensuke, art is a way to share happiness with people all over the world. ②He sees life as a journey to discover an answer to the question: Who am I as a person and as an artist?

1

③I've always loved painting. ④During a spring break in high school, I visited Belgium for two weeks. ⑤I spent my time painting on the streets. ⑥People who passed by seemed happy to see my work, even though I couldn't understand their language. I realized the power of art to bring people together.

In college, I had a dream. ⑦I wanted people all over the world to recognize me as a great artist. After graduating, I went to London to become famous.

In London, I lived and worked part-time in a guest house. I didn't have much money. ⑧No gallery accepted my paintings.

⑨My street artist friends and I thought it was cool to look angry. They were expressing their anger at social injustice, and their anger was real. ⑩But I was from an ordinary family living an ordinary life. I wasn't angry at all.

I was in London for two years, but still I wasn't a famous artist. ⑪I decided I had to find a different way of expressing myself.

このセクションの内容

ミヤザキケンスケさんは大学卒業後、世界の人々に（A.　　　　　）とし
て認められたいという夢を抱いてロンドンに渡ったが、彼の絵を受け入れて
くれる画廊はなかった。ストリート・アーティストたちが描く絵からは社会
的な不公平に対する本物の（B.　　　）が感じられたが、ごくふつうの生活
を送ってきたミヤザキさんには、そうしたものはなかった。彼は（C.　　　）
ための違った方法を見つけなければならなかった。

① **For Miyazaki Kensuke, art is a way to share happiness with people all over the world.**

▶ a way to ～で「～する方法［手段］」という意味になる。

▶ share ～ with ... は「～を…と分かち合う、共有する」という意味。

✐ 次の英文を日本語に直しなさい。

Mike shares a room with his brother.

② **He sees life as a journey to discover an answer to the question: Who am I as a person and as an artist?**

▶ see ～ as ... で「～を…とみなす［考える］」という意味。asのあとには名詞のほか、形容詞や分詞が置かれることもある。

▶ コロン (:) 以下は、the questionの具体的内容を示している。2つのasは、どちらも「～として」という意味の前置詞。

③ **I've always loved painting.**

▶ I've always loved ～は「以前からずっと～が大好きだった」という意味。この have loved は〈継続〉を表す現在完了形。

✐（　）内の語を適切な形に変えなさい。

エマは以前からずっとイタリアに行ってみたいと思っていた。

Emma (always want) to visit Italy.

④ **During a spring break in high school, I visited Belgium for two weeks.**

▶ duringは、during a spring break「春休み中に」のように、「（特定の期間・出来事）の間中、～の間に」という意味を表す。

▶ for ～は「～の間」という〈期間〉を表す。この文からは、ミヤザキケンスケさんは「高校時代の春休み中の2週間、ベルギーを訪ねた」ことがわかる。

⑤ **I spent my time painting on the streets.**

▶ spend ～ (in) V-ing は「…することに～（時間）を費やす」という意味。

✑ ( ) 内の語を適切な形に変えなさい。

ジョンは何日もかけてその古い時計を直した。

John (spend) many days (repair) the old clock.

⑥ **People who passed by seemed happy to see my work, even though I couldn't understand their language.**

▶ who は〈人〉を先行詞とする主格の関係代名詞。この文では、who passed by が先行詞 People に説明を加えている。　⇒p.48 G-❶

✑ 次の英文を日本語に直しなさい。

I have an American friend who loves Japanese anime.

▶ pass by は「通り過ぎる」という意味。

▶ seemed happy to 〜は「〜してうれしそうだった」という意味。〈seem + 形容詞〉は「〜のように思われる」。to see my work は原因・理由を表す不定詞の副詞的用法。

▶ even though 〜は、「たとえ〜でも」という意味の接続詞。

⑦ **I wanted people all over the world to recognize me as a great artist.**

▶〈want + O（人）+ to 〜〉で「（人）に〜してほしい」という意味。people all over the world は、不定詞 to recognize の意味上の主語。

▶ recognize 〜 as ... は「〜を…と認める」という意味。

⑧ **No gallery accepted my paintings.**

▶〈no + 名詞〉は「１つの[１人の] 〜も…ない」という全否定を表す。

⑨ **My street artist friends and I thought it was cool to look angry.**

▶ think (that) 〜「〜と考える」の that が省略されている。

▶ it was cool to 〜は、it が不定詞の内容を受ける形式主語構文。

⑩ **But I was from an ordinary family living an ordinary life.**

▶ living は現在分詞の形容詞的用法。living an ordinary life が直前の an ordinary family を後ろから修飾している（後置修飾）。　⇒p.49 G-❷

✑ ( ) 内の語を適切な形に変えなさい。

舞台で踊っている少女たちをご覧なさい。

Look at the girls (dance) on the stage.

⑪ **I decided I had to find a different way of expressing myself.**

▶ decide (that) 〜で「〜と決心する、〜と判断する」という意味。

▶ a way of V-ing で「〜する方法」という意味。a way to 〜とほぼ同じ意味。

このセクションの内容 の答え→　A. 偉大な画家　B. 怒り　C. 自分を表現する

□ happen to ~

□ orphan [ɔ́ːrfən]

□ Nairobi [naɪróʊbi]

□ Kenya [kénjə]

□ urge [ɔ́ːrdʒ]

□ dragon [drǽgən]

□ be happy with ~

□ frighten [fráɪtən]

□ refuse [rɪfjúːz]

□ imaginary [ɪmǽdʒənèri]

□ baobab [béɪəbæb]

□ according [əkɔ́ːrdɪŋ]

□ according to ~

□ turning [tɔ́ːrnɪŋ]

□ a turning point

□ career [kəríər]

□ collaboration [kəlæbəréɪʃən]

□ in collaboration with ~

□ make up one's mind

2

①In London, I happened to watch a TV program about a school for orphans and street children in Nairobi, Kenya. The children looked unhappy. ②I suddenly felt an urge to go to Kenya and paint something for those children.

③It wasn't easy, but finally in 2006, I got to Kenya, found the school, and was able to paint for the children. I painted an angry dragon. I was happy with it, but a teacher complained, "④The children are frightened by the dragon. ⑤Some of them refuse to come to school." ⑥The children thought that it was a big snake. They did not know that dragons are imaginary.

⑦I asked them, "What would *you* like me to paint?"

"Lions!" "Baobabs!"

⑧I asked the children to help me, and we had a lot of fun painting together. ⑨According to the teachers, the children became more active than before.

⑩That was a turning point in my career. ⑪Creating happiness through painting in collaboration with others is my thing. ⑫I made up my mind to do a painting project every year in different parts of the world.

このセクションの内容

ミヤザキさんは、2006年に（A.　　　　）を訪れ、孤児やストリート・チルドレンが通う学校で、子どもたちといっしょに絵を描き始めた。ミヤザキさんは、ほかの人たちと（B.　　　　）し合って絵を描くことこそ、自分が得意とすることなのだと気がついた。彼は毎年、世界各地で絵を描く（C.　　　　）を行おうと決心した。

① **In London, I happened to watch a TV program about a school for orphans and street children in Nairobi, Kenya.**

▶ happen to ～は「たまたま［偶然］～する」という意味。

　🖊 次の英文を日本語に直しなさい。

　Bill happened to be out when I called him.

② **I suddenly felt an urge to go to Kenya and paint something for those children.**

▶ feel an urge to ～は「～したい衝動に駆られる」という意味。to go ～は不定詞の形容詞的用法で、an urge の具体的内容を表している。

③ **It wasn't easy, but finally in 2006, I got to Kenya, found the school, and was able to paint for the children.**

▶ 主語の It は、前文②の to go ～ children を指す。

▶ get to ～は「～に着く」という意味。同意語の arrive よりも、そこへ到達するまでに時間や労力を必要とすることを暗示する。

▶ be able to ～は、助動詞 can と同じく、「～できる」という能力を表す。ただし、過去形の was[were] able to ～は、過去のあるときに1回限り可能だったことを表し、could で言いかえることはできない。

　🖊 英文を完成させなさい。

　幸い私はその試験に合格することができた。

　Fortunately, I (　　　) (　　　) (　　　) pass the exam.

④ **The children are frightened by the dragon.**

▶ are frightened by ～は受動態で、「～におびえている」という意味。by 以下は動作主を表す。　　　　　　　　　　　　　　　　　　　⇒p.49 G-❸

▶ 英語の感情表現では、しばしば〈be 動詞＋過去分詞〉が用いられる。（例）be surprised at ～「～に驚く」、be scared of ～「～をこわがる」、be disappointed with[by] ～「～にがっかりする」。これらの過去分詞の多くは、現在では形容詞として扱われる。

　🖊（　）内の語を適切な形に変えなさい。ただし、1語とは限りません。

　人々はその美しい絵画に魅了された。

　People (fascinate) by the beautiful painting.

⑤ **Some of them refuse to come to school.**

▶ them は前文の The children を指す。

▶ 学校の教師の立場から述べているので、go to school ではなく come to school。

▶ refuse to ～は「～することを拒む」という意味。

⑥ **The children thought that it was a big snake.**

このセクションの内容 の答え→　A．ケニア　B．協力　C．プロジェクト

▶ that節の主語itは、文④のthe dragonを指す。

⑦ **I asked them, "What would *you* like me to paint?"**

▶ themは文⑥のThe childrenを指す。

▶ What would you like me to ～?は「あなたたちは私に何を～してほしいのですか」とたずねる文。〈would like + O（人）+ to ～〉は「（人）に～してほしい」という意味。

> ✍ 次の英文を日本語に直しなさい。

I would like you to show me around the park.

⑧ **I asked the children to help me, and we had a lot of fun painting together.**

▶ 〈ask + O（人）+ to ～〉は「（人）に～するように頼む」という意味。the childrenは不定詞to helpの意味上の主語。

▶ have fun V-ingで「～して楽しむ」（≒enjoy V-ing）という意味。

⑨ **According to the teachers, the children became more active than before.**

▶ according to ～で「～によれば」という意味。

▶ became more active than before「以前より活動的になった」。教師から見た子どもたちの様子を、ミヤザキさんといっしょに絵を描くようになる前と後とで比較している。

⑩ **That was a turning point in my career.**

▶ Thatは直前の内容、つまりミヤザキさんとケニアの学校の子どもたちがいっしょに絵を描くことを楽しみ、その結果子どもたちが活動的になったこと。

▶ a turning point in ～で「～における転機」という意味。

⑪ **Creating happiness through painting in collaboration with others is my thing.**

▶ 動名詞を主語とする〈S + V + C〉の文。Creating happiness ～ with others全体が文の主語。

▶ in collaboration with ～は「～と協力して、～と共同で」という意味。日本語では略して「コラボ」というが、英語ではcollaboration。

▶ *one's* thingで「～が得意とすること、好きなこと」という意味。

⑫ **I made up my mind to do a painting project every year in different parts of the world.**

▶ make up *one's* mind to ～は「～しようと決心する」（≒decide to ～）という意味。

> ✍ 次の英文を日本語に直しなさい。

Yuka made up her mind to be a nurse.

- ☐ earthquake [ə́ːɾθkwèɪk]
- ☐ the Great East Japan Earthquake
- ☐ cheer [tʃíər]
- ☐ cheer ~ up
- ☐ usefulness [júːsfəlnəs]
- ☐ in the face of ~
- ☐ disaster [dɪzǽstər]
- ☐ supply [səpláɪ]
- ☐ donate [dóuneɪt]
- ☐ be of help
- ☐ creation [kriéɪʃən]
- ☐ condition [kəndíʃən]
- ☐ find *oneself*
- ☐ Mariupol [mæ̀riúːpəl]
- ☐ Ukraine [juːkréɪn]
- ☐ go on
- ☐ shell [ʃél]
- ☐ destroy [dɪstrɔ́ɪ]

3

In 2011, after the Great East Japan Earthquake, I joined a volunteer group in Sendai. ①Because schools were closed, children had nothing to do. They looked bored. ②I thought my painting project might cheer them up. ③I started working with these children. We painted the walls of a school.

④A barber in Ofunato, Iwate, asked me to paint a sign for his shop. ⑤I not only made the sign, but I also painted his whole shop in bright colors!

⑥I had doubts about the usefulness of my art project, but ⑦I did not want to think that art has no power in the face of disaster. ⑧Money and supplies that people donate can be of great help. ⑨But working together on a painting and sharing the joy of creation can also help. ⑩People can laugh and smile even in the worst conditions.

⑪In 2017, I found myself in Mariupol, Ukraine. ⑫A war was going on. It was a very dangerous place. People were dying every day. ⑬I saw shell holes everywhere and buildings destroyed by bombs.

このセクションの内容

2011年に（A.　　　　　　　　　）が起きたあと、ミヤザキさんは仙台でボランティア活動に加わり、子どもたちといっしょに学校の壁に絵を描いた。（B.　　　　　　　　）に直面したとき、いっしょに絵を描き、（C.　　　　　　　）を分かち合うことによって、芸術は人々の力になると、ミヤザキさんは考えている。2017年、彼は戦時下のウクライナのマリウポリを訪ねた。

① **Because schools were closed, children had nothing to do.**

 ▶had nothing to doで「何もすることがなかった」という意味。to doは直前の代名詞nothingを修飾する形容詞的用法の不定詞。

② **I thought my painting project might cheer them up.**

 ▶助動詞のmay「〜かもしれない」は控えめな推量を表す。この文では主節がI thoughtなので、that節の中の助動詞も過去形のmight（時制の一致）。

 ▶cheer 〜 upは「〜を励ます、元気づける」という意味。themはchildrenを指す。

 　✎ 英文を完成させなさい。

 　私はローズを元気づけるために彼女を夕食に招待した。

 　I invited Rose for dinner to (　　　) (　　　) (　　　).

③ **I started working with these children.**

 ▶start V-ingは「〜し始める」という意味。startは不定詞と動名詞（V-ing）の両方を目的語にとるが、start to 〜は行為の開始に重点があり、start V-ingは行為の継続に重点がある。

④ **A barber in Ofunato, Iwate, asked me to paint a sign for his shop.**

 ▶〈ask + O（人）+ to 〜〉は「（人）に〜するように頼む」の構文。meは不定詞to paintの意味上の主語。

 ▶signは「看板」のこと。signboardとも言う。

⑤ **I not only made the sign, but I also painted his whole shop in bright colors!**

 ▶〈not only 〜 but also ...〉「〜だけでなく…もまた」では、but alsoのあとに続く語句に意味上の重点が置かれる。この文では、「（理髪店の店主から依頼を受けた）看板を作った」ことよりも、「店全体を鮮やかな色で塗った」ことが強調される。

⑥ **I had doubts about the usefulness of my art project**

 ▶have doubts about 〜は「〜に疑いを抱いている」という意味。

⑦ **I did not want to think that art has no power in the face of disaster.**

 ▶do not want to think that 〜で「〜だとは考えたくない」という意味。

 ▶in the face of 〜は「〜に直面して、〜を前にして」という意味。

 ▶disasterは「（大規模な）災害、大惨事」という意味。cf. natural disaster「自然災害」、air disaster「航空機事故」

⑧ **Money and supplies that people donate can be of great help.**

 ▶thatはMoney and suppliesを先行詞とする目的格の関係代名詞。関係代名詞が文の主語を先行詞とする場合、文構造がつかみにくくなるため、注意が必要である。⇒p.48 G-❶

Money and supplies 〔[that] people donate〕 can be of great help.

S(thatの先行詞)　　　　　〔関係代名詞節〕　　V(助動詞＋be動詞)　　　C

▶ be of great helpは「大いに助けとなる」(≒ be greatly helpful)という意味。〈of＋抽象名詞〉は、形容詞と同様の働きをする。

例 Healthcare is of great importance to any country.

(≒ Healthcare is very important to any country.)

「どんな国にとっても医療は非常に重要である」

⑨ **But working together on a painting and sharing the joy of creation can also help.**

▶ 動名詞を主語とする〈S＋V〉の文。working together on a paintingとsharing the joy of creationが接続詞andで結ばれ、文の主語となっている。

▶ work together on ～は「～にいっしょに取り組む」という意味。

⑩ **People can laugh and smile even in the worst conditions.**

▶ even in the worst conditionsで「最悪の状況においても」という意味。even「～でさえ」は、強調したい語句の直前に置かれる。

⑪ **In 2017, I found myself in Mariupol, Ukraine.**

▶ find *oneself* in ～「(気がつくと)～にいる」は、しばしば予想しなかった場所にいることを表す表現。

▶ 文⑫で述べているように、2017年当時、ウクライナのマリウポリでは戦争が起きていた。こうした紛争地に足を踏み入れることはミヤザキさん自身も予想していなかった、ということ。

⑫ **A war was going on.**

▶ go onは「(出来事が)起こる」という意味で、よく進行形で用いられる。

✐ 次の英文を日本語に直しなさい。

I don't know what is going on in the country.

⑬ **I saw shell holes everywhere and buildings destroyed by bombs.**

▶ sawの目的語はshell holesとbuildings destroyed by bombsの2つ。

▶ destroyed by bombsは、直前の名詞buildingsを後ろから修飾する過去分詞句。関係代名詞を使って、buildings which[that] were destroyed by bombsと言いかえることができる。　　　　　　　　⇒p.49 G-❷

✐ (　)内の語を適切な形に変えなさい。

これは300年以上前に建てられた城です。

This is a castle (build) more than 300 years ago.

教科書p.48　Section 4

□ to *one's* surprise
□ nowhere [nóuw(h)èər]
□ come out of nowhere
□ mitten [mítn]
□ (be) based on ~
□ Ukrainian [juːkréiniən]
□ warmth [wɔ́ːrmθ]
□ decorate [dékərèit]
□ decorate ~ with ...
□ Easter [íːstər]
□ represent [rèprizént]
□ peaceful [píːsfl]
□ super [súːpər]

4

　①Mariupol was not a safe place for an art project. ②But to my surprise, when I started painting, children came out of nowhere to join me.

　We painted a big mitten. ③The idea is based on a popular Ukrainian story, *The Magic Mitten*. ④In the story, one snowy night, an old man drops his mitten. ⑤A mouse, a frog, a rabbit, a fox, a wolf, and many other animals climb into the mitten to stay warm.

　⑥In our painting, you see people from all over the world sharing the warmth of a huge mitten. ⑦It is decorated with Easter eggs which represent life and hope. ⑧Our painting shows that people's warm hearts can hatch the egg of hope and bring a peaceful life to us all.

　⑨I still do not have a clear answer to the question: Who am I as a person and as an artist? ⑩But one thing has become clear: my art has the power to make people "super happy."

このセクションの内容

ウクライナのマリウポリで、ミヤザキさんは子どもたちといっしょに、ウクライナでよく知られた物語に由来する絵を描いた。その絵には、（A.　　　　）の中で世界中の人々がいっしょに温まる様子が描かれている。この絵は、人々の温かい心が（B.　　　　）をかえし、私たち全員に（C.　　　　）をもたらすことができることを示している。

① **Mariupol was not a safe place for an art project.**

▶ a safe place for 〜で「〜にとって安全な場所」という意味。*cf.* be safe for drinking「飲んでも安全だ」

② **But to my surprise, when I started painting, children came out of nowhere to join me.**

▶ to *one's* surpriseは「〜が驚いたことには」という意味。one'sは代名詞または固有名詞の所有格。

英文を完成させなさい。

私たちが驚いたことには、だれもその事実を知らなかった。

(　　　) (　　　) (　　　), no one knew the fact.

▶ come out of nowhereは「突然現れる、どこからともなくやって来る」(≒ suddenly appear) という意味。

▶ to join meは〈結果〉を表す不定詞の副詞的用法。「どこからともなく現れて、(絵を描いている) 私のところにやって来た」という状況から、came out of nowhere and joined meと言いかえることができる。

③ **The idea is based on a popular Ukrainian story, *The Magic Mitten*.**

▶ be based on 〜は「〜に基づいている」という意味。

例The movie is based on a best-selling novel.
「その映画はベストセラー小説に基づいている」

▶ イタリック体で書かれた *The Magic Mitten* は物語の名前。直前のa popular Ukrainian storyとは、コンマ (,) をはさんで〈同格〉の関係にある。

④ **In the story, one snowy night, an old man drops his mitten.**

▶ one snowy nightは「雪の降るある夜に」という意味。

▶ mitten「ミトン」は、親指だけが分かれていて、ほかの指が袋状になった手袋のこと。2枚1組で使うが、ここではhis mittenと単数形なので、老人が落としたのはミトンの片方だとわかる。

⑤ **A mouse, a frog, a rabbit, a fox, a wolf, and many other animals climb into the mitten to stay warm.**

▶ the mittenとは、前文で老人が落とした「ミトンの片方」のこと。

▶ to stay warmは〈目的〉を表す不定詞の副詞的用法。

▶ stayは「〜の (状態の) ままでいる」という意味で、〈S + V + C〉の構文を作る。Cの位置に来るのは形容詞のほか、分詞や名詞など。

例He stayed calm even in the face of danger.
「危険に直面しても、彼は冷静であり続けた」

⑥ **In our painting, you see people from all over the world**

sharing the warmth of a huge mitten.

▶ you see people from all over the world sharing ～は〈S + V + O + 現在分詞〉の知覚動詞構文で、「SはOが～しているのを見る」という意味。people from all over the world がO。

> ✐ 次の英文を日本語に直しなさい。

We saw a train crossing the bridge over the river.

⑦ **It is decorated with Easter eggs which represent life and hope.**

▶ be decorated with ～は受動態で、「～で飾られている」という状態を表す。

⇒p.49 G-❸

> ✐ 次の英文を日本語に直しなさい。

The streets were decorated with colorful lights.

▶ which は Easter eggs を先行詞とする関係代名詞。このあとに続く動詞 represent の主語の役割を果たしている。 ⇒p.48 G-❶

⑧ **Our painting shows that people's warm hearts can hatch the egg of hope and bring a peaceful life to us all.**

▶ show that ～は「～ということを示している」という意味。that節の主語は people's warm hearts「人々の温かい心」で、これを受ける動詞は hatch「(卵)をかえす」と bring「～をもたらす」の2つ。

⑨ **I still do not have a clear answer to the question: Who am I as a person and as an artist?**

▶ an answer to the question で「その質問に対する答え」という意味。前置詞に to を使うことに注意。

▶ コロン (:) のあとの疑問文は、直前の the question の具体的内容。なお、この疑問文は、教科書p.42の3行目にすでに出てきていたもの。

⑩ **But one thing has become clear: my art has the power to make people "super happy."**

▶ has become clear は〈完了〉を表す現在完了形で、「(現在までにすでに)明らかになっている」という意味。

▶ コロン (:) のあとに続く文は、one thing の具体的内容。

▶ to make people "super happy" は、直前の the power を修飾する不定詞の形容詞的用法。〈make + O + C〉で「OをCの状態にする」という意味。

▶ super は副詞で、「とても、すごく」の意味を表す。very よりもくだけた表現。

Grammar for Communication

1 | 関係代名詞：who、whose、whom、which、that

関係代名詞は代名詞と接続詞の働きを兼ねる語で、関係代名詞が修飾する語句のことを先行詞と呼ぶ。先行詞が「人」の場合にはwho、whose、whom、「人以外」の場合にはwhichを使う。また、thatとwhoseはどちらの場合にも用いられる。

---

1. who：先行詞「人」、主格
◆ Do you know the girl **who** sang that English song? （＊sangの主語）
（あなたはあの英語の歌を歌った女の子を知っていますか）

2. whose：先行詞「人、人以外」、所有格
◆ He is a boy **whose** father is an astronaut. （＊his fatherのhisの代用）
（彼は父親が宇宙飛行士の少年だ）
◆ She lent me a book **whose** title was very long. （＊its titleのitsの代用）
（彼女は題名がとても長い本を私に貸してくれた）

3. whom：先行詞「人」、目的格 （＊口語ではしばしばwhoで代用される）
◆ They are the singers (**who [whom, that]**) I like very much.
（彼らは私がとても好きな歌手だ） （＊likeの目的語）

4. which：先行詞「人以外」、主格
◆ She has a guitar **which [that]** was made in Spain. （＊wasの主語）
（彼女はスペインで作られたギターを持っている）

5. which：先行詞「人以外」、目的格
◆ This is the bike (**which [that]**) my uncle gave me. （＊gaveの目的語）
（これはおじが私にくれた自転車だ）

■ **特に関係代名詞が文の主語を先行詞とする場合は、主語と動詞の間に関係代名詞節が割り込んで、動詞が後ろに押しやられる形になる。文構造を正しくつかもう。**

◆ The restaurant 〔(**which**) my uncle opened last year〕
  S（whichの先行詞）　　　　　　　〔関係代名詞節〕

has become　popular. （おじが昨年開業したレストランは人気が出ている）
V（助動詞＋動詞）　　C

2 分詞の形容詞的用法

分詞には現在分詞と過去分詞があり、現在分詞は「〜している…」「〜する…」という能動の意味を、過去分詞は「〜された…」「〜される…」という受動の意味を表す。分詞は単独で名詞の前に置かれる (前置修飾) ほか、〈分詞＋修飾語句〉の形で名詞の後ろに置かれもする (後置修飾)。いずれの場合も名詞を修飾しているので、形容詞と同じ働きになる。

1.〈名詞＋現在分詞＋修飾語句〉

◆ She is a student **studying** Persian at this university.

（彼女はこの大学でペルシャ語を勉強している学生だ）

（= She is a student who studies Persian at this university.）

2.〈名詞＋過去分詞＋修飾語句〉

◆ This is a movie **based** on a famous novel.

（これは有名な小説に基づいた映画だ）

（= This is a movie which[that] is based on a famous novel.）

3 受動態：be動詞＋過去分詞

「〜が…する」のように「動作を行う側」（動作主）に焦点を当てた文を能動態、逆に「〜が…される」のように「動作を受ける側」に焦点を当てた文を受動態 (または受け身) と呼ぶ。

◆ Soccer **is loved** around the world.

（サッカーは世界中で愛されている）

◆ These cookies **were baked by** Mary. （＊動作主はby 〜などで表す）

（これらのクッキーはメアリーによって焼かれた）

◆ Butter **is made from** milk.

（バターは牛乳から作られる）

◆ The top of the mountain **is covered with** snow.

（山頂は雪で覆われている）（＊状態を表す受動態）

◆ The wall **will be painted in** green.

（壁は緑色に塗られるでしょう）　＊〈助動詞＋ be ＋過去分詞〉⇒詳細はp.145 G-❷

確認問題

語彙・表現

1 次の語を（　）内の指示にしたがって書きかえなさい。

(1) angry（名詞に）　　　　　　(2) accept（反意語に）

(3) create（名詞に）　　　　　　(4) build（反意語に）

2 第 1 音節にアクセント（強勢）のある語を 2 つ選び、記号で答えなさい。

ア　in-jus-tice　　　　　イ　rep-re-sent　　　　ウ　col-lab-o-ra-tion

エ　Bel-gium　　　　　　オ　earth-quake　　　　カ　ca-reer

3 日本語に合うように、（　）内に適切な語を入れなさい。

(1) そのテレビドラマは実話に基づいている。

The TV drama is (　　　) (　　　) a true story.

(2) 私の祖母は幸せな人生を送りました。

My grandmother (　　　) a happy (　　　).

(3) そのイベントは地元のレストランとの協力で実現した。

The event was realized (　　　) (　　　) with local restaurants.

(4) ステージは美しい花で飾られていた。

The stage was (　　　) (　　　) beautiful flowers.

文のパターン・文法

1 （　）内に適切な関係代名詞を入れなさい。

(1) Bill wants a book (　　　) illustrates how a car engine works.

(2) I have a friend (　　　) mother is a famous writer.

(3) Is this the CD (　　　) you talked about last week?

(4) That is the tallest tower (　　　) Japan has ever built.

2 （　）内の語を適切な形に直しなさい。

(1) One of the languages (speak) in Canada is French.

(2) Do you know the boys (swim) in the river?

(3) The students (talk) to each other under the tree are my classmates.

(4) We have some books (write) for children by that writer.

3 ( ) 内の語句を並べかえて、英文を完成させなさい。

(1) (our tour / visited / was / the first country / on / we) France.

_____ France.

(2) (working / at / the students / look) as volunteers.

_____ as volunteers.

(3) (seen / by / never / taken / any pictures / I've) the photographer.

_____ the photographer.

(4) This is one of (that / collected / the gallery / were / the paintings / by).

This is one of _____.

(5) At the summer festival, (Alice / in Japan / a yukata / wearing / made / was).

At the summer festival, _____.

> **総合**

次のミヤザキさんの文を読んで、あとの問いに答えなさい。

---

①A barber in Ofunato, Iwate, asked me to paint a sign for his shop. I not only made the sign, but I also painted his whole shop in bright colors!

I had doubts about the usefulness of my art project, but I did not want to think that art has no power ②(　　　) (　　　) (　　　) of disaster. ③Money and supplies that people donate can be of great help. But working together on a painting and sharing the joy of (④) can also help. People can laugh and smile even in the worst conditions.

問1 下線部①について、ミヤザキさんが理髪店から頼まれたこと以外にしたことは何でしたか。日本語で説明しなさい。

問2 下線部②が「災害に直面して」という意味になるように、( ) 内に入る最も適切な3語を書きなさい。

問3 下線部③を日本語に直しなさい。

問4 ④の ( ) 内に入る最も適切な語を選びなさい。

ア decision 　 イ creation 　 ウ frustration 　 エ solution

問5 ミヤザキさんが被災地でアート・プロジェクトを行う意義を簡潔に述べている1文を探し、最初と最後の2語を書きなさい。

Digging into Mystery

- ☐ dig [díg]
- ☐ mystery [místəri]
- ☐ Sydney [sídni]
- ☐ presentation [prèzntéiʃən]
- ☐ prehistory [pri:hístri]
- ☐ introduction [intrədʌ́kʃən]
- ☐ cave [kéiv]
- ☐ prehistoric [pri:histɔ́:rik]
- ☐ impress [imprés]
- ☐ remind ~ of ...
- ☐ artifact [á:rtifæ̀kt]
- ☐ earthen [ɔ́:rθən]
- ☐ c. (circa)
- ☐ mysterious [mistíəriəs]
- ☐ take one's eyes away
- ☐ in a moment
- ☐ incidentally [ìnsidéntəli]
- ☐ pattern [pǽtərn]
- ☐ pottery [pátəri]

Four Japanese high school students from Aomori are visiting their sister school in Sydney, Australia. ①They are on a study tour to learn about Australian history and culture. ②They are going to give a presentation about Japanese prehistory. Shota will be the first speaker.

1 Introduction: *Dogu* and Australian cave paintings

Good morning. ③Yesterday you introduced us to some examples of Australian prehistoric paintings. We were very impressed.

④Some of the paintings reminded us of Japan's prehistoric artifacts. The photo on the left is an example of *dogu*. ⑤They are earthen figures created in the Jomon period (*c.* 11,000 B.C. − *c.* 500 B.C.). The Australian cave painting on the right is probably older. ⑥There is something strange and mysterious about both these prehistoric artifacts. You can't take your eyes away.

In a moment, we'll tell you more about Japan's mysterious little *dogu*. ⑦But first, we'd like to share with you what we've learned about life in the Jomon period. ⑧Incidentally, the Jomon period gets its name from the "rope patterns" that appear in its pottery.

⑨People have found Jomon artifacts all over Japan. ⑩Misaki, our next speaker, will tell you about what was discovered at one of the most important sites: Sannai-Maruyama.

このセクションの内容

前日にオーストラリアの（A. 　　　　　）の壁画を見た青森の高校生たちは、それらが日本の縄文時代に作られた（B. 　　　）とある種の共通点を持っていることを指摘した。最初の発表者ショウタはオーストラリアの高校生たちに「縄文時代」という名前は（C. 　　　）に見られる縄目の文様から来ていることを説明した。

① **They are on a study tour to learn about Australian history and culture.**
- ▶ be on a tour で「旅行中である」という意味。
- ▶ to learn 〜 は、tour を修飾する不定詞の形容詞的用法。

② **They are going to give a presentation about Japanese prehistory.**
- ▶ be going to 〜 は「〜することになっている」という近い将来のほぼ確定的な予定を表す。
- ▶ give a presentation about 〜 で「〜についての発表[プレゼンテーション]を行う」という意味。

③ **Yesterday you introduced us to some examples of Australian prehistoric paintings.**
- ▶〈introduce + O（人）+ to 〜〉で「（人）に〜を紹介する」という意味。

④ **Some of the paintings reminded us of Japan's prehistoric artifacts.**
- ▶〈remind + O（人）+ of 〜〉「（人）に〜のことを思い出させる」（≒ make O think of 〜）という意味で、しばしば無生物を主語とする。

✍ 次の英文を日本語に直しなさい。

The song always reminds me of my high school days.

⑤ **They are earthen figures created in the Jomon period (*c.* 11,000 B.C. − *c.* 500 B.C.).**
- ▶ created は過去分詞の形容詞的用法。created in the Jomon period「縄文時代に作られた」が earthen figures「土製の人形」を後ろから修飾している。

✍（ ）内の語を適切な形に変えなさい。

彼は子どもたちが描いた絵に魅了された。

He was fascinated by the pictures (draw) by children.

⑥ **There is something strange and mysterious about both these prehistoric artifacts.**

▶ 〈There is something + 形容詞 + about ～〉で「～には何か…なものがある」という意味。

▶ both these prehistoric artifacts は、教科書 p.61 に掲載されている Photo 1 の土偶、および Photo 2 のオーストラリアの先史時代の壁画の2つを指す。この both は形容詞で、「両方の、双方の」という意味。

⑦ **But first, we'd like to share with you what we've learned about life in the Jomon period.**

▶ we'd like to ～ は「～したいと思う」という意味で、we want to ～ よりも丁寧な表現。

▶ share ～ with ... は「～を…と共有する」という意味。ここでは名詞節の what 以下全体が share の目的語となるため、with you が前に置かれている。

▶ what we've learned の what は関係代名詞で、「～すること」という意味。what は名詞節を作り、文の主語、目的語、補語になる。ここでは動詞 share の目的語になっている。　　　　　　　　　　　　　⇒p.65 G-❷

　　✍ 英文を完成させなさい。

あなたがそこで見たことを私たちに話してください。

Please tell us (　　　) (　　　) (　　　) there.

⑧ **Incidentally, the Jomon period gets its name from the "rope patterns" that appear in its pottery.**

▶ incidentally は「ついでながら、ちなみに」という意味を表す談話標識。

▶ its name および its pottery の its は、どちらも the Jomon period を指す。

▶ that は直前の the "rope patterns" を先行詞とする関係代名詞。動詞 appear の主語となっているので、主格。

⑨ **People have found Jomon artifacts all over Japan.**

▶ have found は現在完了の経験用法で、「これまでに～を発見してきた」という意味。

⑩ **Misaki, our next speaker, will tell you about what was discovered at one of the most important sites: Sannai-Maruyama.**

▶ Misaki と our next speaker は、コンマ (,) をはさんで、同格の関係にある。

▶ what was discovered は「発見されたもの」という意味で、この what は関係代名詞。　　　　　　　　　　　　　　　　　　　　⇒p.65 G-❷

　　✍ 次の英文を日本語に直しなさい。

She made a speech about what she learned through volunteer work.

────────────────────────────

▶ one of the most important sites「最も重要な現場の1つ」。site は「（重要なことが起きた）場所」という意味で用いられる。*cf.* a historic site「史跡」

- ☐ make a guess
- ☐ excavation [èkskəvéɪʃən]
- ☐ throughout [θruáʊt]
- ☐ wooden [wúdn]
- ☐ pillar [pílər]
- ☐ structure [strʌ́ktʃər]
- ☐ evidence [évɪdəns]
- ☐ permanently [pə́ːrmənəntli]
- ☐ hunt [hʌ́nt]
- ☐ berry [béri]
- ☐ pit [pít]
- ☐ a pit house
- ☐ jewelry [dʒúːəlri]
- ☐ made of ~
- ☐ last [lǽst]
- ☐ due to ~
- ☐ climate [kláɪmət]
- ☐ not ~ but ...
- ☐ tourist [túərəst]

2　Life in the Jomon period

Thank you, Shota.

①Since the Jomon people left no written records, researchers have been trying to make a guess about them based on excavations throughout Japan.

One of the most important excavations began in 1992 at the Sannai-Maruyama site in Aomori.

②Researchers found six huge holes in the ground with the remains of wooden pillars. They were the base for some large structure. ③The researchers also found evidence of another huge wooden structure. Probably hundreds of families lived in this village.

We know that people first arrived there 5,900 years ago. ④Before that, they had been moving from one place to another, but then some of them chose to live there permanently. They hunted animals, fished in rivers or in the sea, and picked berries and mushrooms. ⑤They lived in pit houses and knew how to cook in earthen pots. ⑥The Jomon people loved to decorate themselves with jewelry made of bone, stone, and shell.

⑦This village had lasted for 1,000 years before it disappeared, perhaps due to climate change. ⑧Now, lots of people are coming back to this site, not to live there, of course, but as tourists.

Now, Takuya will tell us more about *dogu*.

このセクションの内容

２番目の発表者ミサキは1992年から発掘が始まった青森の三内丸山にある
(A.　　　　) の概要を説明した。この場所に定住することを選んだ縄文時
代の人々は、(B.　　　　) に住み、手に入れた食べ物を土器で調理した。
(C.　　　　) のために消滅するまで、人々が暮らす村は1,000年間存続した。

① **Since the Jomon people left no written records, researchers have been trying to make a guess about them based on excavations throughout Japan.**

　　▶ since は「〜なので」と理由を表す接続詞。

　　▶ left no written records は「書かれた形での記録をまったく残さなかった」
　　　という意味。〈no + 名詞〉は「１つの［１人の］〜もない」と全否定する。

　　▶ have been trying 〜は、過去のある時点から継続する動作を表す現在完了
　　　進行形。

　　　　✍ 次の英文を日本語に直しなさい。

　　　I have been trying to contact John since last night.

_____

　　▶ make a guess は「推測する」という意味。

　　▶ based on 〜は「〜に基づいて」という意味。もとは過去分詞の分詞構文
　　　であるが、現在では慣用的な熟語として用いられる。

　　　　例 Police arrested the man based on material evidence.
　　　　「警察はその男性を物証に基づいて逮捕した」

② **Researchers found six huge holes in the ground with the remains of wooden pillars.**

　　▶ remains は「遺跡」「遺体」の意味でも用いられることが多いが、ここでは
　　　the remains of wooden pillars で「(発掘で見つかった) 木の柱の残骸」のこと。

③ **The researchers also found evidence of another huge wooden structure.**

　　▶ evidence「証拠」は数えられない名詞。*cf.* scientific evidence「科学的証拠」

　　▶ another は「別の、もう１つの」という意味の形容詞。

④ **Before that, they had been moving from one place to another, but then some of them chose to live there permanently.**

　　▶ had been moving は過去完了進行形 (had been V-ing) で、過去のある時
　　　点まで継続していた動作・状態を表す。　　　　　　　　　　⇒p.64 G-❶

　　▶ この文では、「三内丸山遺跡」周辺に人々が最初に住み着いた「5,900年前」
　　　を基準として、それよりも前にずっと継続していた状態を過去完了進行形

で表している。

> ✍ 次の英文を日本語に直しなさい。

Emma had been studying Japanese for three years when she came to Japan.

▶ from one place to another は「ある場所から別の場所へ」という意味。
▶ choose to ～は「～することを選ぶ」という意味。

⑤ **They lived in pit houses and knew how to cook in earthen pots.**

▶ how to ～は「～のし方、～する方法」という意味で、動詞knewの目的語。

> ✍ 英文を完成させなさい。

祖父はコンピュータの使い方を習いたがっている。

My grandfather wants to learn (　　　) (　　　) (　　　) a computer.

⑥ **The Jomon people loved to decorate themselves with jewelry made of bone, stone, and shell.**

▶ love to ～は「～することを非常に好む」という意味。like to ～よりも、好きな度合いが強い。
▶ decorate ～ with ... で「～を…で飾る」という意味。
▶ made of ～「(材料)で作られた」は、過去分詞の形容詞的用法。made of bone, stone, and shell は、直前の jewelry「装身具」を修飾している。
cf. made from ～「(原料)でできた」

⑦ **This village had lasted for 1,000 years before it disappeared, perhaps due to climate change.**

▶ had lasted は過去完了(had + 過去分詞)。過去のある時点を基準に、それまで継続していた動作や状態を表す。この文では、before 以下で述べている「おそらく村が気候変動のために消滅した」過去の時点を基準とし、「それまでの1,000年間ずっと村が存続していた」ことを過去完了で表している。

⇒p.64 G-❶

> ✍ 次の英文を日本語に直しなさい。

He had lived in Tokyo for 20 years before he moved to Sendai.

---

⑧ **Now, lots of people are coming back to this site, not to live there, of course, but as tourists.**

▶ this site は the Sannai-Maruyama site のこと。
▶ not to live there, of course, but as tourists は「もちろんそこに住むためではなく、観光客として」という意味。not ～ but ...は、2つの事柄を対比して、「～ではなく…」と述べる言い方。

このセクションの内容 の答え→　A. 遺跡　B. 竪穴(式)住居　C. 気候変動

Lesson 4

☐ all kinds of 〜
☐ take a look at 〜
☐ cultural [kΛltʃərəl]
☐ Venus [víːnəs]
☐ pregnant [prégnənt]
☐ goddess [gádəs]
☐ pray [préı]
☐ unique [juːníːk]
☐ design [dızáın]
☐ be unique in design
☐ triangular [traɪǽŋgjələr]
☐ mask [mǽsk]
☐ -shaped [ʃéıpt]
☐ obsess [əbsés]
☐ be obsessed with 〜
☐ after all, 〜
☐ figure out 〜
☐ ritual [rítʃuəl]

3　The mystery of *dogu*

Thank you, Misaki.

①The Jomon people created all kinds of artifacts. In our presentation, however, we'd like to talk about *dogu*.

②Let's take a look at five *dogu* which are very important cultural treasures.

The first one, "Jomon Venus," probably represents a pregnant woman. The second one, "Jomon Goddess," looks very modern. ③Some people think that the third one represents a pregnant woman praying for a healthy baby. The last two are unique in design. Look at the triangular mask in the fourth one, and the heart-shaped face in the last one.

④You may wonder why the Jomon people created *dogu*. ⑤Perhaps they were obsessed with *dogu*. ⑥After all, people have found more than 18,000 *dogu* throughout Japan.

⑦Researchers are trying to figure out the true reason behind the creation of *dogu*, but it still remains a mystery. Perhaps they were used for rituals. Or maybe they were just toys. ⑧We don't know what the real purpose of *dogu* was, but we do know that they were an important part of the Jomon people's life.

Finally, our last speaker is Ayumi.

このセクションの内容

３番目の発表者タクヤは、縄文時代の （A.　　　） のうち、特に土偶に注目した。土偶は （B.　　　） に使われていたかもしれないし、ただの玩具であったかもしれない。土偶が作られた本当の （C.　　　） は今なお謎であるが、それらが縄文時代の人々の生活の重要な部分を占めていたことは間違いない。

① **The Jomon people created all kinds of artifacts.**

▶ all kinds of ～は「あらゆる種類の～、さまざまな～」という意味。all sorts of ～もほぼ同じ意味。

② **Let's take a look at five *dogu* which are very important cultural treasures.**

▶ take a look at ～は「～をちょっと見る」という意味。〈take a[an] ＋動作を表す名詞〉は「１回限りの動作・行為を行う」ことを表し、look の前にさまざまな形容詞を置いて用いられる。

　　例 The airport staff took a close look at my passport.
　　「空港職員は私のパスポートをじっくりと見た」

▶ which は直前の five *dogu* を先行詞とする主格の関係代名詞。

③ **Some people think that the third one represents a pregnant woman praying for a healthy baby**

▶ the third one の one は「同種のものの１つ」を表す代名詞で、ここでは one ＝ *dogu*。

▶ praying は動詞 pray「祈る」の現在分詞で、形容詞的用法。praying for a healthy baby が直前の a pregnant woman を修飾している。

　　✍ 次の英文を日本語に直しなさい。

　　Who is the girl playing over there?

④ **You may wonder why the Jomon people created *dogu*.**

▶〈S ＋ V ＋ O（疑問詞節）〉の文。wonder why ～で「なぜ～か不思議に思う」という意味。　　　　　　　　　　　　　　　　　　　　⇒p.65 G-❸

　　✍ 英文を完成させなさい。

　　彼女はなぜあんなに悲しそうなのだろう。

　　I wonder (　　　) (　　　) (　　　) so sad.

⑤ **Perhaps they were obsessed with *dogu*.**

▶ be obsessed with ～は「～にとりつかれている、～で頭がいっぱいである、～に夢中である」という意味。

　　例 She has been obsessed with making sweets lately.

「彼女は最近お菓子作りに夢中だ」

⑥ **After all, people have found more than 18,000 _dogu_ throughout Japan.**

▶このAfter allは「何しろ」という意味で、あとには理由が続く。ここでは、前文の「おそらく人々は土偶に夢中になっていたのだろう」という推測を裏付ける事実として、日本各地から土偶が出土していることを指摘している。

▶have foundは〈完了〉を表す現在完了形。

▶throughoutは「〜の至る所で」という意味を表す前置詞。

⑦ **Researchers are trying to figure out the true reason behind the creation of _dogu_, but it still remains a mystery.**

▶figure outは「（原因など）を解明する、（解決法など）を考え出す」という意味。目的語には、reason「理由」、mystery「謎」、solution「解決法」などの名詞のほか、how to 〜や疑問詞節が来ることもある。

　🖉 次の英文を日本語に直しなさい。

I can't figure out how to solve this problem.

▶itは文前半のthe true reason behind the creation of _dogu_ を指す。

▶remainは「〜のままである」という意味の動詞で、〈S＋V＋C（形容詞・分詞・名詞）〉の形の文を作る。remains a mysteryで「謎のままである」という意味。

⑧ **We don't know what the real purpose of _dogu_ was, but we do know that they were an important part of the Jomon people's life.**

▶butをはさんで、前半は〈S＋V＋O（疑問詞節）〉の間接疑問文。動詞knowのあとに、疑問詞whatが導く疑問詞節が続いている。　⇒p.65 G-❸

What　　was　　the real purpose of _dogu_?
C（疑問詞）　 V 　　　 S

We don't know **what** the real purpose of _dogu_ was.
　　　　　　　｜疑問詞　　　S'　　　　　V'｜
S 　　V 　　　　　O（疑問詞節＝名詞節）

▶but以降は、〈S＋V＋O（that節）〉の形。

▶we do knowのdoは強調を表し、会話では強く発音される。ここではthat節の内容、つまり「土偶について解明されている事柄」を強調するために、knowの直前に置かれている。動詞を強調する場合、三人称単数現在ではdoesが、過去形の文ではdidが用いられる。

　例 I did believe that he would win the race.
　　「彼がそのレースに勝つと私は固く信じていた」

　このセクションの内容 の答え→　A. 遺物　B. 儀式　C. 目的

教科書 p.66 Section 4

□ conclusion [kənklúːʒən]
□ chasm [kǽzm]
□ exert [ɪgzə́ːrt]
□ influence [ínfluəns]
□ well-known [wélnòun]
□ expo [ékspou]
□ inspire [ɪnspáɪər]
□ separate [sépərèit]
□ get to ～
□ come to ～
□ enable [ɪnéɪbl]
□ enable ～to ...
□ look back at ～
□ up close

4 Conclusion: bridging the chasm

①The Jomon culture still exerts great influence on us today. Okamoto Taro, a well-known Japanese artist, created the Tower of the Sun for the Osaka Expo in 1970. ②It was inspired by the *dogu* with a heart-shaped face.

③Yamaoka Nobutaka, a movie director, had spent five years visiting 100 Jomon sites before filming a movie about the Jomon culture. He says, "④There is a great chasm separating the Jomon period and us. ⑤But as we get to know more about it, we come to see something that enables us to look at ourselves in new ways." ⑥When you look at these *dogu*, try to imagine that they are looking back at you through 10,000-year-old eyes.

You sparked our interest in Australia's prehistoric art. ⑦We hope we've sparked your interest in Japan's. ⑧Next year we hope some of you can come to visit us in Aomori. We'll go together to Sannai-Maruyama. ⑨You'll see the Jomon culture up close.

Thank you. ⑩If you have any questions, we'd be happy to answer them.

このセクションの内容

最後の発表者アユミは、縄文文化が今日の私たちに与えている（A.　　　　）について考察した。例えば岡本太郎の『（B.　　　　）』は、ハート型の顔をした土偶からインスピレーションを受けた作品である。また、縄文文化に関する（C.　　　）を制作した山岡信貴は、縄文時代について知るにつれて、私たちは自分自身を新たな目で見ることができると語っている。

① **The Jomon culture still exerts great influence on us today.**

▶ exert influence on ～で「～に影響を及ぼす」という意味。

② **It was inspired by the *dogu* with a heart-shaped face.**

▶ It は前文の the Tower of the Sun「太陽の塔」を指す。

▶ was inspired は受動態の過去形で、「インスピレーションを受けた」という意味。by 以下は動作主を表す。

▶ with a heart-shaped face は「ハート型の顔をした」という意味。この with は「(性質・外見として) ～をもった」という意味。*cf.* a dress with a flower pattern「花柄のワンピース」

③ **Yamaoka Nobutaka, a movie director, had spent five years visiting 100 Jomon sites before filming a movie about the Jomon culture.**

▶ had spent は過去完了。この文では、before 以下で述べている出来事よりもさらに過去で起きていたことを表す〈大過去〉の用法。

✎ ( )内の語を適切な形に変えなさい。ただし、1語とは限りません。

ミユキは東京に来る前に、3年間ロンドンで暮らしていた。

Miyuki (live) in London for three years before she (come) to Tokyo.

▶ spend ～ (in) V-ing は「…することに～ (時間)を費やす」という意味。

▶ before filming は〈前置詞 + V-ing(動名詞)〉で、「撮影する前に」という意味。before he filmed a movie ～と言いかえられる。

④ **There is a great chasm separating the Jomon period and us.**

▶ There is ～ V-ing. で「V している～がある」、つまり「～が V している」という意味の構文。現在分詞は「～」の位置に来る名詞句の状態や様子を説明している。この文は、現在進行形を使って以下のように言いかえることができる。

A great chasm is separating the Jomon period and us.

⑤ **But as we get to know more about it, we come to see something that enables us to look at ourselves in new ways.**

▶接続詞の as は「～するにつれて」という意味で、2つの物事が互いに影響し合いながら進行することを表す。

▶ get to ～は「～するようになる」という意味。to のあとには know や understand など、〈知覚〉を表す動詞が来る。

✎ 次の英文を日本語に直しなさい。

Mike and Bill are getting to understand each other.

_____

▶ come to ～は「～するようになる」という意味。

このセクションの内容 の答え→　A. 影響　B. 太陽の塔　C. 映画

▶ that は代名詞の something を先行詞とする主格の関係代名詞。

▶ 〈enable + O + to ～〉で「O が～することを可能にする」という意味。しばしば無生物主語をとる。

> ✎ 次の英文を日本語に直しなさい。

The Internet has enabled us to gather information in a short time.

⑥ **When you look at these *dogu*, try to imagine that they are looking back at you through 10,000-year-old eyes.**

▶ try to ～は「～しようと努める」という意味。

▶ imagine that ～は「～と想像する」という意味。they = these *dogu*

▶ look back at ～で「(相手が) ～に視線を返す」という意味。

▶ through 10,000-year-old eyes「1 万年の時を経た目を通して」という意味。

⑦ **We hope we've sparked your interest in Japan's.**

▶ We hope (that) ～で「～と願う」という意味。ここでは that 節の that が省略されている。

▶ we've sparked は〈完了〉を表す現在完了。spark *one's* interest in ...「…に対する～の興味を起こさせる」という意味。

▶ Japan's のあとには、前文の Australia's prehistoric art と共通する prehistoric art が省略されている。

⑧ **Next year we hope some of you can come to visit us in Aomori.**

▶ これも we hope (that) ～「～と願う」の文。

▶ come to visit us in Aomori「青森の私たちを訪ねて来る」という意味。話者がいる場所へ「行く」場合、動詞は go ではなく come を用いる。

⑨ **You'll see the Jomon culture up close.**

▶ up close は「間近で、すぐ近くで」という意味。

> ✎ 次の英文を日本語に直しなさい。

Many animals can be seen up close in the zoo.

⑩ **If you have any questions, we'd be happy to answer them.**

▶ we'd (= we would) be happy to ～で「喜んで～したい」と話者の希望を控え目に述べる言い方。

> 例 I'd be glad to show you around the city of Kyoto.
> 「喜んで京都の街をご案内いたします」

▶ them は if 節の中の any questions を指す。

Grammar for Communication

1　過去完了：had＋過去分詞／過去完了進行形：had been V-ing

過去完了は過去のある時点までの動作や状態の完了・結果、経験、継続を表す。
現在までの動作や状態の完了・結果、経験、継続を表す現在完了の基準となる時点を現在から過去のある時点にそのまま移動させたと考えればよい。
また、過去完了は過去のある時点よりもさらに過去に起こったことを表すことができる。これを「大過去」という。

1. 完了・結果
◆We **had spent** almost all our money when we arrived at the store.
（私たちは店に着いたときにはほとんどすべてのお金を使っていた）
◆John **had** just **left** the office when I called him.
（私がジョンに電話したとき、彼はちょうど会社を出たところだった）

2. 経験
◆She **had seen** the movie three times before she saw it that night.
（彼女はその夜その映画を見るまでに、それを3回見ていた）
◆**Had** you ever **read** a Japanese novel before you came to Japan?
（日本に来る前に日本の小説を読んだことがありましたか）

3. 継続
◆He **had lived** in Nagoya for ten years before he came to Tokyo.
（彼は東京に来る前に名古屋に10年間住んでいた）
◆She **had been** sick for a week when she went to the doctor.
（医者に診てもらったとき、彼女は1週間具合を悪くしていた）
◆The boys **had been practicing** soccer for two hours when it began to rain.
（雨が降り始めたとき、少年たちは2時間サッカーを練習していた）
＊過去のある時点までの動作の継続は、過去完了進行形（had been V-ing）で表す。

4. 大過去
◆We found the ball that we **had lost** in the park.
（私たちは公園で失くしていたボールを見つけた）
◆I took a taxi to the station, but the train **had** already **left**.
（私は駅までタクシーを飛ばしたが、列車はすでに出発していた）

2 | 関係代名詞 what

関係代名詞の what は先行詞をその中に含んでいる。先行詞は具体的ではなく、漠然と「もの、こと」の意味を表す。つまり、この what は the thing(s) which [that] に言いかえられる。

I told him **what** I had heard from you.（きみから聞いたことを彼に話した）
＝I told him the thing(s) which [that] I had heard from you.

what 節は名詞節を作り、文の中で主語、目的語、補語の働きをする。

1. 主語

◆**What** is necessary now is to work together.
　　　　S　　　　　　　　V　　　　C
（今必要なことは協力することだ）

2. 目的語

◆Do you remember **what** he said to us?
　S　 V　　　　　　　O
（彼が私たちに言ったことを覚えていますか）

◆I'm interested in what he is doing now.
　　　　　　　前置詞　　　　O
（私は彼が今やっていることに興味がある）

3. 補語

◆That is **what** I was looking for.（あれは私が探していたものだ）
　S　 V　　　　C

3 | S＋V＋O (O＝疑問詞節/if節)

疑問詞（why / what / who / which / when / how など）や接続詞 if（～かどうか）は節（S＋V …）を従えて、全体として名詞節の役割を果たすことができる。ここでは目的語として用いられている。

◆They wonder **when** we're going to do it.
　（彼らは私たちがいつそれをするのだろうかと思っている）

◆I'd like to know **where** she got the bag.
　（私は彼女がどこでそのバッグを買ったのかを知りたい）

◆I don't know **if** he will come to the party tomorrow.
　（私は彼が明日パーティーに来るかどうか知らない）

確認問題

語彙・表現

1 次の語を（　）内の指示にしたがって書きかえなさい。

(1) introduce（名詞に）　　　　(2) mystery（形容詞に）

(3) prehistory（形容詞に）　　　(4) earth（形容詞に）

2 次の各組で下線部の発音がほかと異なる語を1つずつ選び、記号で答えなさい。

(1) ア　Sydney　　　イ　dig　　　ウ　climate　　　エ　ritual

(2) ア　chose　　　イ　chasm　　　ウ　cave　　　エ　cultural

3 日本語に合うように、（　）内に適切な語を入れなさい。

(1) ちょっとこのグラフを見ましょう。

Let's (　　　　) (　　　　) (　　　　) at this graph.

(2) 私たちは次に何が起こるかを推測した。

We (　　　　) (　　　　) (　　　　) about what would happen next.

(3) 研究者たちはその壁画を間近で観察した。

The researchers studied the cave paintings (　　　　) (　　　　).

(4) 列車はその事故のために10分遅れで到着した。

The train arrived 10 minutes late (　　　　) (　　　　) the accident.

文のパターン・文法

1 次の過去完了形は、a.完了、b.結果、c.継続、d.経験、e.大過去のうちのどの用法にあたるか、記号で答えなさい。

(1) The ship had reached the island before the sunset.　　　　(　　)

(2) She had been to France three times by then.　　　　(　　)

(3) We had known each other for two years when we went to college.

(　　)

(4) He gave me a book that he had bought in London.　　　　(　　)

2 （　）内の語句を並べかえて、英文を完成させなさい。

(1) Don't put off till tomorrow (can / today / what / do / you).

Don't put off till tomorrow _____.

(2) Is this (asked / what / to / you / buy / me)?

Is this _____?

(3) We can't (an accident / will / when / happen / tell).

We can't _____.

(4) Do you (to / will / know / if / the party / come / David) tonight?

Do you _____ tonight?

3 〔 〕内の指示にしたがって、英文を書きかえなさい。

(1) Where is Anne going to spend her vacation? 〔I wonder ～の文に〕

I wonder _____.

(2) How did Emma get to know the man? 〔書き出しに続けて SVO の文に〕

I don't know _____.

(3) Kevin has been listening to the radio for two hours.

〔「私が訪ねたとき、ケビンは～していた」という文に〕

Kevin _____

_____.

総合

次のタクヤの文を読んで、あとの問いに答えなさい。

---

①You may wonder why the Jomon people created *dogu*. ②Perhaps they were obsessed with *dogu*. After all, people have found more than 18,000 *dogu* throughout Japan.

Researchers are trying to figure out the true reason behind the creation of *dogu*, but ③it still remains a mystery. Perhaps they were used for rituals. Or maybe they were just toys. We don't ④(was / the real purpose / know / of *dogu* / what), but we (⑤) know that they were an important part of the Jomon people's life.

問1 下線部①を日本語に直しなさい。

問2 タクヤが下線部②のように考える理由は何ですか。日本語で説明しなさい。

問3 下線部③が指す内容を本文中のひと続きの英語8語で答えなさい。

問4 下線部④の ( ) 内の語句を並べかえて、英文を完成させなさい。

問5 ⑤の ( ) 内に入る最も適切な語を選びなさい。

　　ア don't　　イ did　　ウ do　　エ didn't

Lesson 5　Roots & Shoots

- ☐ root [rúːt]
- ☐ shoot [ʃúːt]
- ☐ Jane Goodall [dʒéɪn gúdɔːl]
- ☐ chimpanzee [tʃìmpænzíː]
- ☐ conserve [kənsə́ːrv]
- ☐ interview [íntərvjùː]
- ☐ Dolittle [dúːlɪtl]
- ☐ Tarzan [táːrzən]
- ☐ somehow [sʌ́mhàʊ]
- ☐ someday [sʌ́mdèɪ]
- ☐ in order to ~
- ☐ observe [əbzə́ːrv]
- ☐ behavior [bɪhéɪvjər]
- ☐ determined [dɪtə́ːrmɪnd]
- ☐ advantage [ədvǽntɪdʒ]
- ☐ take advantage of ~

①Jane Goodall is famous not only for her work with chimpanzees but also for her effort to conserve nature. Here, Ken interviews her about her life and work.

1

Ken: Dr. Goodall, ②thank you for taking time for this interview. ③I know that you spent many years studying chimpanzees in Africa. ④When did you first decide to go to Africa?

Jane: ⑤It was after I had read the Doctor Dolittle and the Tarzan books. When I was 11, ⑥I knew that somehow I would go to Africa to live with animals, study them, and write books about them.

Ken: ⑦I'm sure there are lots of young people who want to work with animals someday. How can they prepare themselves?

Jane: ⑧There are a lot of things you can do in order to understand animals. ⑨It is very important that you watch them and observe their behavior. ⑩It is also important that you write notes and ask questions. ⑪If you are really determined, you'll have to work really hard. ⑫Take advantage of every opportunity, and don't give up.

このセクションの内容

ケンは（A.　　　　　　　）の研究で有名なグドール博士にインタビューしている。博士は11歳のときに、すでに（B.　　　　　　）行きを心に決めていた。動物の研究を目指す若者には、あらゆる（C.　　　　　　）を生かして、決してあきらめないようにと勧めている。

① **Jane Goodall is famous not only for her work with chimpanzees but also for her effort to conserve nature.**

▶ be famous for ～「～で有名だ」。*cf.* be famous as ～「～として有名だ」

例 This park is famous for its beautiful cherry blossoms.
「この公園は美しい桜の花で有名である」

▶ not only A but also B「AだけでなくBも」。AとBには文法的に対等の関係にある要素を置く。この文の場合、AとBはどちらも〈前置詞＋名詞〉。

✎ 次の英文を日本語に直しなさい。

The pianist is popular not only in Japan but also abroad.

_____

▶ work with ～は「～の研究」という意味。このwithは「関連・関係」を表す前置詞。

② **thank you for taking time for this interview**

▶ thank you for V-ingは「～してくれてありがとう」という意味。

✎ 英文を完成させなさい。

今日は私たちのパーティーにおいでいただき、ありがとうございます。

(　　　) (　　　) (　　　) (　　　) to our party today.

▶ take time for ～は「～のために時間を取る」という意味。

③ **I know that you spent many years studying chimpanzees in Africa.**

▶ know that ～「～ということを知っている」。that節はknowの目的語。

▶〈spend + O（時間）+ V-ing〉「～するのにO（時間）を費やす、O（時間）を費やして～する」

✎ (　　)内の語を適切な形に変えなさい。

私たちは何時間もかけてその仕事を終えた。

We (spend) many hours (finish) the work.

④ **When did you first decide to go to Africa?**

▶ firstは副詞で「最初に、初めて」（≒ for the first time）の意味。この意味では通例、動詞の直前に置かれる。

⑤ **It was after I had read the Doctor Dolittle and the Tarzan books.**

▶ Itは直前のケンの質問を受けて「最初にアフリカに行く決心をしたとき」のこと。

▶ had readは過去完了で、過去のある時点よりもさらに過去に起きたことを表す。グドール博士がアフリカへ行く決心をした時点を基準にすると、after以下はそれより前の出来事なので、動詞を過去完了形（大過去）にする。

このセクションの内容 の答え→ A. チンパンジー B. アフリカ C. 機会　　　69

⑥ **I knew that somehow I would go to Africa to live with animals, study them, and write books about them**

　▶ somehow「なんとかして、どうにかして」

　▶ 主節の動詞 knew（過去形）に合わせて、that 節の中の助動詞 will も時制の一致によって過去形 would となる。

　▶ to live、(to) study、(to) write は〈目的〉を表す不定詞の副詞的用法。

⑦ **I'm sure there are lots of young people who want to work with animals someday.**

　▶ I'm sure (that) 〜は「きっと〜だと思う」という話者の確信を表す。

　▶ who は lots of young people を先行詞とする主格の関係代名詞。

⑧ **There are a lot of things you can do in order to understand animals.**

　▶ a lot of things のあとに目的格の関係代名詞 that[which] が省略されている。

　▶ in order to 〜は「〜するために」という目的を表す。so as to 〜で表すこともできる。

> ✎ 次の英文を日本語に直しなさい。

You should study English hard in order to study abroad.

⑨ **It is very important that you watch them and observe their behavior.**

　▶〈It 〜 that ...〉で「…は〜だ」という意味の構文。It は形式的な主語で、真の主語は that 以下。ほぼ同じ内容を It is very important for you to watch them and observe their behavior. と言いかえ可能。　⇒p.81 G-❷

> ✎ 次の英文を日本語に直しなさい。

It is amazing that our team won the game.

⑩ **It is also important that you write notes and ask questions.**

　▶〈It 〜 that ...〉の形式主語構文。　⇒p.81 G-❷

⑪ **If you are really determined, you'll have to work really hard.**

　▶ will have to 〜は have to 〜の未来形で、「〜しなければならないだろう」という意味。

⑫ **Take advantage of every opportunity, and don't give up.**

　▶ take advantage of 〜「〜を生かす、活用する」。ここでは make use of 〜 とほぼ同じ意味。

　▶〈don't ＋動詞の原形〉は否定の命令文で、「〜してはいけない」という意味。give up は「あきらめる」という意味。

2

☐ fieldwork [fíːldwὲrk]
☐ in any way
☐ humans
☐ chimp
☐ have a lot in common
☐ brain [bréın]
☐ one another
☐ I mean
☐ cruel [krúːəl]
☐ male [méıl]
☐ community [kəmjúːnəti]
☐ territory [térətὸːri]
☐ loving [lΛvıŋ]
☐ Mel [mél]
☐ Spindle [spíndl]
☐ In what way?
☐ ask for ~
☐ indeed [ındíːd]
☐ caring [kéərıŋ]

Ken: ①You did a lot of fieldwork, observing chimpanzees in the wild. ②Are they in any way like humans?

Jane: ③Chimps and humans have a lot in common, sharing 98.6 percent of DNA. ④Their brains are very much like ours and much of their behavior is like ours. ⑤The members of a chimp family are very close, often helping one another. They can feel sad, happy, afraid, and angry.

Ken: ⑥What about their character — I mean, are they friendly? Are they cruel?

Jane: ⑦They are usually friendly, but they can be cruel, just like humans.

Ken: Really?

Jane: ⑧The males sometimes attack chimps from another community to protect their territories. But they can be very kind and loving too. ⑨Once, when he was about three years old, a chimp called Mel lost his mother and was left alone. ⑩We all thought he'd die. ⑪But, to our surprise, a 12-year-old male chimp called Spindle took care of him.

Ken: ⑫In what way?

Jane: ⑬Mel would ride on his back and share his nest at night. ⑭He shared his food if Mel asked for it. Chimps can indeed be loving and caring.

このセクションの内容

チンパンジーと人間には多くの (A.　　　) がある。DNA、(B.　　　)、行動などである。チンパンジーは家族が (C.　　　) で、感情もある。性格は残酷なこともあるが、たいていは友好的で、愛情深く思いやりがある。

① **You did a lot of fieldwork, observing chimpanzees in the wild.**

▶ observing 〜 wildは〈付帯状況〉を表す分詞構文。「〜しながら…する」というように、2つの動作が同時に行われることを表す。　⇒p.80 G-❶

✐ 次の英文を日本語に直しなさい。

Mary came to us, talking with her friends.

② **Are they in any way like humans?**

▶ in any wayは「何らかの点[方法]で」という意味。

▶ likeは前置詞で「〜に似ている」という意味。

▶ humansは、動物や想像上の生物などと区別して、「人間」という意味を表す。human beingsともいう。

③ **Chimps and humans have a lot in common, sharing 98.6 percent of DNA.**

▶ have a lot in commonは「多くの共通点がある」という意味（≒ be very much alike）

▶ sharing 〜 DNAは分詞構文で、文前半で述べている「チンパンジーと人間に共通している」ものを具体的に述べている。　⇒p.80 G-❶

④ **Their brains are very much like ours and much of their behavior is like ours.**

▶前置詞のlike「〜に似ている」を用いて、チンパンジーと人間の脳と行動が類似していることを述べた文。

▶最初のoursはour brains、2番目のoursはour behaviorのこと。

▶ much of 〜は「〜（数えられない特定のもの）の多く」。*cf.* many of 〜「〜（数えられるもの）の多く」

⑤ **The members of a chimp family are very close, often helping one another.**

▶ often helping one anotherは〈付帯状況〉を表す分詞構文。ここでは「チンパンジーの一家のメンバーは〜で、しばしば…する」と、前半の内容の結果として起こる事柄を追加している。　⇒p.80 G-❶

▶ one anotherは「お互い（に）」という意味。*cf.* each other

✐ 英文を完成させなさい。

インターネットは私たち相互のコミュニケーションのあり方に変化をもたらした。

The Internet has affected how we communicate with (　　　) (　　　).

⑥ **What about their character — I mean, are they friendly?**

▶ What about 〜?は「〜についてはどうですか」とたずねる言い方。

　このセクションの内容　の答え→　A. 共通点　B. 脳　C. 親密

⑦ **They are usually friendly, but they can be cruel, just like humans.**

▶ can be 〜は〈可能性・推量〉を表し、「〜であることもある[あり得る]」という意味を表す。

┃ ✍ 次の英文を日本語に直しなさい。 ┃

Sometimes kindness can be cruel.

⑧ **The males sometimes attack chimps from another community to protect their territories.**

▶ The males は特定の集団 (community) を構成するオスのチンパンジーのこと。

▶ to protect their territories「自分たちの縄張りを守るために」。

⑨ **Once, when he was about three years old, a chimp called Mel lost his mother and was left alone.**

▶ he はあとの a chimp called Mel を指している。

▶ called Mel は chimp を後ろから修飾する過去分詞の形容詞的用法。

▶ be left alone は leave 〜 alone「〜を一人にする」の受動態で、「一人残される」という意味。

⑩ **We all thought he'd die.**

▶ thought のあとに接続詞 that が省略されている。

▶ he'd は he would の短縮形。would は時制の一致による助動詞 will の過去形。

⑪ **But, to our surprise, a 12-year-old male chimp called Spindle took care of him.**

▶ to our surprise「私たちが驚いたことには」は、文全体を修飾する副詞句。

▶ called Spindle は chimp を後ろから修飾する過去分詞の形容詞的用法。

⑫ **In what way?**

▶ In what way? は「どのようにしてですか？」と方法をたずねる表現。How? としても、ほぼ同じ意味。ここでは、In what way <u>did Spindle take care of Mel</u>? の下線部分が省略されていると考える。

⑬ **Mel would ride on his back and share his nest at night.**

▶ 助動詞 would は「〜したものだ」という〈過去の習慣〉を表す。ここでは、and でつながれた ride と share の両方の動詞にかかる。

▶ nest は「(鳥・昆虫・小動物の) 巣」のこと。チンパンジーはふつう樹木の高いところに枝を集めて巣を作る。

▶ ride on one's back で「〜の背中に乗る」という意味。

⑭ **He shared his food if Mel asked for it.**

▶ ask for 〜は「〜を求める、〜を要求する」という意味。it は his food を指す。

Lesson 5

☐ conservation [kànsərvéiʃən]

☐ comment [kάment]

☐ besides [bɪsáɪdz]

☐ drug [drʌ́g]

☐ disease [dɪzíːz]

☐ cure [kjúər]

☐ without V-ing

☐ connected [kənéktɪd]

☐ make up ～

☐ go wrong

☐ one time

☐ grain [ɡréɪn]

☐ rats increased in number

☐ as much ～ as ...

☐ be in danger of ～

☐ environment [ɪnváɪərənmənt]

☐ along with ～

3

Ken: ①You travel all over the world, giving talks about the conservation of nature. Do you have any comment?

Jane: ②Yes, we humans must understand that wild animals have the right to live. They need wild places. ③Besides, there are some kinds of living things that we must not destroy. ④Many drugs for human diseases come from plants and insects. When we destroy a wild area, ⑤maybe we are destroying the cure for cancer without knowing it.

Ken: I see.

Jane: Everything in nature is connected. ⑥Plants and animals make up a whole pattern of life. ⑦If we destroy that pattern, all kinds of things can go wrong.

Ken: ⑧Could you say more about that?

Jane: Sure. ⑨One time in England, rabbits were destroying farmers' grain. The farmers killed the rabbits. ⑩Then foxes didn't have enough to eat and they started killing the farmers' chickens. The farmers then killed the foxes, and ⑪rats quickly increased in number and destroyed just as much grain as the rabbits had eaten. ⑫We humans are in danger of destroying our environment and ourselves along with it.

このセクションの内容

グドール博士は、自然保護のためには人間は、野生動物には生きる（A.　　　　）があることを理解すべきだと語る。自然界のものはすべてつながっているので、人間は（B.　　　　）を破壊すると同時に（C.　　　　）をも破滅させてしまう危険にさらされている。

① **You travel all over the world, giving talks about the conservation of nature.**

▶ giving ～nature は〈付帯状況〉を表す分詞構文。「～しながら…する」というように、2つの動作が同時に行われることを表す。　　　　⇒p.80 G-❶

▶ give talks about ～は「～について講演を行う」という意味。このtalkは「講演、演説」という意味の名詞。「1回の講演」はa talkになる。

　　例 The scientist gave a talk about the global climate change.
　　「その科学者は地球の気候変動について講演を行った」

② **Yes, we humans must understand that wild animals have the right to live.**

▶ we と humans は同格の関係。we を humans で言いかえている。⇒p.81 G-❸

▶ the right to live は「生きる権利」という意味。to live は the right を修飾する不定詞の形容詞的用法。

③ **Besides, there are some kinds of living things that we must not destroy.**

▶ 副詞の besides は、「さらに～、そのうえ～」のように情報を付け加えるときに用いる。in addition とほぼ同じ意味。文頭に置くときは Besides, ～のように、直後にコンマ (,) を打つ。

▶ some kinds of living things は「いくつかの種類の生き物」という意味。これ全体が関係代名詞 that の先行詞となっている。

④ **Many drugs for human diseases come from plants and insects.**

▶ come from ～は「～に由来する、～で作られている」という意味。

⑤ **maybe we are destroying the cure for cancer without knowing it**

▶ without V-ing は「～することなしに、～しないで」という意味。it は直前の we ～ cancer の内容を指している。

⑥ **Plants and animals make up a whole pattern of life.**

▶ plants and animals で「動植物」という意味。日本語と英語では順番が逆であることに注意。

▶ make up ～は「～を構成する」という意味。

　　✍ 次の英文を日本語に直しなさい。

　　Water makes up more than half of our body.

⑦ **If we destroy that pattern, all kinds of things can go wrong.**

▶ that pattern とは、前文で述べている「動植物が作り上げている生物全体のパターン」のこと。

このセクションの内容 の答え→ A. 権利　B. 環境　C. 自分たち自身

▶ go wrong は「うまくいかなくなる、失敗する」(≒ not work well) という意味。この go は「〜になる」という状態の変化を表す。

⑧ **Could you say more about that?**

▶ that は直前のグドール博士の発言 Everything in nature 〜 can go wrong. を指している。

⑨ **One time in England, rabbits were destroying farmers' grain.**

▶ one time は「ある時、かつて」という意味で、once とほぼ同じ意味。*cf.* one day「ある日」

▶ grain は「穀物、穀類」という意味で、数えられない名詞。

⑩ **Then foxes didn't have enough to eat and they started killing the farmers' chickens.**

▶ enough は、ここでは代名詞で「十分な量」という意味。to eat はそれを修飾する不定詞の形容詞的用法。

⑪ **rats quickly increased in number and destroyed just as much grain as the rabbits had eaten**

▶ increase in 〜は「〜の点で大きくなる、増大する」という意味。ここでは in のあとに number「数」とあるので「ネズミの数が増えた」という意味になる。

  例 Internet crimes are increasing in number these days.
  「最近はインターネット犯罪の件数が増えている」
  (≒ The number of Internet crimes is increasing these days.)

▶ as much 〜 as ... は「…と同じ量の〜（物質名詞）」という意味。as many 〜 as ...「…と同じ数の〜（可算名詞）」との使い分けに注意。

  ✐ 次の英文を日本語に直しなさい。

  We can eat as much pizza as we want in this restaurant.

⑫ **We humans are in danger of destroying our environment and ourselves along with it.**

▶ We humans は We = humans の同格関係。補足や言いかえのために、(代) 名詞と名詞を並列して、同格関係を表すことができる。　　　⇒p.81 G-❸

▶ be in danger of 〜は「〜の危険にさらされている、〜の恐れがある」という意味。of のあとには名詞・動名詞 (V-ing) がくる。

  例 The bridge is in danger of collapsing.
  「その橋は崩壊する恐れがある」

▶ it は our environment を指している。

教科書 p.84　Section 4

- ☐ lie in ～
- ☐ That's why ～
- ☐ begin with ～
- ☐ Tanzania [tènzəníːə]
- ☐ work *one's* way through ～
- ☐ break through ～
- ☐ sunlight [sʌ́nlàɪt]
- ☐ wag [wǽg]
- ☐ that's what ～ is all about
- ☐ consequence [kɑ́nsəkwèns]
- ☐ what to ～
- ☐ billion [bíljən]
- ☐ make a difference

4

Ken: Are you worried about our future?

Jane: Yes, I am.　①But my hope lies in young people.　②That's why I started Roots & Shoots.　③It began with a group of high school students in Tanzania in 1991.　④It is called Roots & Shoots because roots can work their way through rocks to reach water.　⑤And shoots can break through a wall to reach the sunlight.　⑥The rocks and wall are the problems humans have caused to our earth.

Ken: Is it a kind of club for young people?

Jane: Yes.　We now have groups all over the world and each group chooses three projects: one to help people, one to help animals, one to help the environment.　⑦The world is a better place when a sad person smiles at you, when a dog wags its tail for you, or when you give water to a thirsty plant.　⑧That's what Roots & Shoots is all about.

Ken: Some final words?

Jane:　⑨People should think about the consequences of the little choices they make each day.　⑩What to buy?　What to eat?　What to wear? You are just one person, but ⑪what you do affects the whole world.　⑫The changes you make may be small, but ⑬if a thousand, then a million, finally a billion people all make those changes, this is going to make a big difference.

Ken: Dr. Goodall, ⑭thank you very much for sharing your ideas with us.

このセクションの内容

グドール博士は将来を（A.　　）に期待してルーツ・アンド・シューツを始めた。それは人、動物、（B.　　）を支援している。個人が毎日の行動を通して起こす変化は小さくても、多くの人々がそうした変化を起こせば、それは最後には大きな（C.　　）をもたらすことになる。

① **But my hope lies in young people.**

▶ lie in ～は「～にある、存在する」という意味。

例 You should understand that happiness lies in yourself.
「幸福はあなた自身の中にあることを理解すべきだ」

② **That's why I started Roots & Shoots.**

▶ That's why ～は「そういうわけで～である」という意味を表す構文。why は関係副詞で、先行詞 the reason が省略されている。

✐ 英文を完成させなさい。

そういうわけで私は毎朝、朝食にパンを食べるのです。

（　　）（　　）I eat bread for breakfast every morning.

③ **It began with a group of high school students in Tanzania in 1991.**

▶ begin with ～は「～から始まる」という意味。

例 Scientists say that the universe began with a big bang.
「宇宙はビッグバンから始まったと科学者たちは言っている」

④ **It is called Roots & Shoots because roots can work their way through rocks to reach water.**

▶ It は Roots & Shoots のグループそのもの、またはその活動内容を指す。〈call ＋ A ＋ B〉「A（人・もの）を B（名前）と呼ぶ」の受動態は〈A is called B〉の形。

▶ work *one's* way through ～は「～の中［間］をゆっくり進む」という意味。

▶ to reach water は〈結果〉を表す不定詞の副詞的用法。

⑤ **And shoots can break through a wall to reach the sunlight.**

▶ break through ～は「～を突き通す、突き破る」という意味。

▶ to reach the sunlight は〈結果〉を表す不定詞の副詞的用法。

⑥ **The rocks and wall are the problems humans have caused to our earth.**

▶ the problems のあとに目的格の関係代名詞 that[which] が省略されている。

▶ cause ～ to ... は「…に対して～をもたらす」という意味。

例 The typhoon caused serious damage to the area.
「その台風はその地域に深刻な被害をもたらした」

⑦ **The world is a better place when a sad person smiles at you, when a dog wags its tail for you, or when you give water to a thirsty plant.**

▶ The world is a better placeのあとに、when ～, when ..., or when －の形で３つのwhen節を続け、世界がよりよい場所になるのはどのようなときかを具体的に述べている。

▶ wag *one's* tailは「(犬などが) 尾を振る」という意味。

⑧ **That's what Roots & Shoots is all about.**

▶ that's what ～ is all aboutは「それが～の関係[目的と]しているところだ、それこそが～だ」という意味。このwhatは関係代名詞。

▶ thatは直前の文 (The world is ～ a thirsty plant.) の内容を指している。

⑨ **People should think about the consequences of the little choices they make each day.**

▶ think about ～は「～について (時間をかけて慎重に) 考える」という意味。

▶ the little choicesのあとに目的格の関係代名詞that[which]が省略されている。

▶ make a choiceは「選択を行う」という意味。

⑩ **What to buy? What to eat? What to wear?**

▶ what to ～は「何を～すべきか」という意味。前文のthe little choicesの内容を具体的に述べている。

⑪ **what you do affects the whole world**

▶ whatは関係代名詞で、what you doで「あなたがすること」という意味。これ全体が名詞節として文の主語となっている。

⑫ **The changes you make may be small**

▶ The changes you makeは「あなたが生み出す変化」という意味で、これ全体が文の主語。The changesのあとに目的格の関係代名詞that[which]が省略されている。

⑬ **if a thousand, then a million, finally a billion people all make those changes, this is going to make a big difference**

▶ a thousand「千の」、a million「100万の」、a billion「10億の」の順にだんだん数が大きくなっている。これら３つの数詞は、どれも名詞のpeopleを修飾する。

▶ make a differenceは「違いを生む、重要である、影響する」という意味。

⑭ **thank you very much for sharing your ideas with us**

▶ thank you for V-ingは「～してくれてありがとう」という意味。

▶ share ～ with ...は「～を…と分かち合う」という意味。

このセクションの内容 の答え→ A. 若者 B. 自然環境 C. 変化

Grammar for Communication

1 | 分詞構文

〈V-ing (現在分詞) + ...〉が副詞的に文を修飾するものを分詞構文という。分詞構文は〈付帯状況〉、〈時〉、〈原因・理由〉などを表す。これらのうちどれを表すかは、分詞自体ではなく、その前後関係によって決まる。分詞構文は、文頭、文中、文末のいずれの場所にも置くことができる。

◆ Walking along the river, I met a woman with a large dog.
（川沿いを歩いていると、大きな犬を連れた女の人に会った）

この分詞構文は接続詞を使って、

◆ When[While] I was walking along the river, I met a woman with a large dog.

のように言いかえられることから、〈時〉を表すと判断できる。

---

1. 付帯状況：「〜しながら…する」（2つの動作が同時に行われる場合）、「〜して、そして…する」（動作が続けて起こる場合）

◆ Mary went out, **singing** a song.（メアリーは歌を歌いながら出て行った）

◆ A young woman came up to me, **asking** me the way to the post office.
（1人の若い女性が私に近づいてきて、私に郵便局への道をたずねた）
= A young woman came up to me, and asked me the way to the post office.

2. 時：「〜すると」、「〜している間に」など

◆ **Looking** out of the window, I saw some birds flying away.
（窓の外を見ると、数羽の鳥が飛び去って行くのが見えた）
= When I looked out of the window, I saw some birds flying away.

◆ **Talking** with her friends, she forgot to call her father.
（友だちと話している間に、彼女は父親に電話をかけるのを忘れた）
= While she was talking with her friends, she forgot to call her father.

3. 原因・理由：「〜なので」、「〜するので」など

◆ **Being** in a hurry, we took a taxi to the station.
（急いでいたので、私たちは駅までタクシーで行った）
= As[Since] we were in a hurry, we took a taxi to the station.

◆ **Knowing** nothing about gardening, I asked for my grandmother's advice.
（園芸については何も知らなかったので、私は祖母の助言を求めた）
= Because[As] I knew nothing about gardening, I asked for my grandmother's advice.

2	〈It 〜 that ...〉「…は〜だ」

形式主語 it は to 不定詞のほかに that 節の内容を受けることもできる。

◆ **It** is important **that** you should take enough sleep every day.
（あなたが毎日十分な睡眠をとることが大切だ）

この文は That you should take enough sleep every day is important. とすることもできるが、英語ではこのような場合、it を形式主語として文の先頭に置き、真の主語である that 節を後ろに回すのがふつうである。

◆ **It** is really surprising **that** he finished this work in just a week.
（彼がこの作品をたった1週間で仕上げたとは本当に驚きだ）

◆ **It** is possible **that** I gave her the wrong directions.
（私は彼女に間違った道順を教えたかもしれない）

3	同格

名詞 (句) のあとに、それを補足説明したり、言いかえたりする語句を置くことがある。この場合、それらの2つの語句は「同格」の関係にあるという。同格を表すものには、名詞 (句)、名詞節、疑問詞節、前置詞などがある。

---

1. 〈(代) 名詞＋同格の語句〉

◆ **We** Japanese often eat rice.（私たち日本人はよく米を食べる）

◆ **Peter,** an old friend of mine, visited my office yesterday.
（昨日旧友の1人であるピーターが私のオフィスを訪ねてきた）

2. 〈the ＋名詞＋ that 節〉

◆ **The news** that he became a doctor made us very happy.
（彼が医者になったという知らせに私たちはとても喜んだ）

3. 〈名詞＋疑問詞節〉

◆ We had no **idea** when they would come to see us.
（私たちは彼らがいつ私たちに会いに来るかまったくわからなかった）

4. 〈名詞＋ of ＋名詞／V-ing〉

◆ John was born in **the city** of Boston in the U.S.
（ジョンはアメリカのボストンという都市で生まれた）

◆ We have **a chance** of winning the game.
（私たちにはその試合に勝つチャンスがある）

確認問題

語彙・表現

1 次の語を（　）内の指示にしたがって書きかえなさい。
(1) love（形容詞に）　　　(2) conservation（動詞に）
(3) friend（形容詞に）　　(4) million（これの千倍を表す語に）

2 次の各組で下線部の発音がほかと異なる語を1つずつ選び、記号で答えなさい。
(1) ア　disease　　イ　interview　　ウ　indeed　　エ　fieldwork
(2) ア　male　　イ　brain　　ウ　caring　　エ　grain

3 日本語に合うように、（　）内に適切な語を入れなさい。
(1) 私たちは英語を使うどんな機会も活用すべきです。
We should take (　　　) (　　　) every opportunity to use English.
(2) その2つの国には多くの共通点がある。
Those two countries have a lot (　　　) (　　　).
(3) その家は崩壊する危険がある。
The house is (　　　) (　　　) (　　　) falling down.
(4) 試合のあと、彼らは食べたいだけ食べた。
After the game, they ate (　　　) (　　　) food (　　　) they wanted.

文のパターン・文法

1 次の英文を分詞構文にしなさい。
(1) They looked out of the window, and waved to us.
They looked out of the window, _____.
(2) Because I felt very sleepy, I went to bed early.
_____, I went to bed early.
(3) While Tom was taking a rest, he heard birds singing in the trees.
_____, Tom heard birds singing in the trees.

2 （　）内の語句を並べかえて、英文を完成させなさい。
(1) (she / it / this work / is / that / did / clear) by herself.
_____ by herself.
(2) (the city / living / far away / a village / from / in), he had few visitors.
_____, he had few visitors.

(3) We must look straight at (that / decreasing / the child population / is / the fact).

We must look straight at _____.

3 次の各組の文がほぼ同じ意味になるように、（　）内に適切な語を入れなさい。

(1) The number of tall buildings is increasing in this area.

Tall buildings are increasing (　　　) (　　　) in this area.

(2) He didn't know what he should tell her.

He didn't know (　　　) (　　　) tell her.

(3) Helping one another is important for us.

(　　　) is important (　　　) (　　　) help one another.

(4) Worrying too much is a problem for Emma.

Emma has a problem (　　　) (　　　) too much.

総合

次の文を読んで、あとの問いに答えなさい。

Ken: ①You travel all over the world, giving talks about the conservation of nature. Do you have any comment?

Jane: Yes, we humans must understand that ②(to / have / live / wild animals / the right). They need wild places. (　③　), there are ④some kinds of living things that we must not destroy. Many drugs for human diseases come from plants and insects. When we destroy a wild area, maybe we are destroying the cure for cancer without knowing it.

Ken: I see.

問1　下線部①を日本語に直しなさい。

問2　下線部②が「野生の動物たちは生きる権利をもっている」という意味になるように、（　）内の語句を並べかえなさい。

問3　③の（　）内に入る最も適切な語を選びなさい。

　　　ア　However　　　イ　Beside　　　ウ　Then　　　エ　Besides

問4　下線部④の生き物を滅ぼすとどのようなことが起こるか、日本語で説明しなさい。

問5　多くの薬は何を原料にしていますか。本文中のひと続きの英語3語で答えなさい。

You and Your Smartphone — Who's in Charge?

教科書p.94　Section 1

- ☐ charge [tʃáːrdʒ]
- ☐ be in charge
- ☐ not always
- ☐ for the better
- ☐ misuse [mìsjúːs]
- ☐ it's (about) time to ~
- ☐ examine [ɪgzǽmɪn]
- ☐ whether [(h)wéðər]
- ☐ in a ~ way
- ☐ bend [bénd]
- ☐ private [práɪvət]
- ☐ no longer
- ☐ estimate [éstɪmèɪt]
- ☐ rapidly [rǽpɪdli]
- ☐ population [pàpjəléɪʃən]
- ☐ rate [réɪt]
- ☐ average [ǽvərɪdʒ]
- ☐ on average
- ☐ teenager [tíːnèɪdʒər]
- ☐ in one's ~s
- ☐ indicate [índɪkèɪt]
- ☐ digital [dídʒɪtəl]

①Smartphones are changing our lives — but not always for the better. There are dangers of misuse. ②It's about time to examine carefully whether we are using smartphones in a healthy way.

1

③Everywhere we look, we see people bending over their smartphones. They are in their own private world. ④This kind of scene has become so common that we no longer find it strange.

⑤It is estimated that more than four billion people in the world are using smartphones. ⑥In Japan, the number of people who own smartphones has been increasing rapidly. In 2011, only 14.6% of the total population was using smartphones. ⑦By 2018, the rate had increased to 64.7%. ⑧On average, Japanese teenagers spend 143 minutes a day using smartphones just for the Internet, while people in their 20s spend 129 minutes for the same purpose. ⑨These figures indicate that we are now living in a new culture where the digital world meets the real world.

このセクションの内容

スマートフォンの利用者は全世界で（A.　　　　　）以上いると推定されている。日本ではスマートフォンで（B.　　　　　）を利用する1日あたりの平均時間が、10代の若者では143分、20代では129分である。これらの数字は、私たちはデジタル世界が（C.　　　　　）と出会う新しい文化の中で生きていることを示している。

① Smartphones are changing our lives — but not always for the better.

▶ ダッシュ（―）のあとの not always は、「いつも～とは限らない」という部分否定。

> ✎ 次の英文を日本語に直しなさい。
> Newspapers don't always tell us the truth.

▶ for the better は「よい方向へ」という意味。but not always for the better は、but <u>they</u>（= smartphones）are not always <u>changing our lives</u> for the better と語句を補って考える。

② It's about time to examine carefully whether we are using smartphones in a healthy way.

▶ It's（about）time to ～ で「（そろそろ）～すべきときだ」という意味。

> ✎ 英文を完成させなさい。
> そろそろ結論を出すときです。
> (　　　) (　　　) to make a decision.

▶ 接続詞の whether は「～かどうか」という意味を表し、〈whether + S + V〉の形の名詞節を作る。この文では、whether we ～ a healthy way が名詞節で、動詞 examine「調べる、検討する」の目的語になっている。whether ～ or not とすることもある。

> ✎ 次の英文を日本語に直しなさい。
> I don't know whether his story is true (or not).

③ Everywhere we look, we see people bending over their smartphones.

▶ 〈everywhere + S + V〉で、「どこで[へ] ～しても」という意味。

▶ see people bending over their smartphones は知覚動詞構文。〈see + O + V-ing〉で「O が～しているのを見る」という意味を表す。　⇒p.97 G-❷

> ✎ 次の英文を日本語に直しなさい。
> I saw a man fishing in the river.

④ This kind of scene has become so common that we no longer find it strange.

▶ has become は〈結果〉を表す現在完了形。この文は、〈so ～ that ...〉「とても～なので…」の構文。

▶ no longer は「もはや～ではない」という意味。

▶ find it strange は〈find + O + C〉「O を〜だと考える［思う］」という意味。it は This kind of scene、つまり「どこを見ても人々が体をかがめてスマートフォンを使っている光景」を指す。

⑤ **It is estimated that more than four billion people in the world are using smartphones.**

▶ It is estimated that 〜は「〜と推定される」という意味。it は形式主語で、真の主語は that 節である。

⑥ **In Japan, the number of people who own smartphones has been increasing rapidly.**

▶ the number of people who 〜で「〜する人々の数」という意味。who は people を先行詞とする主格の関係代名詞。the number of 〜は単数扱い。

⑦ **By 2018, the rate had increased to 64.7%.**

▶ had increased は、2018年（＝過去のある時点）までに完了していた事柄を表す過去完了形。increase to 〜で「〜まで増加する」という意味。

▶ 64.7% は sixty-four point seven percent と読む。

⑧ **On average, Japanese teenagers spend 143 minutes a day using smartphones just for the Internet, while people in their 20s spend 129 minutes for the same purpose.**

▶ on average は「平均して」という意味の熟語。

▶ spend 〜 V-ing は「…することに〜（時間）を費やす」という意味。

▶ 接続詞の while は、2つの事柄を対比させて、「〜、その一方で…」という意味を表す。

⑨ **These figures indicate that we are now living in a new culture where the digital world meets the real world.**

▶ These figures は前文で挙げているスマートフォンの使用時間を示す2つの数字を指す。

▶ indicate that 〜は「〜ということを示す」という意味。

▶ where は直前の a new culture を先行詞とする関係副詞。where は〈場所〉を表す名詞以外に、situation「状況」や case「場合」など、範囲や広がりをもつ抽象名詞を先行詞とすることがある。　⇒p.96 G-❶

　　✍ 次の英文を日本語に直しなさい。

　　Those people are in a situation where they can't get enough water.

▶ 動詞の live は、「住んでいる」という意味では進行形にしないのがふつう。ただし、「ある場所に一時的に住んでいる」状況を表す場合は、現在進行形を用いることがある。

教科書p.96　Section 2

□ go by
□ decade [dékeɪd]
□ relate [rɪléɪt]
□ amuse [əmjúːz]
□ media [míːdiə]
□ constant [kánstənt]
□ contact [kántækt]
□ stay in constant contact
　with ～
□ even if ～
□ halfway [hæfwéɪ]
□ halfway across the world
□ technology [teknáləʤi]
□ pleasant [plézənt]
□ benefit [bénɪfɪt]
□ practical [prǽktɪkəl]
□ instance [ínstəns]
□ for instance
□ emergency [ɪmə́ːrʤənsi]
□ find *one's* way
□ app [ǽp]
□ monitor [mánətər]
□ calorie [kǽləri]
□ burn [bə́ːrn]

2

①Not a day goes by that we don't use our smartphones.　②Over the past decade, they have made us do many things differently — the way we relate to people, the way we amuse ourselves, and the way we take care of things in our daily lives.

③Texting, emailing, social media, and video chatting let us stay in constant contact with our friends and families, even if they are living halfway across the world.　With our smartphones, we can watch movies when we want to watch them.　We can listen to music.　We can play video games.　④Smartphone technology has indeed made our lives richer and more pleasant.

⑤Besides all of those benefits, smartphones offer many practical services.　⑥For instance, we don't have to go to a bank to do our banking business.　⑦In an emergency, police officers and firefighters can immediately find where their help is needed.　⑧We also use smartphones to find our way around town, to call a taxi, or to check the prices of sneakers.　⑨Some apps even let us monitor how far we walked and how many calories we burned during the day.

このセクションの内容

過去10年間に、スマートフォンは私たちの（A.　　　　）の過ごし方を変えてしまった。スマートフォンのさまざまな利点のおかげで、私たちの生活はより豊かで（B.　　　）ものとなった。それだけでなく、スマートフォンは私たちに多くの（C.　　　　）を提供してくれる。

① **Not a day goes by that we don't use our smartphones.**

▶ Not a day goes by that we don't 〜「1日たりとも私たちが〜しない日はない」という意味。二重否定となり、逆に強い肯定を表す。that は a day を先行詞とする関係副詞で、when の代用である。

▶ go by は「(時間が)過ぎる、経過する」(≒ pass)という意味。

② **Over the past decade, they have made us do many things differently — the way we relate to people, the way we amuse ourselves, and the way we take care of things in our daily lives.**

▶ over the past decade は「過去10年間に」という意味。前置詞の over は過去から現在までの時間の経過を表し、この文のように、しばしば〈継続〉を表す現在完了形といっしょに用いられる。

▶ have made us do は使役構文。〈make + O + C(原形不定詞)〉で「O に〜させる」という意味を表す。us と do の間には、〈主語 + 動詞〉の関係が成り立つ。　　　　　　　　　　　　　　　　　⇒p.97 G-❷

✍ 次の英文を日本語に直しなさい。

Her pretty smile always makes us feel happy.

_____

▶ ダッシュ(-)の後に続く3つの〈the way + S + V〉は、「S が V する仕方[方法]」という意味。いずれも many things の具体例。

▶ relate to 〜で「〜にかかわる」という意味。

▶ amuse oneself で「楽しむ」という意味。

▶ take care of things in our daily lives は「私たちの日常生活において物事に対処する」という意味。

③ **Texting, emailing, social media, and video chatting let us stay in constant contact with our friends and families, even if they are living halfway across the world.**

▶ Texting, 〜 and video chatting 全体がこの文の主語。

▶ let us stay の let は使役動詞で、〈let + O + C(原形不定詞)〉「O を〜させておく、O が〜するのを許す」という構文を作る。us と stay の間には、〈主語 + 動詞〉の関係が成り立つ。　　　　　　　　　　　　　　　　　⇒p.97 G-❷

✍ 次の英文を日本語に直しなさい。

Many dog owners let their dogs play in the park.

_____

▶ stay in constant contact with 〜で「〜と絶えず連絡を取り合う」(≒ keep in close touch with 〜)という意味。

このセクションの内容 の答え→ A. 日常生活　B. 楽しい　C. 実用的なサービス

▶ even if ～は「たとえ～でも」という意味。この2語で接続詞の働きをする。

✐ 次の英文を日本語に直しなさい。

He goes for a walk every morning even if it rains.

_____

▶ halfway across the world は「地球の反対側に（←地球を半周したところに）」（≒ on the other side of the world）という意味。

▶ 現在進行形の are living は「ある場所に一時的に住んでいる」ことを表す。

④ **Smartphone technology has indeed made our lives richer and more pleasant.**

▶〈make + O + C（形容詞）〉「Oを～の状態にする」という意味。ここでは has indeed made で、〈結果〉を表す現在完了。

⑤ **Besides all of those benefits, smartphones offer many practical services.**

▶ besides は前置詞で「～のほかに、～に加え」という意味。

▶ all of those benefits は、直前の段落（教科書p.96の6～12行目）で述べているスマートフォンのさまざまな利点を指す。

⑥ **For instance, we don't have to go to a bank to do our banking business.**

▶ for instance は「例えば」という意味。for example と同様、具体例を挙げるときの談話標識として用いられる。

▶ don't have to ～は have to ～の否定形で、「～する必要はない、～しなくてもよい」という意味。

⑦ **In an emergency, police officers and firefighters can immediately find where their help is needed.**

▶ where their help is needed は疑問詞節（間接疑問）で、「どこで彼らの助けが必要とされているか」という意味。これ全体が動詞 find の目的語。

⑧ **We also use smartphones to find our way around town, to call a taxi, or to check the prices of sneakers.**

▶ to find ～ of sneakers は、〈目的〉を表す副詞的用法の不定詞が3つ並列された形。

▶ find one's way は「道を探す」という意味。

⑨ **Some apps even let us monitor how far we walked and how many calories we burned during the day.**

▶ let us monitor は〈let + O + C（原形不定詞）〉「Oを～させておく」の使役構文。

⇒p.97 G-❷

▶ how far we walked と how many calories we burned during the day は、どちらも名詞節（間接疑問）で、動詞 monitor の目的語。

教科書p.98　Section 3

☐ report on ~

☐ negative [négətɪv]

☐ effect [ɪfékt]

☐ entertain [èntərtéɪn]

☐ negatively [négətɪvli]

☐ development [dɪvéləpmənt]

☐ mental [méntəl]

☐ physical [fízɪkəl]

☐ adult [ədʌ́lt]

☐ risk [rísk]

☐ distract [dɪstrǽkt]

☐ buzz [bʌ́z]

☐ attention [əténʃən]

☐ pay attention to ~

☐ in fact

☐ mode [móʊd]

☐ solve [sálv]

☐ those who ~

☐ focus [fóʊkəs]

☐ focus *one's* attention (on
　~)

3

①Smartphones have made our lives richer and more pleasant. ②However, many researchers report on the negative effects of the use of smartphones.

③Using smartphones to entertain very young children may negatively affect their development. ④For full mental and physical development, children need contact with other people and the real world.

⑤It's not only the problem of child development. ⑥Teenagers and adults also face risks. ⑦Smartphones may distract us. ⑧They are always ringing and buzzing to make us pay attention to them. ⑨In fact, they may distract us even when they're on silent mode.

⑩In one study, 800 people were asked to solve math problems. ⑪They were in three groups: (1) those who left their smartphones in another room; (2) those who had their smartphones in their pockets; and (3) those who kept their smartphones right in front of them. ⑫The results: Group 1 did the best; Group 2 came next; Group 3 did the worst. ⑬Smartphones had an effect on how well people were able to focus their attention.

このセクションの内容

スマートフォンの使用は、ほかの人々や現実の世界との (A.　　　　) を必要とする幼い子どもたちの精神的・肉体的な (B.　　　　) に悪影響を与える。また、スマートフォンは、私たちの (C.　　　　) を失わせてしまう。

① **Smartphones have made our lives richer and more pleasant.**

▶〈make + O + C（形容詞）〉「Oを〜の状態にする」の構文。形容詞の比較級を2つ並べたricher and more pleasant全体がC。

▶ have madeは、〈結果〉を表す現在完了。

② **However, many researchers report on the negative effects of the use of smartphones.**

▶ report on 〜は「〜について報告する」という意味。ここではtell about 〜とほぼ同じ意味。

▶ the negative effects of 〜は「〜の悪影響、弊害」という意味。

③ **Using smartphones to entertain very young children may negatively affect their development.**

▶ Using smartphones 〜 young children全体が、この文の主語。

④ **For full mental and physical development, children need contact with other people and the real world.**

▶ 文頭のFor full 〜 physical developmentは〈目的〉を表す前置詞句。

▶ need contact with 〜は「〜との接触を必要とする」という意味で、withの目的語はother peopleとthe real worldの2つ。

⑤ **It's not only the problem of child development.**

⑥ **Teenagers and adults also face risks.**

▶ not only 〜 but（also）...は、2つのものを対比して、butのあとに来るものを強調する。ここでは、文⑤と⑥の2つの文にまたがって使われている。スマートフォンが及ぼす悪影響は、「子どもの成長」だけでなく、「10代の若者たちや大人」にも及ぶ、ということ。

▶ faceは動詞で、「〜に直面する」という意味。

⑦ **Smartphones may distract us.**

▶ 助動詞mayは控えめな推量を表す。

⑧ **They are always ringing and buzzing to make us pay attention to them.**

▶ are always ringing and buzzingのように、alwaysと現在進行形を組み合わせて、繰り返し頻繁に起こる出来事を表すことができる。

＿✍ 次の英文を日本語に直しなさい。＿

John is always worrying about small things.

――――――――――――――――――――――――――

▶ to make 以下は〈結果〉を表す不定詞の副詞的用法。

▶〈make + O + C（原形不定詞）〉は「O を（強引に）〜させる」という意味の使役構文。make us pay attention to them で、「その結果私たちがそれらに注意を向けることになる」という意味。

⑨ **In fact, they may distract us even when they're on silent mode.**

▶ in fact は「実際」という意味。前文の内容を補足したり、強調したりするために用いられる談話標識の 1 つ。

▶ they はどちらも smartphones を指す。

▶ even は強調したい語（句）の直前に置かれ、「〜さえも」という意味を表す。

⑩ **In one study, 800 people were asked to solve math problems.**

▶〈ask + O + to 〜〉の受動態は〈be 動詞 + asked + to 〜〉。ここでは動作主が示されていないが、スマートフォンに関する実験を行った研究者と考えられる。

＿✍ 英文を完成させなさい。＿

キャロルはそのパーティーでスピーチをするように頼まれた。

Carol (　　　) (　　　) (　　　) make a speech at the party.

⑪ **They were in three groups: (1) those who left their smartphones in another room; (2) those who had their smartphones in their pockets; and (3) those who kept their smartphones right in front of them.**

▶ 主語の They は前文の 800 people を指す。

▶ three groups の内訳は、コロン (:) のあとの (1) 〜 (3) に具体的に書かれている。

▶ those who 〜は「〜する人々」（≒ people who 〜）という意味。

⑫ **The results: Group 1 did the best; Group 2 came next; Group 3 did the worst.**

▶ did the best「いちばん成績がよかった」⇔ did the worst「いちばん成績が悪かった」。worst は形容詞 bad の最上級。the worst の形で、名詞としても用いられる。比較級は worse。

⑬ **Smartphones had an effect on how well people were able to focus their attention.**

▶ have an effect on 〜は「〜に影響を及ぼす」という意味。

▶ how well 〜 their attention は疑問詞節（間接疑問）で、前置詞 on の目的語になっている。

▶ focus *one's* attention は「意識を集中させる」という意味。

☐ mentally [méntəli]
☐ rely [rɪláɪ]
☐ rely on ～
☐ replace [rɪpléɪs]
☐ laziness [léɪzinəs]
☐ to make matters worse
☐ spread [spréd]
☐ ability [əbíləti]
☐ independently [ìndɪpéndəntli]
☐ impact [ímpækt]
☐ limit [límət]
☐ moderation [mɑ̀dəréɪʃən]

4

①Smartphones make our lives so easy that we could become mentally lazy. ②We no longer even try to remember meetings and dates. We use our smartphones to connect to the Internet. ③We rely on the Internet for the news, for our school reports, and for understanding world events. ④For some of us, the Internet is so easy to use that it has replaced books and newspapers as our main source of information: another form of mental laziness.

⑤To make matters worse, sometimes the Internet spreads lies. ⑥We don't know what to believe and what not to believe. ⑦Believing everything we see on the Internet is not only lazy, it is also dangerous. ⑧We must develop the ability to think independently. ⑨Our smartphones can't teach us that skill.

⑩We are living in a new culture where the digital world is meeting the real world. ⑪And we are only beginning to understand the impact that smartphones have on our mental and social lives. ⑫Until we come to a better understanding of the impact of these new technologies, maybe we should think about limiting our use of smartphones. ⑬"Moderation in all things" might not be a bad idea.

このセクションの内容

スマートフォンのおかげで私たちの生活は便利になったが、それは同時に私たちを精神的に（A.　　　）にしてしまった。インターネットは時として（B.　　　）を拡散させる。私たちはインターネット上の情報を何でも信じてしまうのではなく、（C.　　　）で考える力を養うべきである。

① **Smartphones make our lives so easy that we could become mentally lazy.**

▶〈make＋O＋C（形容詞）〉「Oを〜の状態にする」の文型に〈so 〜 that ...〉「とても〜なので…」が組み合わさっている。

② **We no longer even try to remember meetings and dates.**

▶no longerは「もはや〜ない」という否定を表す。

③ **We rely on the Internet for the news, for our school reports, and for understanding world events.**

▶rely on 〜 for ...で「…を〜に頼る」という意味。depend on 〜 for ...とほぼ同じ意味。この文では、3つのfor ...が並列されている。

　✎ 英文を完成させなさい。

警察は容疑者に関する情報を地元の住民に頼っている。

Police rely (　　　) local residents (　　　) information on possible suspects.

④ **For some of us, the Internet is so easy to use that it has replaced books and newspapers as our main source of information: another form of mental laziness.**

▶〈so 〜 that ...〉「とても〜なので…」の構文。that it(＝ the Internet) hasからof informationまでがthat節で、インターネットが簡単に使える結果として起きていることを述べている。

▶be easy to 〜は「〜しやすい、〜するのが簡単である」という意味。

▶コロン (:) のあとのanother form of mental laziness「精神的な怠惰のもう1つの形態」は、コロンの前で述べている状況を言い表している。

⑤ **To make matters worse, sometimes the Internet spreads lies.**

▶to make matters worseは「さらに悪いことには」という意味。

⑥ **We don't know what to believe and what not to believe.**

▶what to believeは「何を信じるべきか」、what not to believeは「何を信じるべきではないか」という意味。これら2つの〈疑問詞＋to 〜〉がknowの目的語。

⑦ **Believing everything we see on the Internet is not only lazy, it is also dangerous.**

▶動名詞で始まるBelieving everything 〜 the Internet全体がこの文の主語。動名詞が文の主語になる場合は単数扱いなので、これを受けるbe動詞はis。

▶everythingのあとに目的格の関係代名詞that[which] が省略されている。

▶〈S is not only 〜, it is also ...〉で「Sは〜であるというだけでなく…でもある」という意味。〈not only 〜 but (also) ...〉の変形。itはBelieving everything 〜 the Internetを指す。

⑧ **We must develop the ability to think independently.**

▶ the ability to ～で「～する能力」という意味。to think ～はabilityを後ろから修飾する形容詞的用法の不定詞。

▶ think independentlyは、ここでは「ネットの情報に頼らずに自分の頭で物事を考える」ということ。

⑨ **Our smartphones can't teach us that skill.**

▶〈teach + O（人）+ O（物事）〉で「（人）に物事を教える」という意味。

▶ that skillは、前文で述べている「自分の頭で物事を考える（think independently）ために必要な技能、スキル」を指す。

⑩ **We are living in a new culture where the digital world is meeting the real world.**

▶この文は、教科書p.94の16～17行目とほぼ同じ。　⇒p.86 文⑨解説

▶whereは直前のa new cultureを先行詞とする関係副詞。　⇒p.96 G-❶

⑪ **And we are only beginning to understand the impact that smartphones have on our mental and social lives.**

▶ we are only beginning to understand ～は、「私たちはようやく～を理解し始めたところである」という意味。

▶ thatはthe impact「影響」を先行詞とする目的格の関係代名詞。

⑫ **Until we come to a better understanding of the impact of these new technologies, maybe we should think about limiting our use of smartphones.**

▶ come to a better understanding of ～は「～をよりよく理解するようになる」という意味。

▶ these new technologiesは、スマートフォンで利用できるさまざまな技術のこと。

▶ maybe we should ～は「～したほうがいいかもしれない」と、何かを控えめに勧める表現。

▶ think about V-ingで「～することを検討する」という意味。

⑬ **"Moderation in all things" might not be a bad idea.**

▶ moderationは「節度（を持つこと）」という意味。Moderation in all things. は「何事もほどほどに」という意味の決まった表現。

▶ might not be a bad ideaは「～は悪くないかもしれない」という意味。このmightは控えめな助言を表す。

✎ 次の英文を日本語に直しなさい。

It might be a good idea to think about buying a new car.

Grammar for Communication

1 　　関係副詞：where、when、why、how

関係副詞にはwhere、when、why、howがあり、先行詞の名詞が表す意味に
応じて使い分ける。

関係副詞	先行詞
where	「場所」を表す語 (place、house、townなど)
when	「時」を表す語 (time、day、yearなど)
why	「理由」を表す語 (reason)
how	the way「方法」(＊通例省略)

＊howの場合、the way howとなることはなく、the wayかhowのどちらかが省略される。
＊関係副詞は〈前置詞＋関係代名詞〉で言いかえることができる場合がある。

1. 先行詞：場所

◆ This is the school **where** (＝**in which**) my mother studied when she
was a child. （これが私の母が子どものときに学んだ学校である）

2. 先行詞：時

◆ Do you remember the day **when** (＝ **on which**) we first met?
（私たちが初めて会った日を覚えていますか）

3. 先行詞：理由

◆ This is the reason **why** (＝ **for which**) I didn't go there yesterday.
（これが私が昨日そこに行かなかった理由だ[こういうわけで私は昨日そこ
に行かなかった]）

4. how ～は「方法、仕方」を表す

◆ That is **how** the accident happened. （そのようにして事故は起こった）

■ 関係副詞または先行詞が省略されることがある。

◆ This is **where** they lived 10 years ago.(＝ This is the place they lived
10 years ago.)
（ここは彼らが10年前に住んでいたところである）

◆ I still remember **when** he left this city.(＝ I still remember the time he
left this city.)
（彼がいつこの都市を去ったのかを私はまだ覚えている）

◆This is **why** I asked him the question. (= This is the reason I asked him the question.)
（これが私が彼にその質問をした理由である）

2 S＋V＋O＋C（C＝原形不定詞／分詞）

〈S＋V＋O＋C〉のCの位置に原形不定詞（toのない不定詞）や分詞（現在分詞・過去分詞）がくることがある。この場合、Oはあとに続く原形不定詞や分詞の意味上の主語となり、OとCの間には〈主語＋動詞〉の関係が成り立つ。この文型を作る主な動詞には、使役動詞（make、have、let）や知覚動詞（see、hear、feelなど）がある。

文型	使役動詞	知覚動詞
〈S＋V＋O＋C（原形不定詞）〉	make、have、let	see、hear、feelなど
〈S＋V＋O＋C（分詞）〉	have、get、make	see、hear、feelなど

① **使役動詞：make、have、let**
　　◆My father **made** me **clean** the garden. （父は私に庭を掃除させた）
　　◆Mr. Brown **had** his students **write** a short story.
　　　（ブラウン先生は生徒たちに短い物語を書かせた）
　　◆Please **let** me **know** when you will leave Japan.
　　　（いつ日本を発つか私に知らせてください）
　　＊letは「人に（本人が望むとおりに）〜させてやる、人が〜するのを許す」という意味。

② **知覚動詞：hear、see、feelなど**
　　◆I **saw** an old man **walking** across the street. 　（＊動作全体のうちの一部を見る）
　　　（私は1人の老人が通りを横断しているのを見た）
　　◆I **saw** an old man **walk** across the street. 　（＊初めから終わりまで動作全体を見る）
　　　（私は1人の老人が通りを横断するのを見た）
　　◆Mike **heard** his name **called**.
　　　（マイクは自分の名前が呼ばれるのを聞いた）

③ **〈S＋V＋O＋C（分詞）〉の構文を作るその他の動詞**
　　◆How do you **want** your eggs **cooked**?
　　　（卵はどのように料理してほしいですか）
　　◆They **found** themselves **lost** in the deep forest.
　　　（彼らは深い森の中で道に迷ったことに気づいた）

確認問題

語彙・表現

1 次の語を（　）内の指示にしたがって書きかえなさい。

(1) able（名詞に）　　　　　　　(2) mental（副詞に）

(3) please（形容詞に）　　　　　(4) positive（反意語に）

2 次の各組で下線部の発音がほかと異なる語を1つずつ選び、記号で答えなさい。

(1) ア　spr<u>ea</u>d　　　イ　<u>e</u>stimate　　ウ　m<u>e</u>dia　　エ　d<u>e</u>cade

(2) ア　ph<u>y</u>sical　　イ　rel<u>y</u>　　　ウ　l<u>i</u>mit　　エ　d<u>i</u>gital

3 日本語に合うように、（　）内に適切な語を入れなさい。

(1) 何事も常に計画通りに行くとは限らない。

Everything does (　　　) (　　　) go as planned.

(2) たとえ離れて暮らしていても、私たちは情報を共有することができる。

We can share information (　　　) (　　　) we live far away from each other.

(3) さらに悪いことには雨が激しく降り始めた。

To make (　　　) (　　　), it began to rain hard.

(4) アメリカ人は週に平均して約34時間働く。

Americans work about 34 hours (　　　) (　　　) a week.

文のパターン・文法

1 （　）内に適切な関係副詞を入れなさい。

(1) I would like to know the reason (　　　) you said that to them.

(2) The village (　　　) my mother was born is on the Japan Sea.

(3) Can you tell me the time (　　　) we should be at the station?

(4) That was (　　　) we were able to finish the job so quickly.

2 （　）内の語を適切な形に直しなさい。形を変えなくてよい場合は、そのまま書きなさい。

(1) When I looked out of the window, I saw a woman (stand) under a tree.

(2) The boy began to cry when he found himself (leave) alone in the room.

(3) I've heard this song (sing) at the concert several times.
(4) Could you let me (know) when Jack comes back?

3 （ ）内の語句を並べかえて、日本語に合う英文を作りなさい。
(1) 海辺にいた人々は太陽が昇るのを見た。
Those (on the beach / the sun / were / rise / who / saw).
Those ＿＿＿＿＿＿＿＿＿＿＿＿＿＿＿＿＿＿＿＿＿ .
(2) 彼は秘書に会議用資料をコピーしてもらった。
(the document / copy / he / his secretary / had) for the meeting.
＿＿＿＿＿＿＿＿＿＿＿＿＿＿＿＿＿＿＿ for the meeting.
(3) あなたはなぜこの店がずっと閉まったままなのかを知っていますか。
Do you (closed / has / this store / why / remained / know)?
Do you ＿＿＿＿＿＿＿＿＿＿＿＿＿＿＿＿＿＿＿ ?
(4) 私はこのようにしてその問題を自力で解決したのです。
(how / this / the problem / solved / is / I) by myself.
＿＿＿＿＿＿＿＿＿＿＿＿＿＿＿＿＿＿＿ by myself.

総合

次の文を読んで、あとの問いに答えなさい。

①Using smartphones to entertain very young children may negatively affect their development. For full mental and physical development, children need contact with other people and the real world.
It's not only the problem of child development. Teenagers and adults (②) face risks. Smartphones may distract us. They are always ringing and buzzing to ③(them / attention / make / pay / to / us). In fact, they may (④) us even when they're on silent mode.

問1 下線部①を日本語に直しなさい。
問2 ②の（ ）内に入る最も適切な語を選びなさい。
ア just イ also ウ still エ too
問3 下線部③の（ ）内の語を並べかえて、英文を完成させなさい。
問4 ④の（ ）内に入る適切な1語を本文中から探して答えなさい。
問5 子どもたちが精神的・肉体的に成長するために必要なものとは何ですか。日本語で説明しなさい。

Living in Alaska

教科書p.112　Section 1

- ☐ Alaska [əlǽskə]
- ☐ a great number of ~
- ☐ wildlife [wáɪldlàɪf]
- ☐ distant [dístənt]
- ☐ freshman [fréʃmən]
- ☐ come across ~
- ☐ Shishmaref [ʃíʃmərèf]
- ☐ at first
- ☐ remote [rɪmóʊt]
- ☐ go and visit ~
- ☐ tiny [táɪni]
- ☐ mayor [méɪər]
- ☐ reply [rɪpláɪ]
- ☐ invite ~ to ...
- ☐ Eskimo [éskɪmòʊ]
- ☐ caribou [kǽrəbùː]
- ☐ hunting [hántɪŋ]
- ☐ lead *one's* ~ life
- ☐ out-of-the-way [àʊtəvðəwéɪ]
- ☐ just as ~

Hoshino Michio (1952-1996) is a well-known nature photographer. ①He produced a great number of wonderful photos of wildlife in Alaska. Here, he talks about Alaska, its people, and "distant nature."

1

②When I was a freshman in college, I came across a photo that changed my life. ③It was a beautiful photo of a small village called Shishmaref on a small island in Alaska. ④At first, I couldn't believe that people could live in such a remote place. ⑤However, when I found the village on the map, I got interested and had an urge to go and visit this tiny village.

I decided to write a letter, but I didn't know anyone in the village. ⑥So I wrote "Dear Mayor of Shishmaref," asking him to introduce me to some family who might let me stay. ⑦Half a year later, I received a reply inviting me to visit.

In 1973, I went to Shishmaref and spent the summer with an Eskimo family. ⑧I ate the same food as they did, and even went caribou hunting with them. ⑨The local people often called me "Eskimo boy"! ⑩It seemed that every day brought me new experiences.

⑪Living in Alaska, I discovered that people lead their everyday lives even in such an out-of-the-way place, just as we do back in Japan.

【このセクションの内容】

星野道夫氏は大学1年生のときに、1枚の写真を通して、（A.　　　　）
の小さな島にあるシシュマレフという美しい村の存在を知った。1973年、
彼は（B.　　　　）から招待を受け、シシュマレフを訪ねた。彼はそこで
（C.　　　　）の家族とひと夏を過ごした。

① **He produced a great number of wonderful photos of wildlife in Alaska.**

▶ a great number of ～で「多くの～」（≒ many ～、a lot of ～）という意味。*cf.* a large number of ～「多くの」、a considerable number of ～「かなりの数の～」

【✍ 次の英文を日本語に直しなさい。】

The country has attracted a large number of tourists since the 1980s.

② **When I was a freshman in college, I came across a photo that changed my life.**

▶ come across ～は「～を偶然見つける、（人）に出くわす」という意味。
▶ that は直前の a photo を先行詞とする主格の関係代名詞。

③ **It was a beautiful photo of a small village called Shishmaref on a small island in Alaska.**

▶ 主語の It は前文の a photo ～ my life を指す。
▶ called ～は a small village を後ろから修飾する過去分詞の形容詞的用法。

④ **At first, I couldn't believe that people could live in such a remote place.**

▶ at first で「最初は、初めは」という意味。

【✍ 次の英文を日本語に直しなさい。】

At first, Jane didn't like Japanese food very much.

▶ believe that ～で「～ということを信じる」という意味。
▶ such a ～は直前に出てきた人やものを指して、「そのような～」という意味を表す。such a remote place = a small village ～ in Alaska

⑤ **However, when I found the village on the map, I got interested and had an urge to go and visit this tiny village.**

▶ get interested in ～は「～に興味がわく」という意味。〈get + 形容詞〉は「～になる」という〈状態の変化〉を表す。

▶ had an urge to ～は「～したい衝動に駆られた」という意味。to ～は urge を修飾する不定詞の形容詞的用法。

▶ go and *do* で「～しに行く」という意味。and のあとには〈目的〉を表す動詞が続く。*cf.* go and get something to eat「何か食べ物を買いに行く」

⑥ **So I wrote "Dear Mayor of Shishmaref," asking him to introduce me to some family who might let me stay.**

▶ asking ～は分詞構文で、シシュマレフ村の村長宛に手紙を書いた目的を述べている。

▶ 〈ask + O（人）+ to ～〉は「（人）に～するように頼む」という意味。

▶ who は some family を先行詞とする主格の関係代名詞。

▶ let me stay は〈let + O（人）+ 原形不定詞〉の使役構文で、「私を泊めてくれる」という意味。

⑦ **Half a year later, I received a reply inviting me to visit.**

▶ inviting ～は a reply を後ろから修飾する現在分詞の形容詞的用法。

⑧ **I ate the same food as they did, and even went caribou hunting with them.**

▶ ate the same food as they did「彼ら（が食べるの）と同じ食べ物を食べた」。〈the same ～ as + S + V〉で「SがVするのと同じ～」という意味を表す。この as は関係代名詞とよく似た働きをしているため、疑似関係代名詞と呼ばれることがある。

⑨ **The local people often called me "Eskimo boy"!**

▶ 〈call + O + C〉「OをCと呼ぶ」の構文。

⑩ **It seemed that every day brought me new experiences.**

▶ 〈It seems that ～〉で「～と思われる」という話者の主観的な判断や印象を表す。

⇒p.112 G-❶

✎ 英文を完成させなさい。

彼はアメリカの歴史に興味を持っているように思われる。

（　　　）（　　　）（　　　）he is interested in American history.

⑪ **Living in Alaska, I discovered that people lead their everyday lives even in such an out-of-the-way place, just as we do back in Japan.**

▶ Living in Alaska は分詞構文で、「～しているときに」という意味を表す。While[When] I was living in Alaska と言いかえ可能。

▶ just as we do back in Japan は「私たちが日本にいるときにそうするのとまったく同じように」という意味。do は直前に出てきた動詞句の代わりをする代動詞で、ここでは do = lead our everyday lives。

このセクションの内容 の答え→　A．アラスカ　B．村長　C．エスキモー

2

☐ graduate from ~

☐ work for ~

☐ ~ or so

☐ as it turned out

☐ elsewhere [éls(h)wèər]

☐ Grand Canyon
　　[grǽndkǽnjən]

☐ Yellowstone [jéloustòun]

☐ vast [vǽst]

☐ expanse [ıkspǽns]

☐ wilderness [wíldərnəs]

☐ rather [rǽðər]

☐ seasonal [síːznəl]

☐ Fairbanks [féərbæ̀nks]

☐ a little past ten

☐ temperature [témpərətʃər]

☐ degree [dıgríː]

☐ melt [mélt]

☐ horizon [həráızən]

☐ day and night

①After graduating from college, I worked for a photographer for two years.　In 1978, I went to Alaska again.　②My plan was to stay for five years or so, taking photographs.　③But as it turned out, I've been living there for 18 long years!

Why do I like Alaska so much?　Well, of course, it has great nature.　④Elsewhere in America, there are great national parks like Grand Canyon and Yellowstone.　⑤But just outside of these parks, there are cities and towns.　⑥In Alaska, there is only the vast expanse of wilderness.

⑦You may think that it is always winter in Alaska, but the fact is that there are rather clear seasonal changes.　I live in Fairbanks.　The sun rises a little past ten in the morning in January, and then sinks before two in the afternoon.　⑧The average low temperature is about 24 degrees below zero. ⑨As the days get longer, people sense the coming of spring.　⑩Snow begins to melt, ice breaks up on the rivers, and the whole world seems to change.　⑪In summer, the sun is above the horizon day and night; the average high in July is 23 degrees.　In autumn, people prepare for winter.　⑫Many people make jam from berries they pick in the forest.

このセクションの内容

1978年に再びアラスカを訪れた星野氏は、その魅力は広大な（A.　　　）が続く大自然にあると語る。彼はそのアラスカで写真を撮りながら（B.　　　）年間生活している。一般の人々の予想に反して、アラスカにははっきりとした（C.　　　）の変化がある。

① **After graduating from college, I worked for a photographer for two years.**

▶ After graduating は前置詞 after のあとに動名詞 V-ing が続いた形。接続詞としての after を使って、After I graduated from college と言いかえられる。

▶ work for ～ は「～のために働く」という意味。*cf.* work for a big company「大手企業で働く［に勤める］」

② **My plan was to stay for five years or so, taking photographs.**

▶ 〈S + V（be 動詞）+ C（不定詞）〉の文。to stay 以下は、S（My plan）の具体的内容を述べている。

▶ or so は数を表す語句のあとに置いて、「～かそこらで」という意味を表す。

　　✍ 次の英文を日本語に直しなさい。

　　He'll be back in twenty minutes or so.

_____

▶ taking photographs は付帯状況を表す分詞構文で、「写真を撮りながら」という意味。5年間アラスカでどう過ごす計画だったかを具体的に述べている。

③ **But as it turned out, I've been living there for 18 long years!**

▶ as it turned out は「結局のところ（～だ）」という意味。星野氏は当初の計画では5年間アラスカに滞在する予定だったが、「結局のところ、すでに18年間もの長い間アラスカに住んでいる」と述べている。

▶ I've been living there は、過去のある時点から現在まで継続している一時的な状態を表す現在完了進行形。〈have been + V-ing（現在分詞）〉で「ずっと～している」という意味を表す。

④ **Elsewhere in America, there are great national parks like Grand Canyon and Yellowstone.**

▶ Elsewhere in America は「アメリカのほかの場所では」という意味。アラスカは1959年にアメリカ合衆国49番目の州として加えられた。全米で最も面積の大きな州であるが、人口は約73万5千人（2019年現在）で、人口密度は全50州のうち最小である。

⑤ **But just outside of these parks, there are cities and towns.**

▶ there are ～構文。この文では、場所を表す語句が文頭にきている。

▶ these parks は前文の great national parks を指す。

⑥ **In Alaska, there is only the vast expanse of wilderness.**

▶ 〈there is[are] ～〉構文で「～」の位置にくるのは、不特定のものを表す名詞で、ふつう〈the + 名詞〉はこない。ここでは、アラスカという特定の州に広がる荒野について述べているため、例外的に the が付いている。

⑦ **You may think that it is always winter in Alaska, but the fact**

is that there are rather clear seasonal changes.

▶ the fact is that ～は〈S + is + C (that節)〉の構文で、「実際は～だ」という
意味。　　　　　　　　　　　　　　　　　　　　　　⇒p.113 G-❷

　📝 英文を完成させなさい。

問題はその計画には多大なコストがかかるということだ。

The (　　　) (　　　) (　　　) the project costs much.

▶ ratherは後ろに続く形容詞を修飾して、「かなり」という程度を表す。

⑧ **The average low temperature is about 24 degrees below zero.**

▶ The average low temperature は「平均最低気温」という意味。

▶ 温度 (temperature) の「～度」は、～ degree(s) で表す。

▶ below zero は「零下」という意味。

⑨ **As the days get longer, people sense the coming of spring.**

▶ 接続詞のasは「～するにつれて」という意味。2つの物事が互いに関連し
合いながら進行することを表す。

▶ senseは「～を感じ取る」という意味の動詞。cf. sense danger「危険を察
知する」

⑩ **Snow begins to melt, ice breaks up on the rivers, and the
whole world seems to change.**

▶ seem to ～は「～のように思われる」という意味。the whole world以下は、
it seems that the whole world changesと言いかえることができる。

⇒p.112 G-❶

　📝 英文を完成させなさい。

彼の意見は私のとは違うように思えた。

His opinion (　　　) (　　　) (　　　) different from mine.

⑪ **In summer, the sun is above the horizon day and night; the
average high in July is 23 degrees.**

▶ above the horizon は「水平線上に」という意味。

▶ day and night は「夜も昼も」という意味。

▶ the average high はthe average high temperature「平均最高気温」のこ
と。文⑧でthe average low temperature「平均最低気温」が出てきてい
るため、共通部分のtemperatureが省略されている。

⑫ **Many people make jam from berries they pick in the forest.**

▶ make ～ from ... は「…（原料）から～を作る」という意味。cf. make ～
of ...「…（材料）で～を作る」

▶ berries「ベリー類」のあとに目的格の関係代名詞that[which]が省略され
ている。theyは同じ文のMany peopleを指す。

□ Bering Sea [bèərɪŋ síː]
□ Point Hope [pɔ́ɪnt hóup]
□ hunter [hʌ́ntər]
□ on top of ～
□ iceberg [áɪsbə̀ːrg]
□ the right moment
□ sail out
□ umiak [úːmiæ̀k]
□ successful [səksésfəl]
□ villager [vílɪdʒər]
□ onto [ántə/ántu]
□ give thanks for ～
□ once ～
□ elder [éldər]
□ prayer [préər]
□ cut ～ up
□ instruction [ɪnstrʌ́kʃən]
□ in the end
□ push ～ back

3

①Eskimos go whale hunting in April when the ice on the Bering Sea starts to break up. ②In 1983, I went whale hunting for the first time at Point Hope. ③The hunters wait on top of an iceberg for the whales. ④When the right moment arrives, they sail out on boats called "umiak."

⑤They are not always successful in whale hunting. ⑥But if they are lucky, all the villagers come running to pull the whale onto the ice. ⑦I still remember seeing an old Eskimo lady come dancing and singing, to give thanks for the gift from the sea.

⑧Once the whale is placed on the ice, an elder of the village says a prayer. ⑨Then the young people start cutting it up, carefully following the elder's instructions. ⑩The meat is shared by all the villagers, and in the end they push the huge head bone of the whale back into the sea, saying, "Come back again next year!"

このセクションの内容

星野氏は1983年に、ベーリング海に面したホープ岬で、エスキモーによる
（A.　　　　）を体験した。漁が成功したときは、村民たちが総出でクジラ
を仕留めた仲間たちを迎え、長老の指示に従って、クジラが解体される。
（B.　　　）を村民たちで分け合ったあと、最後に（C.　　　　）を海に戻す。

① **Eskimos go whale hunting in April when the ice on the Bering Sea starts to break up.**
- ▶ go whale huntingは「クジラを捕りに出かける」。
- ▶ start to ～は「～し始める」という意味。

② **In 1983, I went whale hunting for the first time at Point Hope.**
- ▶ for the first timeは「初めて」という意味。

③ **The hunters wait on top of an iceberg for the whales.**
- ▶ wait on top of an iceberg for the whalesは「氷山の上でクジラが現れるのを待つ」という意味。wait for ～「～を待つ」と on top of ～「～の上で」が組み合わされている。

  例 There is a small house on top of the hill.
  「丘の上に小さな家が1軒建っている」

④ **When the right moment arrives, they sail out on boats called "umiak."**
- ▶ When the right moment arrivesは「絶好のタイミングが訪れると」という意味。arriveは「(時期が) 到来する」の意味でも用いられる。

  ✎ 次の英文を日本語に直しなさい。

  The day of departure finally arrived.

- ▶ sail outは「出航する、海へ出る」という意味。
- ▶ called ～はboatsを後ろから修飾する過去分詞の形容詞的用法。

⑤ **They are not always successful in whale hunting.**
- ▶ are not always ～は「いつも～とは限らない」という部分否定。

  ✎ 次の英文を日本語に直しなさい。

  Expensive things are not always good.

⑥ **But if they are lucky, all the villagers come running to pull the whale onto the ice.**
- ▶ all the villagers come runningは〈S + V + C (分詞)〉の形で、「村人たち全員が走ってやって来る」という意味。runningは主語all the villagersの様子・状態を説明している。 ⇒p.113 G-❸

  ✎ ( )内の語を適切な形に変えなさい。

  少女たちは歌いながらやって来た。

  The girls (come) (sing).

- ▶ to pullは〈目的〉を表す不定詞の副詞的用法。pull ～ onto ...で「～を…の上に引き上げる」という意味。

⑦ **I still remember seeing an old Eskimo lady come dancing and singing, to give thanks for the gift from the sea.**

▶ remember V-ingは「〜したことを覚えている」という意味。

✐ 次の各英文を下線部に注意して日本語に直しなさい。

I <u>remember locking</u> the door.

_____

<u>Remember to lock</u> the door.

_____

▶ seeing an old Eskimo lady come dancing and singingは〈V + O + C（原形不定詞）〉「Oが〜するのを見る」の構文。

✐ 次の英文を日本語に直しなさい。

I saw a bear come out of the forest.

_____

▶ come dancing and singingは「踊ったり歌ったりしながらやって来る」という意味。　　　　　　　　　　　　　　　　　　　⇒p.113 G-❸

⑧ **Once the whale is placed on the ice, an elder of the village says a prayer.**

▶ 接続詞のonceは「ひとたび〜すると」という意味。

▶ elderは「（部族などの）長老」という意味。elderはoldの比較級の1つ。

⑨ **Then the young people start cutting it up, carefully following the elder's instructions.**

▶ start V-ingは「〜し始める」という意味。

▶ cut 〜 upは「切り裂く、切り刻む」という意味。itは前文のthe whaleを指す。

▶ carefully following 〜は分詞構文で、「〜しながら」という付帯状況を表す。

✐ 次の英文を日本語に直しなさい。

She set up her new computer, following the instructions.

_____

⑩ **The meat is shared by all the villagers, and in the end they push the huge head bone of the whale back into the sea, saying, "Come back again next year!"**

▶ is shared by 〜は受動態で、by all the villagersは動作主を表す。

▶ in the endは「最後に」という意味。

　例 Mari's parents allowed her to work part-time at the bakery in the end.
　　「真理の両親は結局、彼女がパン屋でアルバイトをすることを認めた」

▶ push 〜 backは「〜を（もとの場所に）戻す」という意味。

▶ saying 〜は分詞構文で、「〜しながら」という付帯状況を表す。

□ nearby [nìərbáɪ]
□ come to (one's) mind
□ be home to ~
□ the beginning of time
□ attract [ətrǽkt]
□ movement [múːvmənt]
□ tens of thousands of ~
□ Arctic [áːrktɪk]
□ imagination [ɪmæ̀dʒɪnéɪʃən]
□ at this very moment
□ all sorts of ~
□ carry on ~
□ set ~ free
□ enrich [ɪnrítʃ]
□ concerned [kənsɔ́ːrnd]
□ as far as one is concerned

4

①Living in Alaska for many years, I've come to think that there are two types of nature: nature nearby and distant wild nature. ②Having a small park nearby makes us feel comfortable. That is very important. ③Distant nature, however, is what comes to my mind when I think about Alaska.

④Alaska has been home to wildlife since the beginning of time. ⑤I am most attracted by the seasonal movement of the caribou across the vast expanse of wilderness. Tens of thousands of them travel in Arctic Alaska every year.

⑥Thinking of distant nature, I sometimes wonder what will happen if the caribou and other wildlife disappear. Some people say, "⑦Who cares? ⑧Nobody goes that far just to look for caribou."

⑨Indeed, even if all the caribou die, your daily life will not change. ⑩But you might lose something important, and that is "distant nature in your imagination." ⑪Just imagine that at this very moment all sorts of wildlife are carrying on their lives out there. Isn't it wonderful? ⑫This act of imagination can set you free and enrich your life. ⑬As far as I'm concerned, distant nature is just as important as nature nearby.

このセクションの内容

星野氏は、自然には（A.　　　）と（B.　　　）の2種類があると考えている。（B.　　　）の中で生きている野生の生き物たちが失われても、私たちの日常生活に変化はないかもしれないが、私たちの（C.　　　）の中で息づく（B.　　　）は失われてしまう。

① **Living in Alaska for many years, I've come to think that there are two types of nature: nature nearby and distant wild nature.**

▶ Living in Alaska for many years は〈状態の継続〉を表す分詞構文。

▶ come to ～は「～するようになる」という意味。現在完了形の I've come to ～は「長い間アラスカに住んでいるうちに～と考えるようになった（現在もそう考えている）」という〈結果〉を表している。

② **Having a small park nearby makes us feel comfortable.**

▶〈S + make + O + C（原形不定詞）〉で「SがOを～させる」の文型。動名詞の Having ～ nearby 全体が主語。

③ **Distant nature, however, is what comes to my mind when I think about Alaska.**

▶ what は「～すること」という意味を表す関係代名詞で、名詞節を作る。この文では、what comes to my mind 全体が be 動詞の補語となっている。

▶ come to *one's* mind は「（人の）心[頭]に浮かぶ」という意味。

④ **Alaska has been home to wildlife since the beginning of time.**

▶ be home to ～は「（生物などの）生息地である」という意味。ここでは「有史以来」（since the beginning of time）の〈状態の継続〉を表す現在完了形 has been home の形で使われている。

⑤ **I am most attracted by the seasonal movement of the caribou across the vast expanse of wilderness.**

▶ be most attracted by ～は「～に最も心を引かれる」という意味。「私（＝星野氏）」という同一人物においての比較なので、most には the を付けない。

  例 Rika is the cutest of all the girl students. （＊ほかの女子生徒との比較）
  「すべての女子生徒の中でリカがいちばんかわいい」

  例 Rika is cutest in pink dress. （＊同一人物に関する服装の違いによる比較）
  「リカはピンク色の服を着ているときがいちばんかわいい」

⑥ **Thinking of distant nature, I sometimes wonder what will happen if the caribou and other wildlife disappear.**

▶ Thinking of distant nature は分詞構文で、「遠い自然を思うとき」という意味。When I think of distant nature とほぼ同じ意味。

▶ wonder what will happen は〈S + V + O（疑問詞節）〉の構文で、「何が起こるだろうかと思う」という意味。

⑦ **Who cares?**

▶ Who cares? は「だれが気にするものか」という意味。修辞疑問文と呼ばれるもので、形は疑問文であるが、内容的には「だれも気にしない」（≒

このセクションの内容 の答え→　A．身近な自然　B．遠い自然　C．想像力

Nobody cares.) という強い否定を表す。

> ✍ 次の英文を日本語に直しなさい。

Who knows what will happen tomorrow?

---

⑧ Nobody goes that far just to look for caribou.

▶ Nobody goesは「だれも行かない」という全否定を表す。

▶ that farは「そんな遠いところに」という意味。このthatは副詞で、「それほど、そんなに」という意味を表す。

▶ just to look for ~は〈目的〉を表す不定詞の副詞的用法。

⑨ Indeed, even if all the caribou die, your daily life will not change.

▶ even if ~は「たとえ~でも」という意味。

▶ indeedは「実際 (は)」(≒ in fact) という意味。直前に述べた内容を強調したり、補足したりする働きをする談話標識の１つ。

⑩ But you might lose something important, and that is "distant nature in your imagination."

▶ mightは「~かもしれない」と可能性を控えめに述べる助動詞。

▶ thatは直前のsomething importantを指す。

⑪ Just imagine that at this very moment all sorts of wildlife are carrying on their lives out there.

▶ at this very momentは「まさに今この瞬間に」(≒ just right now) という意味。veryは「まさにこの~」という〈強調〉を表す。

▶ all sorts of ~は「ありとあらゆる~」(≒ all kinds of ~) という意味。

▶ carry on ~は「~を続ける」(≒ continue ~) という意味。

▶ out there「そこでは」。例えばAlaskaのような「遠く離れた自然」を指す。

⑫ This act of imagination can set you free and enrich your life.

▶ This act of imaginationは、文⑪でJust imagine that ~「ちょっと~と想像してみてください」と筆者が勧めている「想像する行為」を指す。

▶ set ~ freeは「~を自由にする」という意味。

> ✍ 次の英文を日本語に直しなさい。

She set the bird in the cage free.

---

⑬ As far as I'm concerned, distant nature is just as important as nature nearby.

▶ As far as I'm concernedは「私の考えでは」(≒ in my view) という意味。

▶ just as important as ~は「~と同じくらい大切である」という意味。

Grammar for Communication

1 | seem to ～ ; it seems that ～

〈S＋seem to ～〉で「Sは～のように思える」という話者の主観的な判断や印象を表す。

She is a professional pianist. （＊客観的な事実）
（彼女はプロのピアニストである）

She seems to be a professional pianist. （＊話者の主観的な印象）
（彼女はプロのピアニストであるように思われる）

〈S＋seem to ～〉の文は〈It seems (that) ～〉の形で言いかえられる。

He seems to be happy about his exam results.

It seems (that) he is happy about his exam results.
（彼は試験の結果に満足しているように思われる）

(1) もとの文の主語がthat節の主語となる。
(2) 不定詞はthat節の主語に応じた形の動詞に変える。

◆Everything **seems to** be quiet. （すべてが静かであるように思われる）
　　= **It seems (that)** everything is quiet.
◆They **seemed to** be very busy. （彼らはとても忙しそうだった）
　　= **It seemed (that)** they were very busy.
◆The boy **seemed to** be lost in the forest. （少年は森で道に迷ったようだった）
　　= **It seemed (that)** the boy was lost in the forest.

〈It seems that ～〉の文では、to ～ を加えて話者を示すことがある。

◆**It seems** to me **that** she has not recovered from the shock.
　　（彼女はまだショックから立ち直っていないように私には思われる）

印象・感想をたずねるとき、疑問詞にはwhatを用いる。

◆What **seems to** be the problem[trouble]?
　　（どうなさいましたか） （＊医者が患者に症状をたずねるときの表現）
　　— I've had a terrible headache since this morning.
　　（今朝から頭痛がひどいのです）

2　S + is + C (C = that節)

〈S + V + C〉のCの位置にthat節がくることがある。この構文で主語となる名詞には、fact、point、problem、reason、truthなどがある。

◆ **The problem is that** he often breaks his promise.
（問題は彼がよく約束を破るということだ）
◆ **The fact was that** they didn't go there that afternoon.
（実は彼らはその日の午後にそこには行かなかったのだ）
◆ **The truth is that** I have never wanted to leave this country.
（本当は私はこれまでに一度もこの国を出たいと思ったことはない）
◆ **The reason** for his being angry **is that** we didn't invite him to the party.
（彼が怒っている理由は私たちが彼をパーティーに招かなかったことだ）
◆ **The point is that** you should do your best.
（要するにあなたは最善を尽くすべきだということだ）

3　S + V + C (C =分詞)

〈S + V + C〉のCには分詞 (現在分詞・過去分詞) が用いられることもある。この構文を作る動詞にはkeep、come、get、remainなどが用いられる。

◆ The horses **kept running** in the field.
（馬たちは野原を走り続けた）
◆ Anne **came singing** happily.
（アンは楽しそうに歌いながらやって来た）
◆ My bike **got stolen** last night.　*stolen　steal「〜を盗む」の過去分詞
（私の自転車は昨夜盗まれた）
◆ The poor fox **remained caught** in the trap.　*trap「わな」
（そのかわいそうなキツネはわなにかかったままだった）

〈S + V + C (＝分詞)〉を使った定型表現として、〈go + 現在分詞〉「〜しに行く」や〈get + 現在分詞〉「〜し始める」がある。
◆ Rika **went swimming** in the sea yesterday. （昨日リカは海に泳ぎに行った）
◆ Shall we **get going** now? （そろそろ出かけましょうか）

確認問題

語彙・表現

1 次の語を ( ) 内の指示にしたがって書きかえなさい。

(1) move （「移動」を表す名詞に）　　(2) imagine （名詞に）

(3) season （形容詞に）　　(4) success （形容詞に）

2 第1音節にアクセント (強勢) のある語を2つ選び、記号で答えなさい。

ア　re-ply　　　　　イ　ex-panse　　　　ウ　dis-tant

エ　de-gree　　　　オ　tem-per-a-ture　　カ　ho-ri-zon

3 日本語に合うように、( ) 内に適切な語を入れなさい。

(1) 私たちはあと10分かそこらで空港に着きます。

We'll arrive at the airport in ten minutes (　　) (　　).

(2) 最初、彼女はその大型犬のことがこわかった。

(　　) (　　), she was afraid of the big dog.

(3) その島には珍しい動物が生息している。

The island is (　　) (　　) some rare animals.

(4) 彼が森を散歩しているときによい考えが浮かんだ。

A good idea (　　) to (　　) (　　) while he was walking in the forest.

文のパターン・文法

1 ( ) 内の語を適切な形に直しなさい。

(1) The boy came (run) toward me.

(2) They kept (laugh) as they watched the funny man dancing.

(3) You should remain (seat) until the plane stops completely.

(4) Masaki went (ski) in Hokkaido last winter.

2 次の各組の文がほぼ同じ意味になるように、( ) 内に適切な語を入れなさい。

(1) She seems to want something to drink.

(　　) seems (　　) she (　　) something to drink.

(2) Nami seemed to be nervous before the important game.

(　　) (　　) Nami (　　) nervous before the important game.

(3) We're in trouble because we cannot contact Mike.

(　　) (　　) is (　　) we cannot contact Mike.

3 ( )内の語句を並べかえて、英文を完成させなさい。

(1) (was / we / little time / that / the problem / had).

_____.

(2) (is / nobody / the truth / saw / that) the person that night.

_____ the person that night.

(3) (be / seemed / a success / the party / to).

_____.

(4) (the man / eat / it / nothing / that / to / seemed / had).

_____.

(5) (a shower / she / caught / got / in) on her way back home.

_____ on her way back home.

総合

次の文を読んで、あとの問いに答えなさい。

> Thinking of distant nature, I sometimes wonder what will happen if the caribou and other wildlife disappear. Some people say, "①Who cares? Nobody goes that far just to look for caribou."
>
> Indeed, even if all the caribou die, your daily life will not change. But you might lose ②something important, and that is "distant nature in your imagination." Just imagine that at this very moment ③(   ) (   ) (   ) wildlife are carrying on their lives out there. Isn't it wonderful? This act of imagination can set you free and (④) your life. ⑤As far as I'm concerned, distant nature is just as important as nature nearby.

問1 下線部①はどのようなことが起きても「かまわない」と言っているのですか。日本語で具体的に説明しなさい。

問2 下線部②が具体的に指す内容を本文中のひと続きの英語5語で答えなさい。

問3 下線部③が「あらゆる種類の野生生物」という意味になるように、( )内に入る最も適切な3語を書きなさい。

問4 ④の( )内に入る最も適切な語を選びなさい。
ア enrich　　イ attract　　ウ melt　　エ introduce

問5 下線部⑤を日本語に直しなさい。

Lesson 8　Not So Long Ago

□ exhibition [èksɪbíʃən]
□ feature [fíːtʃər]
□ ancient [éɪnʃənt]
□ progress [prɑ́grəs]
□ achieve [ətʃíːv]
□ freedom [fríːdəm]
□ equality [ɪkwɑ́ləti]
□ tens of millions of ~
□ go through ~
□ particularly [pərtíkjələrli]

①A group of high school students is visiting a photo exhibition featuring the 20th century. A museum guide speaks to the students.

1

Today I'm going to take you back to the 20th century. ②It may seem to you like ancient history, but in fact, it really was not so long ago. ③The 300 photographs in this exhibition show us the history of the past century.

④The 20th century was an age of great progress in science and communications. ⑤People's lives became richer and more comfortable. ⑥People achieved greater freedom and equality, and seemed to be closer to the dream of living a happy life.

⑦But it was also an age of terrible wars, and tens of millions of people lost their lives. ⑧The photos here will show you what people like you and me went through in the 20th century. ⑨As you look at them, ask yourself: "⑩How would you feel if these were photos of your own family and friends?" ⑪Some will shock you; some may make you sad or angry. But they will also give you a message for our future. ⑫First of all, I would like to show you two photographs which are particularly important to us.

このセクションの内容

20世紀は科学と通信の分野でめざましい進歩が見られた一方、悲惨な
(A.　　　) の時代でもあった。この20世紀を振り返る写真展には
(B.　　　) 枚の写真が展示されている。それらの写真からはショック、
悲しみや怒りを感じると同時に、(C.　　　　　　　) も伝わってくる。

① **A group of high school students is visiting a photo exhibition featuring the 20th century.**
  ▶ featuring 〜は feature「〜を特集する、呼び物にする」の現在分詞形で、a photo exhibition を後ろから修飾する形容詞的用法。

② **It may seem to you like ancient history, but in fact, it really was not so long ago.**
  ▶〈seem（＋to＋人）＋like 〜〉は「（人にとっては）〜のように思える」という意味。
  ▶ 文中に主語として使われている it は、どちらも前文の the 20th century を指す。
  ▶ in fact は、文と文の論理的な関係を示す談話標識の1つ。but のあとに置かれると、直前の内容を訂正して、「実際は、それどころか」という意味を表す。
  ▶ 本課のタイトルにもなっている not so long ago は、「それほど昔のことではない」という意味。

③ **The 300 photographs in this exhibition show us the history of the past century.**
  ▶〈show ＋ O₁（人）＋ O₂（事柄）〉で「（人）に事柄を見せる［教える］」という意味。
  ▶ the past century「前世紀」は21世紀から見た20世紀のこと。

④ **The 20th century was an age of great progress in science and communications.**
  ▶ progress in 〜は「〜における進歩」という意味。

⑤ **People's lives became richer and more comfortable.**
  ▶ lives は名詞 life「生活」の複数形。[láɪvz] と発音する。

⑥ **People achieved greater freedom and equality, and seemed to be closer to the dream of living a happy life.**
  ▶ 主語の People は achieved と seemed の両方の主語。seem to be 〜は「〜であるように思われる」という話者の主観的な印象を表す。
  ▶ be close to 〜は「〜に近い」という意味。
  ▶ the dream of V-ing は「〜するという夢」という意味。of は「〜という…」の意味で、同格を表す。動名詞の living は前置詞 of の目的語。
  ▶ live a happy life は「幸福な生活［人生］を送る」という意味。live と life は同じ語源に由来する語。動詞と同じ語源の名詞がその動詞の目的語になるとき、それを「同族目的語」と呼ぶ。
    例 I dreamed a wonderful dream.
    「私は素晴らしい夢を見た」

⑦ **But it was also an age of terrible wars, and tens of millions of people lost their lives.**
  ▶ it は文④の The 20th century を指している。

このセクションの内容 の答え→ A．戦争　B．300　C．未来へのメッセージ

▶ million は「100万」という意味。〈tens of millions of ＋ 複数名詞〉で「何千万もの〜」（≒ a great number of 〜）という意味になる。

✎ 英文を完成させなさい。

何千万もの人々がその試合をテレビで見た。

(　　　) (　　　) (　　　　) (　　　　) people watched the game on TV.

▶ lose *one's* life で「命を落とす」という意味。

⑧ **The photos here will show you what people like you and me went through in the 20ᵗʰ century.**

▶〈show ＋ O₁（人）＋ O₂（疑問詞節）〉で「（人）に〜であるかを示す」という意味。　⇒p.128 G-❷

✎ 次の英文を日本語に直しなさい。

This picture shows us how the people at that time lived.

▶ what 節内の go through 〜は「〜を通り抜ける、（試練・困難など）を体験する」という意味。

例 These countries went through several wars in the 19ᵗʰ century.
「これらの国々は19世紀にいくつかの戦争を経験した」

⑨ **As you look at them, ask yourself**

▶ them は前文の The photos here、つまり「写真展」で展示されている写真を指している。

⑩ **How would you feel if these were photos of your own family and friends?**

▶ 仮定法過去の文。現在の事実に反することや、現実に起こりそうにもないことを仮定するときに用いる。　⇒p.128 G-❶

✎ 次の英文を日本語に直しなさい。

What would he say if we told him this news?

---

⑪ **Some will shock you; some may make you sad or angry.**

▶ some 〜，some ...は「〜もあれば、…もある」という意味。この文では、some はどちらも some photos のこと。前後の文脈から指すものが明らかな場合、some 単独で用いられる。

▶〈make ＋ O ＋ C〉は「O を C にする」という意味。ここは O が you、C が形容詞の sad と angry。

⑫ **First of all, I would like to show you two photographs which are particularly important to us.**

▶ which は two photographs を先行詞とする主格の関係代名詞。

教科書p.130　Section 2

□ photojournalist
　[fòutoudʒóːrnəlɪst]
□ Joe O'Donnell [dʒóu oʊdánl]
□ interviewer [íntərvjùːər]
□ on *one's* back
□ serious [síəriəs]
□ tip [tip]
□ as if ～
□ asleep [əslíːp]
□ fast asleep
□ in white masks
□ take off ～
□ That is when ～
□ hold ～ by the ...
□ flame [fléim]
□ blood [blʌd]
□ turn around
□ deserve [dizə́ːrv]

2

This photograph was taken by an American photojournalist, Joe O'Donnell, in Nagasaki in 1945. He spoke to a Japanese interviewer about this picture:

"①I saw a boy about 10 years old walking by. ②He was carrying a baby on his back. ③In those days in Japan, we often saw children playing with their little brothers or sisters on their backs, but this boy was clearly different. ④I could see that he had come to this place for a serious reason. ⑤He was wearing no shoes. His face was hard. ⑥The little head was tipped back as if the baby were fast asleep.

"The boy stood there for 5 or 10 minutes. ⑦The men in white masks walked over to him and quietly began to take off the rope that was holding the baby. ⑧That is when I saw that the baby was already dead. ⑨The men held the body by the hands and feet and placed it on the fire.

"⑩The boy stood there straight without moving, watching the flames. ⑪He was biting his lower lip so hard that it shone with blood. ⑫The flame burned low like the sun going down. The boy turned around and walked silently away."

Years later, O'Donnell said: "⑬Children and their mothers did not deserve to die to win a war."

このセクションの内容

ガイドが紹介したのは（A.　　　）年長崎でアメリカ人フォトジャーナリストが撮影した写真である。それは、すでに亡くなっている（B.　　　　）を背負っている少年の写真だった。少年は遺体を包む（C.　　　）を見つめ立ち去った。

119

① **I saw a boy about 10 years old walking by.**

  ▶〈see + O + V-ing〉で「Oが～しているのを見る」という意味。

  ▶ walk by は「そばを通り過ぎる」という意味。

② **He was carrying a baby on his back.**

  ▶ on *one's* back は「(人の)背中に」という意味。

③ **In those days in Japan, we often saw children playing with their little brothers or sisters on their backs**

  ▶ in those days は「その当時」という意味。*cf.* these days「最近、近ごろ」

  ▶〈with + 名詞 + 状態を表す語句〉は〈付帯状況〉を表し、「～(名詞)を…のままにして」という意味を表す。　　　　　　　　　　⇒p.129 G-❸

  > ✍ 次の英文を日本語に直しなさい。

  He began to run with the heavy bag in his hands.

  ⸻

④ **I could see that he had come to this place for a serious reason.**

  ▶ had come は過去完了形。過去のある時点までの〈完了・結果〉を表し、「すでに～していた」の意味。

⑤ **He was wearing no shoes.**

  ▶ 動詞 wear を進行形で使うと、「(ある特定のときに) ～を着ている[はいている、かぶっている、など]」という一時的な服装を表す。

  ▶ 主語や目的語などに〈no + 複数名詞〉を用いた場合、「1つの[1人の] ～もない」という全否定となる。

⑥ **The little head was tipped back as if the baby were fast asleep.**

  ▶ was tipped back は tip back ～「～を後ろに傾ける」の受動態の過去形。

  ▶〈as if + 仮定法過去〉で「まるで～かのように」という意味。仮定法過去では、主語の人称・数に関係なく be 動詞は were を用いるのが原則。⇒p.128 G-❶

  > ✍ 英文を完成させなさい。

  その少女はまるで母親のように弟の世話をしていた。

  The girl took care of her little brother (　　) (　　) she (　　) his mother.

  ▶ fast asleep は「ぐっすり眠って」(≒ sleeping deeply)という意味。

⑦ **The men in white masks walked over to him and quietly began to take off the rope that was holding the baby.**

  ▶ in white masks は「白いマスクをした」(≒ wearing white masks)という意味。

▶ walk over to 〜は「〜のところに歩み寄る」という意味。

▶ take off 〜は「〜を取る、はずす、脱ぐ」という意味。*cf.* put on 〜「〜を着る」

✎ 次の英文を日本語に直しなさい。

My grandfather took off the glasses and put on other glasses.

___

▶ that は the rope を先行詞とする主格の関係代名詞。

⑧ **That is when I saw that the baby was already dead.**

▶ That は前文の、男たちがひもをほどき始めたときのこと。

▶ That is when 〜は「〜はその時だ」(≒ That is the time when 〜)という意味。関係副詞 when の先行詞 the time が省略された形。

⑨ **The men held the body by the hands and feet and placed it on the fire.**

▶ 〈hold +（人）+ by the 〜〉は「（人）の〜（身体の一部）をつかむ」という意味。同様の表現に次のようなものがある。

・〈catch +（人）+ by the arm[sleeve]〉「（人）の腕[袖]をつかむ」
・〈pat +（人）+ on the shoulder[back]〉「（人）の肩[背中]を軽くたたく」
・〈look +（人）+ in the eye[face]〉「（人）の目[顔]をまともに見る」

▶ body は「死体、遺体」という意味。

⑩ **The boy stood there straight without moving, watching the flames.**

▶ stand straight は「まっすぐに立つ」という意味。

▶ without V-ing は「〜することなしに、〜しないで」という意味。

▶ watching the flames は〈付帯状況〉を表す分詞構文。

⑪ **He was biting his lower lip so hard that it shone with blood.**

▶ lower lip は「下唇」という意味。*cf.* upper lip「上唇」

▶ so 〜 that ... は「とても〜なので…だ」という意味。結果を表す that 節の主語 it は his lower lip を指す。

▶ shine with blood は「血で（赤く）光っている」という意味。

⑫ **The flame burned low like the sun going down.**

▶ burn low は「火の勢いが衰える、下火になる」という意味。

▶ go down は「（太陽・月などが）沈む」という意味。ここでは現在分詞の形で用いられ、直前の the sun を修飾している。

⑬ **Children and their mothers did not deserve to die to win a war.**

▶ deserve to 〜は「（報酬・罪など）に値する」という意味。did not deserve to die は「命を落とさなければならないようなことはしなかった」という意味。

▶ to win a war は〈目的〉を表す不定詞の副詞的用法。

Lesson 8

□ Vietnam [vìːetnáːm]

□ the Vietnam War

□ Kim Phuc [kím fúk]

□ in pain

□ burn off ～

□ be gone

□ operation [àpəréiʃən]

□ repair [rɪpéər]

3

①Now let's take a look at this picture. ②I'm sure some of you have seen it before. ③It was taken at the time of the Vietnam War in 1972. ④Here a young girl, Kim Phuc, is running down a road in pain, with her clothes burned off. ⑤This is what she once said about the experience:

"⑥I didn't hear anything, but I saw the fire around me. ⑦And suddenly my clothes were gone because of the fire. And I saw the fire over my body, especially my arm. But my feet weren't burned. I was crying, and I was running out of the fire. ⑧I kept running and running and running.

"⑨I was in the hospital. Fourteen months. ⑩I went through 17 operations to repair the burns over half my body. ⑪And that thing changed my life. ⑫It made me think about how I could help people.

"When my parents first showed me the picture from the newspaper, ⑬I couldn't believe that it was me, because it was so terrible. ⑭I want everybody to see that picture, because in that picture people can see what war is. ⑮It's terrible for the children. You can see everything in my face. ⑯I want people to learn from it."

このセクションの内容

次は（A.　　　　）中の1972年の少女の写真である。少女は服が焼け落ち、痛みの中、走り続けている。14か月の入院、17回もの（B.　　　　）を経験した彼女だが、その写真により、（C.　　　　）がどんなものかをみんなに見てほしいと語っている。

① **Now let's take a look at this picture.**

▶ take a look at 〜は「〜をちょっと見る、〜に目を通す」という1回限りの動作・行為を表す。

> ✍ 次の英文を日本語に直しなさい。

May I take a look at this ring?

② **I'm sure some of you have seen it before.**

▶ I'm sure (that) 〜は「私は〜を確信している」という意味。

▶ have seen は〈経験〉を表す現在完了。

▶ it は前文の this picture を指している。

③ **It was taken at the time of the Vietnam War in 1972.**

▶ at the time of the Vietnam War in 1972は「ベトナム戦争のさなかの1972年に」という意味。at the time of 〜は「〜のときに」という意味。

▶ the Vietnam War など、戦争名を〈場所＋war〉で表すときは、ふつう the を付ける。

④ **Here a young girl, Kim Phuc, is running down a road in pain, with her clothes burned off.**

▶ a young girl と人名の Kim Phuc「キムフック」は、コンマ (,) をはさんで同格の関係。

▶ with her clothes burned off は「衣類を焼き尽くされて」という意味。〈with＋名詞＋過去分詞〉は「〜が…された状態で」という〈付帯状況〉を表す。her clothes と burned off は受け身の関係になっている。　　　⇒p.129 G-❸

> ✍ 英文を完成させなさい。

父は目を閉じてソファーに座っていた。

My father was sitting on the sofa (　　　) his eyes (　　　).

▶ clothes「衣服」は常に複数形で用いられる。

⑤ **This is what she once said about the experience**

▶ what はその中に先行詞を含む関係代名詞で、「〜するもの、〜すること」という意味。

⑥ **I didn't hear anything**

▶ not 〜 anything は「何も〜ない」という意味。この文は I heard nothing. としてもほぼ同じ意味。

⑦ **And suddenly my clothes were gone because of the fire.**

▶ be gone は「なくなる」(≒ be away or lost) という意味。

▶ because of 〜は「〜のために」という意味。

⑧ **I kept running and running and running.**

▶ keep V-ing は「〜し続ける」という意味。ここでは running and running and running と 3 度繰り返すことで、必死に走り続けた様子が強調されている。

⑨ **I was in the hospital.**

▶ be in the hospital は「入院している」という意味。*cf.* be out of the hospital「退院している」

⑩ **I went through 17 operations to repair the burns over half my body.**

▶ go through 〜は「〜を経験する、（手術などを）受ける」という意味。

▶ to repair 〜は〈目的〉を表す不定詞の副詞的用法。

▶ burns はここでは「やけど」という意味の名詞。

▶ over half my body は「全身の半分に及ぶ」という意味。

⑪ **And that thing changed my life.**

▶ that thing とは14か月の入院中に17回の手術を受けたことを指している。

⑫ **It made me think about how I could help people.**

▶ It は前文の that thing と同じく、14か月の入院中に17回の手術を受けたことを指している。

▶〈make + O + 原形不定詞〉は「O に〜させる」という意味。

> ✍ 次の英文を日本語に直しなさい。
>
> Her words made us all think about environmental problems.

▶ think about 〜は「〜について考える」という意味。

▶ how I could help people は疑問詞節で、think about の目的語。

⑬ **I couldn't believe that it was me, because it was so terrible.**

▶ 2つの it はともに、写真に写っている自分の姿のこと。

⑭ **I want everybody to see that picture, because in that picture people can see what war is.**

▶〈want +（人）+ to 〜〉は「（人）に〜してほしい」という意味。

▶ in that picture は強調のために文頭に置かれている。通常の語順では、people can see what war is in that picture となる。

▶ 2つ目の see は「〜を理解する、見て取る」という意味。

▶ what war is「戦争とはどのようなものか」は疑問詞節で、see の目的語。

⑮ **It's terrible for the children.**

▶ It は前文の war を指している。

⑯ **I want people to learn from it.**

▶ learn from it の it は文⑭の that picture を指している。

4

□ photographs tell us ~
□ in the past
□ journalist [dʒə́ːrnəlist]
□ a great many ~
□ I have to show my son ~ and that there should ...
□ need not ~
□ witness [wítnəs]

①So photographs tell us a lot. ②They show us what happened in the past. ③They sometimes show us things we may not wish to see.

The 20th century was a century of war. ④There were two world wars, a cold war, and smaller wars all over the world. ⑤A Japanese journalist even called the 20th century "36,000 days of suffering." ⑥It is perhaps difficult to find any sign of hope in the photos here, but we can if we try.

⑦Kim Phuc's story is a good example. ⑧With warm support from a great many people, she now enjoys a happy family life in Canada. She says, "⑨I have to show my son what happened to his mom, to her country, and that there should never be war again."

⑩When the 21st century began, many of us hoped that we were entering the century of peace, but wars go on. However, there is still time to change. ⑪If we can learn the lessons from the past, history need not repeat itself.

⑫Just remember that what you have witnessed in this exhibition today happened not so long ago.

このセクションの内容

　（A.　　　　）は多くのことを私たちに語っている。20世紀は戦争の時代だったが、この展覧会を通じて戦争を二度と繰り返してはいけないという（B.　　　）が伝わってくる。これが起きたのはそんなに（C.　　　　）のことではないのである。

① **So photographs tell us a lot.**

▶〈tell + O₁（人）+ O₂（もの）〉で「（人）に～を語る［教えてくれる］」という意味。ここでは無生物のphotographsが主語として使われている。

▶a lotは「多くのこと」という意味。

② **They show us what happened in the past.**

▶〈S + V + O₁（人）+ O₂（疑問詞節）〉の文。「（人）に何を～するかを示す［教える］」という意味。　⇒p.128 G-❷

▶Theyは前文のphotographsを指している。

▶in the pastは「過去に（おいて）」という意味。*cf.* in the future「将来」

　　✐ 次の英文を日本語に直しなさい。

　　Natural disasters in the past teach us a lot.

───────────────────────

③ **They sometimes show us things we may not wish to see.**

▶thingsのあとに目的格の関係代名詞that［which］が省略されている。

▶mayは〈推量〉を表す助動詞で、「～かもしれない」という意味。

▶wish to ～は「～したいと思う」という意味。

④ **There were two world wars, a cold war, and smaller wars all over the world.**

▶two world warsとは第一次世界大戦（World War I / the First World War）と第二次世界大戦（World War II / the Second World War）を指す。

▶a cold warは「（一般的に）冷戦（というもの）」という意味。*cf.* the Cold War（米ソの冷戦）

▶all over the worldは「世界中に」という意味。

⑤ **A Japanese journalist even called the 20ᵗʰ century "36,000 days of suffering."**

▶〈call + O + C〉は「OをCと呼ぶ」という意味。Oはthe 20ᵗʰ century、Cは"36,000 days of suffering"。

⑥ **It is perhaps difficult to find any sign of hope in the photos here, but we can if we try.**

▶It is ... to ～の構文で「～することは…だ」の意味。Itはto ～を受ける形式主語。

▶〈any + 単数名詞〉は肯定文で「どんな～でも」という意味。

▶sign of ～は「～の兆し、兆候」という意味。

▶we can if we tryは直前の文との共通部分が省略されている。we can（find some signs of hope）if we try（to find them）と補って考える。

⑦ **Kim Phuc's story is a good example.**

▶exampleとは「見つけようとすれば見つかる希望の兆し」の例のこと。

⑧ **With warm support from a great many people, she now enjoys a happy family life in Canada.**

▶ with は「～を得て」という意味。from ～ people が warm support を修飾している。

▶ a great many ～は「非常に多くの～」(≒ a great number of ～) という意味。

⑨ **I have to show my son what happened to his mom, to her country, and that there should never be war again.**

▶〈S + V + O₁ + O₂ (O₂＝疑問詞節と that 節)〉の文。　　⇒p.128 G-❷

前半：<u>show</u> <u>my son</u> <u>what happened to his mom, to her country,</u>
　　　　V　　O₁　　　　O₂ (O₂＝疑問詞節)

後半：and <u>(show</u> <u>him)</u> <u>that there should never be war again</u>
　　　　　　V　　O₁　　　O₂ (O₂＝that節)

▶ 目的語になる that 節が複数ある場合、最初の that は省略できるが、2つ目以降の that は省略できない。

⑩ **When the 21ˢᵗ century began, many of us hoped that we were entering the century of peace, but wars go on.**

▶ enter the century of peace は「平和の世紀に入る」という意味。教科書 p.134の4行目に出てくる a century of war「戦争の世紀」と対比させた表現。

▶ go on は「続く」という意味。

⑪ **If we can learn the lessons from the past, history need not repeat itself.**

▶ learn a lesson from ～は「～から教訓を学ぶ」という意味。

▶ need not は助動詞 need の否定形で、「～する必要はない」(≒ doesn't have to ～) という意味。

▶ history need not repeat itself は、History repeats itself.「歴史は繰り返す」ということわざを踏まえた表現。

⑫ **Just remember that what you have witnessed in this exhibition today happened not so long ago.**

▶ Just remember that ～は「～ということを忘れないでください」という意味。

▶ what は先行詞を含む関係代名詞で、「～するもの、～すること」という意味の名詞節を作る。ここでは what you have ～ exhibition today 全体が名詞節で、that 節の主語になっている。

　🖋 次の英文を日本語に直しなさい。

　　What we need now is action.

▶ not so long ago は「それほど昔のことではない」という意味。

Grammar for Communication

1 仮定法過去

現在の事実と反することを仮定したり、願望したりするときに仮定法過去を用いる。基本的な形は次の通りである。

・〈If＋S＋動詞の過去形 〜，S＋助動詞の過去形＋動詞の原形 ...〉
  「もし〜ならば、…だろうに」
・〈I wish＋S＋動詞の過去形 〜〉「〜であればいいのに」
・〈as if[though]＋S＋動詞の過去形〉「まるで〜かのように」

◆ **If** I **had** much time，I **could visit** the museum.
  （もし時間がたくさんあったら、美術館を訪れることができるのだが）
  ≒ Because I don't have much time, I can't visit the museum.
  （時間があまりないので、私は美術館を訪れることができない）

◆ What **would** Mike **do if** he **were** here?
  （もしマイクがここにいたらどうするだろうか）
  ★仮定法過去では、主語が1人称、3人称の単数の場合でも、was ではなく were を用いるのが原則。（＊ただし、口語では was を用いることもある。）

◆ **I wish** I **were** as young as you.
  （あなたと同じくらい若ければいいのに）
  ≒ I am sorry[It is a pity] that I am not as young as you.
  （私はあなたほど若くなくて残念だ）

◆ He speaks **as if[though]** he **knew** everything about Tokyo.
  （彼はまるで東京についてなんでも知っているかのような口ぶりである）

2 S＋V＋O₁＋O₂（O₂＝that節／疑問詞節）

that節〈that＋S＋V 〜〉や疑問詞節〈疑問詞＋S＋V 〜〉は名詞節の働きをし、文の主語や動詞の補語、目的語になる。〈S＋V＋O₁＋O₂〉の文型で、間接目的語 (O₁) のあとに続いて、直接目的語 (O₂) の働きをすることもできる。

◆ That experience **taught** him **that** life was not so easy.
  （その経験で、彼は人生がそれほど甘くないことがわかった）

◆ The movie **showed** us <u>how</u> terrible war was.
（その映画は私たちに戦争がいかに恐ろしいかを示してくれた）

◆ This story **will tell** you <u>what</u> you should do to succeed.
（この物語は成功するために何をすべきかをあなたに教えてくれるだろう）

◆ She **has told** me <u>where</u> she is going to go this summer.
（彼女は私に今年の夏どこに行くつもりかを話してくれた）

3 　　付帯状況を表す with 〜

〈with ＋（代）名詞＋形容詞・副詞・分詞・前置詞句など〉の形で、ある動作や状態に伴う付帯状況を表す。「〜しながら」、「〜なので」など、同時の動作・状態や理由を表すことが多い。形容詞・副詞・分詞・前置詞句などが直前の名詞の状態を表す。

1.〈with ＋（代）名詞＋前置詞句〉
◆ The boy was walking **with** his hands **in his pockets**.
（その少年は両手をポケットに入れて歩いていた）

2.〈with ＋（代）名詞＋副詞〉
◆ He was busy working hard **with** his jacket **off**.
（彼はジャケットを脱いで忙しく懸命に働いていた）

◆ My grandmother was reading a newspaper **with** her glasses **on**.
（祖母はメガネをかけて新聞を読んでいた）

3.〈with ＋（代）名詞＋分詞〉
◆ The girl came running toward us **with** her hair **waving** in the wind.
（その少女は風に髪をなびかせながら私たちのほうに駆けてきた）

◆ The man was standing there **with** his hat **covered** with snow.
（その男は、帽子を雪で覆われたままそこに立っていた）

4.〈with ＋（代）名詞＋形容詞〉
◆ He looked at me, **with** his eyes wide **open**.
（彼は目を大きく見開いて私を見つめた）

◆ Don't talk **with** your mouth **full**.
（口いっぱいにほおばったまましゃべってはいけません）

確認問題

語彙・表現

1 第2音節にアクセント (強勢) のある語を2つ選び、記号で答えなさい。

ア　e-qual-i-ty　　　　イ　jour-nal-ist　　　　ウ　wit-ness

エ　prog-ress 名　　　オ　par-tic-u-lar-ly　　カ　ex-hi-bi-tion

2 日本語に合うように、( ) 内に適切な語を入れなさい。

(1) イベントはとても多くの人々で混雑していた。

The event was crowded with (　　　) (　　　) (　　　) people.

(2) そのとき私は自分が大きな間違いを犯していたことに気づいた。

That (　　　) (　　　) I found I had made a big mistake.

(3) 彼女は突然振り返って、私たちにほほ笑んだ。

She (　　　) (　　　) suddenly, smiling at us.

(4) その子どもは母親の袖をしっかりとつかんだ。　*sleeve「袖」

The child (　　　) her mother (　　　) the sleeve.

(5) 私たちが車で湖に向かっている間、トムはぐっすりと眠っていた。

Tom was (　　　) (　　　) while we were driving to the lake.

(6) 彼女は若いころ多くの困難を経験した。

She (　　　) (　　　) a lot of difficulties when she was young.

文のパターン・文法

1 次の各文を、仮定法過去を用いてほぼ同じ意味の文に書きかえなさい。

(1) Because I don't have enough money, I can't buy this CD.

_____

(2) As he doesn't know your phone number, he won't call you.

_____

(3) I am sorry that I cannot speak English as well as you.

_____

(4) She isn't a journalist, but she talks like one.

_____

2 ( ) 内の語句を並べかえて、英文を完成させなさい。

(1) The boy kept (his back / with / walking / on / a heavy bag).

The boy kept _____.

(2) She ran (her hair / the wind / blowing / with / in).
She ran _____ .

(3) This book will (us / the people / tell / live / in / how / the village).
This book will _____ .

(4) The important thing (we / is / what / do / him / will / for).
The important thing _____ .

(5) We (sunny / baseball / if / could / were / now / play / it).
We _____ .

(6) (kinder / he / others / wish / were / I / to).

_____ .

総合

次の文を読んで、あとの問いに答えなさい。

The 20ᵗʰ century was an age of great progress in science and communications. People's lives became richer and more comfortable. People achieved greater ①(free) and equality, and seemed to be closer to the dream of (②) a happy life.

But it was also an age of terrible wars, and ③(_____) (_____) (_____) of people lost their lives. The photos here will show you what people like you and me went through in the 20ᵗʰ century. As you look at them, ask yourself: "④How would you feel if these were photos of your own family and friends?" Some will shock you; some may make you sad or angry. But they will also give you a message for our future. First of all, I would like to show you two photographs which are particularly important to us.

問1　①の語の名詞形を書きなさい。

問2　②の（　）内に入る適語を書きなさい。

問3　下線部③が「何千万もの人々」という意味になるように、（　）内に入る最も適切な3語を書きなさい。

問4　下線部④を日本語に直しなさい。

問5　ここで触れられている写真が「あなた」に教えてくれるものとはどのようなことですか。日本語で説明しなさい。

Our Lost Friend

教科書p.146　Section 1

- ☐ Easter Island [íːstər áɪlənd]
- ☐ Rapa Nui [rɑ́ːpə núːi]
- ☐ giant [dʒáɪənt]
- ☐ statue [stǽtʃuː]
- ☐ moai [mòuáɪ]
- ☐ the British Museum
- ☐ moreover [mɔːróuvər]
- ☐ steal [stíːl]
- ☐ islander [áɪləndər]
- ☐ scatter [skǽtər]
- ☐ hillside [hílsàɪd]
- ☐ damage [dǽmɪdʒ]
- ☐ height [háɪt]
- ☐ (be) in ~ condition
- ☐ permission [pərmíʃən]
- ☐ in short
- ☐ Queen Victoria
  [kwíːn vɪktɔ́ːriə]
- ☐ be known as ~
- ☐ Hoa Hakananai'a
  [hóuə hæ̀kənənáɪə]
- ☐ translate [trǽnsleɪt]
- ☐ take a new turn
- ☐ gain [géɪn]
- ☐ gain control of ~
- ☐ Chile [tʃíli]
- ☐ bring ~ back
- ☐ delegation [dèlɪgéɪʃən]

①Easter Island (Rapa Nui) is famous for its giant statues called moai. But did you know that the most famous statue is in the British Museum? Moreover, it was stolen from the islanders. Here is the story.

1

②The story began when a British ship arrived at Easter Island in 1868. ③The crew saw huge statues scattered on a hillside. ④Most of the statues were damaged, but there was one smaller statue, about 2.4 meters in height, in perfect condition.

⑤The crew took the statue without asking permission from the islanders. ⑥In short, they stole it. ⑦They brought it to England as a gift for Queen Victoria, who donated it to the British Museum. ⑧It is known as Hoa Hakananai'a, Rapa Nui words which can be translated as "Lost Friend."

⑨About 150 years later, the story took a new turn. ⑩In 2017 the Rapa Nui people gained control of their land, which had been part of Chile since 1888. ⑪One of the first things they did was to try to bring Hoa Hakananai'a back to Easter Island. ⑫They formed a delegation to ask the British Museum to let their Lost Friend come home.

132

> **このセクションの内容**
>
> 1868年、イギリスの船がイースター島に着いたとき、船員たちは島に散在している巨大な影像のうちの1体を島民から（A.　　　　）を得ることなく本国に持ち帰った。それから約150年後、現地のラパ・ヌイ語で「ホアハカナナイア」（「(B.　　　　)」の意味)と呼ばれるモアイ像を取り戻そうと、ラパ・ヌイの人々は大英博物館に影像の（C.　　　　）を求めた。

① **Easter Island (Rapa Nui) is famous for its giant statues called moai.**

> ▶ be famous for ～は「～で有名だ」。
>
> ▶ called ～はits giant statuesを後ろから修飾する過去分詞の形容詞的用法。

② **The story began when a British ship arrived at Easter Island in 1868.**

> ▶ arrive at ～は「（比較的狭い場所）に着く、到着する」という意味。
>
> *cf.* arrive in London「ロンドンに到着する」

③ **The crew saw huge statues scattered on a hillside.**

> ▶ crewは「（船・航空機などの）乗組員全員」を指す語。
>
> ▶ scattered ～はhuge statuesを後ろから修飾する過去分詞の形容詞的用法。

④ **Most of the statues were damaged, but there was one smaller statue, about 2.4 meters in height, in perfect condition.**

> ▶ most of ～で「～の大部分、～のほとんど」という意味。
>
> ▶ in ～ conditionで「～な状態の[で]」という意味。
>
> **✐ 次の英文を日本語に直しなさい。**
>
> The patient is in a serious condition.

---

⑤ **The crew took the statue without asking permission from the islanders.**

> ▶ without V-ingで「Vすることなしに、Vせずに」という意味。

⑥ **In short, they stole it.**

> ▶ in shortで「要するに、一言で言えば」という意味。
>
> ▶ itは前文のthe statue、つまり文④のone smaller statueを指す。

⑦ **They brought it to England as a gift for Queen Victoria, who donated it to the British Museum.**

> ▶ 〈, who〉はQueen Victoriaを先行詞とする主格の関係代名詞の非制限用法。

who 以下で、自分に贈られたモアイ像を Queen Victoria が結局どうしたかを補足的に説明している。　　　　　　　　　　　　　　⇒p.145 G-❸

> ✍ 次の英文を日本語に直しなさい。

My sister, who is very good at piano, won first prize in the contest.

---

⑧ It is known as Hoa Hakananai'a, Rapa Nui words which can be translated as "Lost Friend."

▶ It is known as ～で「～として知られている」という意味。It = The statue

▶ Hoa Hakananai'a「ホアハカナナイア」と Rapa Nui words「ラパ・ヌイ語の言葉」は、コンマ (,) をはさんで同格の関係。

▶ which は Rapa Nui words を先行詞とする主格の関係代名詞。which can ～ as "Lost Friend"が関係詞節で、先行詞を説明している。

▶ can be translated as ～は「～と訳すことができる」という意味。助動詞のあとに続く動詞は必ず原形なので、受動態も〈助動詞 + be + 過去分詞〉の形となる。　　　　　　　　　　　　　　　　　　　　　⇒p.145 G-❷

⑨ About 150 years later, the story took a new turn.

▶ take a new turn は「(事態などが) 新たな展開を見せる」という意味。

⑩ In 2017 the Rapa Nui people gained control of their land, which had been part of Chile since 1888.

▶ gain control of ～で「～の支配権を握る」という意味。

▶〈, which〉は their land を先行詞とする主格の関係代名詞の非制限用法。which 以下で、their land に関して補足的に説明している。　　⇒p.145 G-❸

▶ had been は〈had + 過去分詞〉で過去完了。ここでは1888年から島民が自治権を獲得する2017年 (＝基準となる過去の時点) まで、ずっと継続していた状態を表している。

⑪ One of the first things they did was to try to bring Hoa Hakananai'a back to Easter Island.

▶〈S + V (be動詞) + C (不定詞)〉の文型。One of ～ they did 全体が文の主語、また to try ～ Island が C (補語) である。

▶ the first things のあとに目的格の関係代名詞 that[which]が省略されている。

⑫ They formed a delegation to ask the British Museum to let their Lost Friend come home.

▶ ask the British Museum to ～は、〈ask + O + to ～〉で「Oに～するよう頼む」という意味を表す不定詞構文。

▶ let their Lost Friend come home は、〈let + O + 原形不定詞〉で「Oを～させる、Oが～するのを許す」という意味の使役構文。

☐ soul [sóul]

☐ attraction [ətrǽkʃən]

☐ embodiment [ɪmbάdimənt]

☐ ancestor [ǽnsestər]

☐ socket [sάkət]

☐ legend [lédʒənd]

☐ coral [kɔ́ːrəl]

☐ insert [ɪnsɔ́ːrt]

☐ come to life

☐ ambassador [æmbǽsədər]

☐ Great Britain [grèit brítn]

2

　①In November 2018, the delegation of the Rapa Nui people arrived in London to look for Hoa Hakananai'a. They went immediately to the British Museum. ②When they found him, they were deeply moved. ③For them, he represents the living soul of the island. They said, "④He is not just a rock; he's our brother."

　A member of the delegation explained, "⑤For the museum, Hoa Hakananai'a is just an attraction. But for us, he is one of our family. ⑥Once eyes are added to the statues, they become the living embodiment of our ancestors." The moai have large empty eye sockets. ⑦According to legend, when "eyes" made of bright stones and coral are inserted, the moai come to life.

　The leader of the delegation told the museum, "⑧Hoa Hakananai'a has been our ambassador to Great Britain for 150 years. ⑨It's time to let him come home. ⑩We will make a new moai and send him to you."

このセクションの内容

大英博物館を訪れたラパ・ヌイの代表団一行は、「ホアハカナナイア」と感動的な対面を果たし、この像は自分たちにとって島の生ける魂の (A.　　　) であり、また (B.　　　) の一員なのだと訴えた。伝説によれば、その眼窩（がんか）に明るい色の石と (C.　　　) でできた目玉をはめ込むと、モアイ像は蘇るという。

① **In November 2018, the delegation of the Rapa Nui people arrived in London to look for Hoa Hakananai'a.**

▶ arrive in ～は「(比較的広い場所) に着く、到着する」という意味。
cf. arrive at the station「駅に着く」

▶ to look for ～は〈目的〉を表す不定詞の副詞的用法。

② **When they found him, they were deeply moved.**

▶ theyは文①の the delegation of the Rapa Nui peopleを、himはモアイ像の Hoa Hakananai'aを指す。

▶ 受動態の were deeply moved は「深い感動を覚えた」という意味。

③ **For them, he represents the living soul of the island.**

▶ representは「(ものが) ～を表す、～の象徴となる」という意味。

▶ them = the delegation of the Rapa Nui people

▶ he = Hoa Hakananai'a

④ **He is not just a rock; he's our brother.**

▶ not just ～で「ただの～ではない」という意味。

⑤ **For the museum, Hoa Hakananai'a is just an attraction.**

▶ attractionは動詞 attract「(客など) を呼び込む、引き寄せる」の名詞形で、「呼び物」という意味。*cf.* a tourist attraction「観光名所」

⑥ **Once eyes are added to the statues, they become the living embodiment of our ancestors.**

▶ once ～は「ひとたび～すれば、いったん～すれば」という意味の接続詞。

✍ 次の英文を日本語に直しなさい。

Once she starts something, she never gives it up.

――――――――――――――――――――――――――――

▶ add ～ to ...「～を…に付け加える、付け足す」の受動態は、be added to ... となる。

⑦ **According to legend, when "eyes" made of bright stones and coral are inserted, the moai come to life.**

▶ according to ～は「～によれば」という意味。

✍ 次の英文を日本語に直しなさい。

According to today's newspaper, there was a big earthquake in Alaska.

――――――――――――――――――――――――――――

▶ made of ～「(材料) で作られた」は過去分詞の形容詞的用法。made of bright stones and coralは、直前の"eyes"を修飾している。

▶ come to lifeは「息を吹き返す、生き返る、復活する」(≒ become alive) という意味。

このセクションの内容 の答え→　A. 象徴　B. 家族　C. サンゴ

例 The plants and flowers in the garden came to life after a shower.
「にわか雨のあと、庭の草木や花は息を吹き返した」

⑧ Hoa Hakananai'a has been our ambassador to Great Britain for 150 years.

▶ has been 〜は現在完了の〈継続〉用法で、「ずっと〜であり続けている」という意味。文末の for 150 years は〈継続の期間〉を表す。

▶ an ambassador to 〜で「〜に駐在する大使」という意味。ここでは象徴的な意味で用いられている。「駐〜大使」という場合、ambassador は大文字で始めることもある。

例 She served as Ambassador to Japan for more than three years.
「彼女は駐日大使を 3 年間以上務めた」

⑨ It's time to let him come home.

▶ It's time to 〜は「（そろそろ）〜してよいときだ」という意味。It's about time to 〜や It's high time to 〜の形もほぼ同じ意味で用いられる。

＊ 次の英文を日本語に直しなさい。

It's time to make a decision.

▶ let him come home は、〈let ＋ O ＋ 原形不定詞〉で「O を〜させる」という意味の使役構文。

＊ 次の英文を日本語に直しなさい。

Don't let your children play with fire.

⑩ We will make a new moai and send him to you.

▶ will は〈意志未来〉の助動詞で、話者がこれから何かを行う意志を表す。

▶ him は a new moai を指す。

▶ send 〜 to ... は「〜を…に送る」という意味。send は目的語を 2 つとる動詞であり、〈send ＋ O（人）＋ O（もの）〉の構文を作るが、目的語が 2 つとも代名詞の場合は、〈send ＋ O（もの）＋ to ＋ O（人）〉の形がふつう。目的語を 2 つとるほかの動詞（give、teach、tell、lend など）についても同様である。

＊ 英文を完成させなさい。

私は今度彼に会うときにそれを彼に貸してあげるつもりです。

I'll lend it (　　　) (　　　) when I see him next time.

□ discuss [dɪskʌ́s]
□ proposal [prəpóuzəl]
□ loan [lóun]
□ deny [dɪnáɪ]
□ point of view
□ good reasons
□ security [sɪkjúərəti]
□ controlled [kəntróuld]
□ environmental
　　[ɪnvàɪərənméntəl]
□ scholar [skálər]
□ access [ǽkses]
□ argue [áːrgjuː]
□ heritage [hérətɪdʒ]
□ object [ábdʒekt]
□ make sense
□ the fact remains that ～
□ against *one's* will

3

①The British Museum welcomed the delegation and discussed their proposal.　②In the end, the museum offered to let Hoa Hakananai'a return, but only as a loan.　③They refused to give it back permanently.

④The museum did not deny that the moai had been taken without the islanders' permission, so why didn't they immediately agree to return it?

⑤From the point of view of the museum, there are good reasons to keep the statue.　⑥Since Easter Island does not have the security and controlled environmental conditions that the British Museum has, the statue is safer in London.　⑦The statue can now be seen by many more people than on a remote island.　⑧Scholars have easier access to the statue.　⑨Moreover, some people argue that the moai deserves to be a world heritage object.

⑩These reasons make sense.　⑪However, the fact remains that Hoa Hakananai'a was taken without permission and is still held against the people's will.　⑫So, many people — not only the Rapa Nui — question the museum's reasoning.

このセクションの内容

大英博物館は「ホアハカナナイア」を無断で島から持ち出したことを否定しなかったが、ラパ・ヌイの人々に像を（A.　　　）に返還することを拒否した。その理由は、像を今のままロンドンで保管するほうが（B.　　　）であり、離島にあるよりもずっと多くの人々が見ることができるし、（C.　　　）にとっても研究しやすい、というものであった。

① **The British Museum welcomed the delegation and discussed their proposal.**

▶ discussは「〜について議論する、話し合う」（≒ talk about 〜）という意味の他動詞。× discuss about 〜としないように注意する。

② **In the end, the museum offered to let Hoa Hakananai'a return, but only as a loan.**

▶ in the endは「結局、最後には」という意味。

▶ offer to 〜は「〜することを申し出る」という意味。

▶ let Hoa Hakananai'a returnは「ホアハカナナイアが（島に）帰ることを許す」という意味。〈let ＋ O ＋原形不定詞〉「Oを〜させる」の使役構文。

▶ as a loanは「一定期間の貸し出し措置として」という意味。

③ **They refused to give it back permanently.**

▶ refuse to 〜は「〜することを拒否する」という意味。

▶ give it backのitは前文のHoa Hakananai'aを指す。

④ **The museum did not deny that the moai had been taken without the islanders' permission, so why didn't they immediately agree to return it?**

▶ deny that 〜は「〜ということを否定する」という意味。

▶ had been takenは〈had been ＋過去分詞〉で過去完了の受動態。この文では、「（島民に無断で）持ち出された」という〈完了・結果〉を表す。　⇒p.144 G-❶

　　✍ 英文を完成させなさい。

　　彼らは建物が台風によってひどく損傷を受けていたことに気付いた。

　　They found that the building (　　　) (　　　) badly (　　　) by the typhoon.

▶ without one's permissionは「〜の許可なしに」という意味。

⑤ **From the point of view of the museum, there are good reasons to keep the statue.**

▶ point of viewは「見方、観点、見解」という意味。From the point of view of the museumは「博物館の見方からすれば」（≒ From the museum's point of view）という意味になる。複数形はpoints of view。

　　✍ 次の英文を日本語に直しなさい。

　　It is important to look at a problem from another point of view.

_____

▶ good reasonsは「もっともな理由」（≒ valid reasons）という意味。

▶ to keep 〜は直前のgood reasonsを修飾する不定詞の形容詞的用法。

⑥ **Since Easter Island does not have the security and**

controlled environmental conditions that the British Museum has, the statue is safer in London.

▶ since は「〜なので」という理由を表す接続詞。

▶ that は the security 〜 conditions を先行詞とする目的格の関係代名詞。that the British Museum has が関係詞節で、先行詞を説明している。

▶ the statue is safer in London は、後ろに than in Easter Island を補って、「モアイ像は（イースター島にいるよりも）ロンドンにいるほうが安全だ」と考える。

⑦ **The statue can now be seen by many more people than on a remote island.**

▶ can be seen は助動詞を含む受動態。〈助動詞 can + be + 過去分詞〉で「〜されることができる」という意味。by many more people は動作主。

⇒p.145 G-❷

▶ many more 〜は「さらに［ずっと］多くの〜」という意味の比較表現。ここでは、モアイ像は「離島にいるよりも（ロンドンにいるほうが）ずっと多くの人々に（よって）見られることができる」と述べている。

⑧ **Scholars have easier access to the statue.**

▶ have easier access to 〜で「〜により接近しやすい、〜をより利用しやすい」という意味。前文と同様に、モアイ像がロンドンの大英博物館にいる場合と離島にいる場合とを比較している。

⑨ **Moreover, some people argue that the moai deserves to be a world heritage object.**

▶ argue that 〜は「〜と主張する」という意味。

▶ deserve to 〜は「〜する価値がある」という意味。

⑩ **These reasons make sense.**

▶ These reasons は、文⑥〜⑨で述べている、モアイ像が現在のままロンドンの大英博物館に保管されているほうがよいとする理由のこと。

▶ make sense は「道理にかなう、筋が通っている」という意味。

⑪ **However, the fact remains that Hoa Hakananai'a was taken without permission and is still held against the people's will.**

▶ the fact remains that 〜は「〜という事実は依然として残っている→〜もまた事実である」という意味。that 節は the fact の具体的内容を述べている。

▶ against one's will は「〜の意志に反して」という意味。

⑫ **So, many people ― not only the Rapa Nui ― question the museum's reasoning.**

▶ not only 〜は「〜だけでなく」という意味。

▶ question は動詞で、「〜を疑問に感じる」という意味。

□ critic [krítɪk]

□ artwork [ɑ́ːrtwə̀ːrk]

□ colonial [kəlóuniəl]

□ Parthenon Marbles
　[pɑ́ːrθənàn mɑ́ːrblz]

□ Greece [gríːs]

□ Rosetta Stone [rouzétə stòun]

□ Benin Bronzes
　[bəníːn bránzɪz]

□ present-day [prézəntdéi]

□ Nigeria [naɪdʒíəriə]

□ some

□ precedent [présɪdənt]

□ rightful [ráɪtfəl]

□ priceless [práɪsləs]

□ one can argue that ～

□ entire [entáɪər]

□ display [dɪspléi]

□ a large number of ～

□ desire [dɪzáɪər]

4

①Critics say that the real reason the British Museum refuses to return the Rapa Nui's Lost Friend is quite different.

②Hoa Hakananai'a is not the only artwork that was taken without permission. ③The British Museum got many of its artworks during the colonial period (the late 16th through the early 20th century). ④The list includes the Parthenon Marbles from Greece, the Rosetta Stone from Egypt, and the Benin Bronzes from present-day Nigeria. And then there are some 23,000 Chinese artworks. ⑤The owners are asking for the return of their stolen treasures. ⑥If the museum returns the Lost Friend, it would set a precedent.

⑦Museums all over the world face similar problems. ⑧Who is the rightful owner of works of art that are hundreds or even thousands of years old? These works are now part of our priceless world heritage. ⑨And even if the rightful owners can be found, can they be trusted to keep these works safe? ⑩One can argue that great art belongs to the entire world and should be displayed where it can be safely viewed by the largest number of people.

⑪However, for the Rapa Nui people, these questions are less important than the simple human desire to bring home their lost family member, their Lost Friend.

このセクションの内容

大英博物館の所蔵品の中には、「ホアハカナナイア」以外にも、植民地時代に無断で持ち出した（A.　　　　）が数多く含まれており、モアイ像の返還要求に応じれば、それが（B.　　　　）となってしまうため、博物館は返還を拒否したのだという（C.　　　　）の声もある。

① **Critics say that the real reason the British Museum refuses to return the Rapa Nui's Lost Friend is quite different.**

▶ Critics say that ～で「～と批判する声もある」という決まった表現。

▶ that節の中の文は〈S + V (is) + C（形容詞 different）〉で、the real reason ～ Lost Friend全体がthat節の主語。

▶ the real reasonのあとに関係副詞whyが省略されている。the British Museum ～ Lost Friend全体が関係詞節で、先行詞のthe real reasonを説明している。

② **Hoa Hakananai'a is not the only artwork that was taken without permission.**

▶ that は the only artwork「唯一の芸術作品」を先行詞とする主格の関係代名詞。先行詞がonlyや形容詞の最上級などで修飾されている場合、関係代名詞はwhich よりもthatを用いることが多い。

③ **The British Museum got many of its artworks during the colonial period (the late 16th through the early 20th century).**

▶ many of ～は「～の多く」という意味。itsはThe British Museumを指す。

④ **The list includes the Parthenon Marbles from Greece, the Rosetta Stone from Egypt, and the Benin Bronzes from present-day Nigeria.**

▶ The listは、前文で述べている「大英博物館がその多くを植民地時代に手に入れた芸術作品」のリストのこと。

⑤ **The owners are asking for the return of their stolen treasures.**

▶ ask for ～「～を求める、要求する」という意味。

▶ stolenはsteal「～を盗む」の過去分詞の形容詞的用法（前置修飾）。

⑥ **If the museum returns the Lost Friend, it would set a precedent.**

▶ itはif節の内容、つまり「大英博物館が『失われた友人』を返還すること」を指す。

▶ wouldは控えめな推量を表す。

⑦ **Museums all over the world face similar problems.**

▶ similar problemsとは、「（大英博物館が抱えているのと）同じような問題」ということ。

⑧ **Who is the rightful owner of works of art that are hundreds or even thousands of years old?**

▶ thatは works of art「芸術作品」を先行詞とする主格の関係代名詞。

▶ hundreds or even thousands of ～は「何百、あるいは何千もの～」という意味。

⑨ **And even if the rightful owners can be found, can they be trusted to keep these works safe?**

▶ can be foundおよび can they be trusted ～?は、助動詞を含む受動態。疑問文は〈助動詞＋主語＋be＋過去分詞 ～?〉の形。　⇒p.145 G-❷

▶〈keep＋O＋C〉は「OをCの状態に保つ」という意味。

⑩ **One can argue that great art belongs to the entire world and should be displayed where it can be safely viewed by the largest number of people.**

▶ One can argue that ～は「～とも言える」（≒It is possible to argue that ～）という意味。

▶ should be displayedは助動詞を含む受動態。　⇒p.145 G-❷

▶ whereは接続詞で、「～するところで[に]」という意味の副詞節を作る。関係副詞のwhereと間違えないように注意。

　✐ 次の英文を日本語に直しなさい。

　Put the dictionary back where it was.

▶ it can be safely viewed by ～は、助動詞を含む受動態。itは同じ文のgreat artを指し、by ～は動作主を表す。　⇒p.145 G-❷

▶ the largest number of ～は「最大限の数の～」という意味。a large number of ～「多くの～」（≒a great many ～）の最上級。

⑪ **However, for the Rapa Nui people, these questions are less important than the simple human desire to bring home their lost family member, their Lost Friend.**

▶ these questionsは、文⑧および⑨で提起された2つの疑問を指す。

▶ less important than ～は「～ほど重要ではない」という意味。〈less＋形容詞＋than ～〉は「～ほど…ではない」という意味を表す比較表現。

▶ desire to ～は「～したいという願い」という意味。

▶ their lost family memberと their Lost Friendは、どちらもラパ・ヌイ語でHoa Hakananai'aと呼ばれているモアイ像のこと。

Grammar for Communication

---

1 受動態の完了形：have [has、had] been＋過去分詞

受動態はさまざまな時制と組み合わせて使うことができる。受動態の現在完了形は〈have[has] ＋ been ＋過去分詞〉、受動態の過去完了形は〈had ＋ been ＋過去分詞〉の形になる。

The building <u>has been destroyed</u> many times.
（その建物は何度も破壊された）

現在完了形	(have[has]	＋過去分詞)
受動態	(be動詞	＋過去分詞)
受動態の現在完了形	(have[has] ＋ been	＋過去分詞)

---

1. 経験

◆I **have been invited** to his house twice.
（私は彼の家に2度招かれたことがある）

2. 完了

◆**Have** you **been introduced** to her parents yet?
（あなたはもう彼女の両親に紹介されましたか）

◆The rocks on the road **had already been taken** away before we arrived there.
（道路上の岩は私たちがそこに着く前に、すでに取り除かれていた）

3. 結果

◆The milk **has been drunk** by my brother.
（ミルクは兄［弟］によって飲まれてしまった）

4. 継続

◆This book **has been read** all over the world for a long time.
（この本は長い間世界中で読まれている）

5. 大過去「(過去のあるときまでに) 〜されていた」

◆They found that the diamond in the box **had been replaced** with a fake.
（彼らは箱の中のダイヤモンドが偽物とすり替えられていたことに気づいた）

2 | 助動詞＋be＋過去分詞

助動詞を含む受動態は〈助動詞＋be＋過去分詞〉の形となる。否定形、過去形（mustとshouldを除く）がある。

◆ This box **can be used** as a chair.
（この箱はいすとして使うことができる）

◆ Not a star **could be seen** that night because it was very cloudy.
（その夜はとても曇っていたので星は1つも見られなかった）

◆ The results **will be announced** tomorrow afternoon.
（結果は明日の午後発表されるだろう）

◆ A new planet **may be discovered** in the future.
（将来、新しい惑星が発見されるかもしれない）

◆ All these rules **must be observed** by every student.
（これらすべての規則はすべての生徒によって守られなくてはならない）

◆ **Should** this job **be finished** by the end of this month?
（この仕事は今月末までに仕上げられるべきですか）

3 | 関係代名詞の非制限用法

〈先行詞＋コンマ (,)＋関係代名詞〉の形で、直前の語句に説明を加える関係代名詞の用法を「非制限用法」と呼ぶ。非制限用法の関係代名詞は目的格でも省略できない。また、関係代名詞のthatおよびwhatには、非制限用法がない。

◆ He has a daughter**, who** wants to be a nurse.（＊娘は1人だけいる）
（彼には娘が1人いて、彼女は看護師になりたがっている）

　　比較 He has a daughter who wants to be a nurse.（＊ほかに娘がいる可能性あり）
　　（彼には看護師になりたがっている娘が1人いる）

◆ Jane brought a cake to the party**, which** she baked by herself.
（ジェーンはパーティーにケーキを持参したが、それは彼女が自分で焼いたものだった）

◆ Carol**, whose** father works for a bank, knows a lot about the world economy.
（キャロルは父親が銀行に勤めているが、世界経済にとても詳しい）

確認問題

語彙・表現

1 次の語を（　）内の指示にしたがって書きかえなさい。

(1) steal（過去分詞に）　　　　　(2) attract（名詞に）

(3) high（名詞に）　　　　　　　(4) admit（反意語に）

2 第1音節にアクセント（強勢）のある語を2つ選び、記号で答えなさい。

ア　an-ces-tor　　　イ　se-cur-i-ty　　　ウ　am-bas-sa-dor

エ　pro-pos-al　　　オ　dis-cuss　　　　カ　dam-age

3 日本語に合うように、（　）内に適切な語を入れなさい。

(1) 音楽が始まると、子どもたちは生き生きしだした。

The children (　　　　) to (　　　　) when music started.

(2) その中古車はとてもよい状態だとわかった。

I found the used car (　　　　) very good (　　　　).

(3) 私たちはその計画にたくさんのボランティアを必要としている。

We need a (　　　　) (　　　　) of volunteers for the project.

(4) 彼らは彼女の失われた記憶を取り戻そうとした。

They tried to (　　　　) (　　　　) her lost memory.

文のパターン・文法

1 （　）内に適切な関係代名詞を入れなさい。

(1) My father gave me a camera on my birthday, (　　　　) I had long wanted.

(2) I have a friend in America, (　　　　) father teaches math at a high school.

(3) He has a big brother, (　　　　) loves climbing mountains.

(4) The package, (　　　　) was full of books, was sent from London.

2 次の各組の文がほぼ同じ意味になるように、（　）内に適切な語を入れなさい。

(1) You must clean the classroom within 10 minutes.

The classroom (　　　) (　　　) (　　　) within 10 minutes.

(2) My sister has just baked those cookies.

Those cookies (　　　) just (　　　) (　　　) by my sister.

(3) You should keep your legs warm.

Your legs (　　　) (　　　) (　　　) warm.

3 （　）内の語句を並べかえて、英文を完成させなさい。

(1) (seen / your room / be / the mountain / can / from)?

_____?

(2) (been / many tourists / by / the old city / visited / has).

_____.

(3) (not / the problem / solved / been / has) yet.

_____ yet.

(4) Our teacher (to / might / shocked / the fact / be / know).

Our teacher _____.

> **総合**

次の文を読んで、あとの問いに答えなさい。

---

　①From the (　　　) (　　　) (　　　) of the museum, there are good reasons to keep the statue. Since Easter Island does not have the security and controlled environmental conditions that the British Museum has, the statue is (　②　) in London. ③The statue can now be seen by many more people than on a remote island. Scholars have easier access to the statue. Moreover, some people argue that the moai deserves to be a world heritage object.

　These (　④　) make sense. However, the fact remains that Hoa Hakananai'a was taken without permission and is still held against the people's will. ⑤So, many people — not only the Rapa Nui — question the museum's reasoning.

問1　①が「博物館の見方からすれば」という意味になるように、（　）内に入る最も適切な3語を書きなさい。

問2　②の（　）内に入る最も適切な語を選びなさい。

　　ア　safer　　　イ　older　　　ウ　smaller　　　エ　greater

問3　下線部③を日本語に直しなさい。

問4　④の（　）内に入る適切な1語を本文中から探して答えなさい。

問5　下線部⑤について、大英博物館がホアハカナナイアをラパ・ヌイの人々に返還しない理由が批判されるのはなぜですか。日本語で説明しなさい。

Lesson 10 Good Ol' Charlie Brown

教科書p.162　Section 1

- ☐ ol'
- ☐ Charlie Brown [tʃáːrli bráun]
- ☐ PEANUTS [píːnʌts]
- ☐ cartoon [kɑːrtúːn]
- ☐ cartoonist [kɑːrtúːnɪst]
- ☐ Charles M. Schulz
  　[tʃáːrlz ém ʃúlts]
- ☐ publish [pʌ́blɪʃ]
- ☐ Snoopy [snúːpi]
- ☐ Lucy [lúːsi]
- ☐ Linus [láɪnəs]
- ☐ hundreds of millions of ～
- ☐ the best-known of all
- ☐ beagle [bíːgl]
- ☐ capture [kǽptʃər]

The first *PEANUTS* cartoon appeared in 1950. ①The cartoonist, Charles M. Schulz, died in 2000, but old cartoons continue to be published, and everybody knows the *PEANUTS* characters, especially Snoopy.

1

　　Charlie Brown. Lucy. Linus. Snoopy. ②They have appeared in magazines and newspapers for over 70 years. ③They have hundreds of millions of fans around the world.

　　④People who don't know the names of their next-door-neighbor's children know Charlie Brown, the little "loser" who never stops believing that he can win; ⑤Lucy, the little girl who always gives people advice; ⑥Linus, the small boy who always has his security blanket with him; and, ⑦the best-known of all, Snoopy, the beagle who thinks that he is a fighter pilot or a great writer. ⑧They are the main characters in the *Peanuts* cartoons.

　　⑨Why are these cartoons so popular? ⑩Why has *Peanuts* captured the hearts of people all over the world?

　　⑪Let's look at a few *Peanuts* cartoons and see if we can find answers to these questions.

このセクションの内容

漫画家の（A.　　　　　　　　）のマンガ『（B.　　　　　）』は半世紀以上、2000年に彼が亡くなってからもなお世界中で読み続けられている。このマンガの（C.　　　　　）の理由、魅力を探るべく、いくつかの作品を見てみよう。

① **The cartoonist, Charles M. Schulz, died in 2000, but old cartoons continue to be published**

▶ The cartoonist と Charles M. Schulz はコンマ (,) をはさんで〈同格〉の関係。

▶ continue to ～は「～し続ける」(≒ continue V-ing) という意味。

▶ to be published は〈to be ＋過去分詞〉で不定詞の受動態。

✎ 英文を完成させなさい。

その物語は何世紀にもわたって読まれ続けた。

The story continued (　　　) (　　　) (　　　) for centuries.

② **They have appeared in magazines and newspapers for over 70 years.**

▶ They は『ピーナッツ』に登場するキャラクター、Charlie Brown、Lucy、Linus、Snoopy を指している。

▶ have appeared は〈継続〉を表す現在完了。

▶ for over 70 years「70年以上にわたって」は〈継続〉の期間を表している。この over は「～以上」(≒ more than) という意味。

③ **They have hundreds of millions of fans around the world.**

▶ hundreds of millions of ～は「何億という～」という意味。

▶ around the world は「世界中に」(≒ all over the world) という意味。

✎ 次の英文を日本語に直しなさい。

Hundreds of millions of people around the world watched the movie.

④ **People who don't know the names of their next-door-neighbor's children know Charlie Brown, the little "loser" who never stops believing that he can win**

▶ 1文に主格の関係代名詞 who が2つ含まれた文。1つ目の who は People が先行詞。People who ～ next-door-neighbor's children 全体がこの文の主語となっている。

▶ 2つ目の who は the little "loser" を先行詞とする主格の関係代名詞。この the little "loser" は、know の目的語 Charlie Brown と〈同格〉の関係である。

▶ stop V-ing は「～することをやめる」という意味。*cf.* stop to ～「～するために立ち止まる」

✎ 次の英文を日本語に直しなさい。

The children who were in the field wouldn't stop running around.

▶ that he can win は believing の目的語となる名詞節。he = Charlie Brown

⑤ **Lucy, the little girl who always gives people advice**

▶ Lucy と the little girl who ～は〈同格〉の関係。who は the little girl を先行詞とする主格の関係代名詞。

⑥ **Linus, the small boy who always has his security blanket with him**

▶ Linus と the small boy who ～は〈同格〉の関係。who は the small boy を先行詞とする主格の関係代名詞。

⑦ **the best-known of all, Snoopy, the beagle who thinks that he is a fighter pilot or a great writer**

▶ the best-known of all は最上級を用いた慣用表現で、「すべての中で最もよく知られている、とりわけ有名なもの」(≒ the most famous of all) という意味。

▶ Snoopy, the beagle who ～は、直前の the best-known of all と〈同格〉の関係。

▶ who は the beagle を先行詞とする主格の関係代名詞。beagle「ビーグル犬」は人ではないが、ここはマンガの登場人物として擬人化されているため、人が先行詞の場合と同様に who が使われている。

▶ that 以下は thinks の目的語となる名詞節。

⑧ **They are the main characters in the *Peanuts* cartoons.**

▶ They は Charlie Brown、Lucy、Linus、Snoopy を指している。

⑨ **Why are these cartoons so popular?**

▶ these cartoons は前文の the *Peanuts* cartoons を指す。

⑩ **Why has *Peanuts* captured the hearts of people all over the world?**

▶ has ～ captured は〈完了・結果〉を表す現在完了。

⑪ **Let's look at a few *Peanuts* cartoons and see if we can find answers to these questions.**

▶ Let's look at ～ and see ... で 2 つの動詞が並列されている。

▶ see if ～で「～かどうか調べる、確かめる」という意味。if 以下は名詞節で、see「～を確かめる、検討する」の目的語。

> ✍ 次の英文を日本語に直しなさい。

Let's see if there are enough chairs for the meeting.

▶ answers to ～は「～に対する答え」という意味。「答え」や「解決法」を表す名詞は、前置詞 to と結びつく傾向がある。*cf.* the best solution to this problem「この問題の最良の解決法」

▶ these questions とは、前出の文⑨ Why are these cartoons so popular? と文⑩ Why has *Peanuts* captured the hearts of people all over the world? の 2 つの質問のこと。

- ☐ Violet [vάiələt]
- ☐ little
- ☐ barbershop [bɑ́ːrbərʃùp]
- ☐ no matter＋疑問詞
- ☐ compete [kəmpíːt]
- ☐ compete with ～
- ☐ episode [épəsòud]
- ☐ focus on ～
- ☐ heart-warming
  [hɑ́ːrtwɔ̀ːrmiŋ]
- ☐ aspect [ǽspekt]
- ☐ put ～ into ...
- ☐ incident [ínsidənt]
- ☐ childhood [tʃáildhùd]

2

①It is Father's Day and Charlie Brown and his friend Violet are talking about their fathers. ②Violet says that her father is richer than Charlie Brown's dad, and that he is better at sports. ③Charlie Brown has little to say. ④He just asks Violet to come with him to his father's barbershop. ⑤He tells her that no matter how busy his father is, he always has time to give him a big smile because he likes him. ⑥Violet has nothing more to say. She simply walks away. ⑦Her father's money and athletic ability cannot compete with a father's simple love for his son.

⑧Many *Peanuts* episodes would focus on such heart-warming aspects of family life. ⑨Charles M. Schulz, the cartoonist who created *Peanuts*, would put people and incidents from his childhood into his cartoons. ⑩And this may be part of the reason why the *Peanuts* cartoons are so popular among people all over the world.

このセクションの内容

父の日のマンガをはじめ、『ピーナッツ』の多くは家庭生活の
(A.　　　　　　　　) に焦点を当てている。作者は自分の (B.　　　　)
時の人々や出来事をマンガに取り入れており、これがこのマンガの
(C.　　　　　) の理由の１つなのかもしれない。

① **It is Father's Day and Charlie Brown and his friend Violet are talking about their fathers.**

▶ このItは〈日時〉を表す文の主語なので、日本語には訳さない。

② **Violet says that her father is richer than Charlie Brown's dad, and that he is better at sports.**

▶ Violet says that 〜, and that ... の形。sayの目的語として2つのthat節が置かれる場合、1つ目のthatは省略できるが、2つ目のthatは省略できない。

> ✎ 次の英文を日本語に直しなさい。

He said he would be here early tomorrow, and that he would come alone.

▶ be better at 〜は「〜がより得意である」という意味。be good at 〜のgoodが比較級になったもので、better at sportsのあとにthan Charlie Brown's dadが省略されている。

③ **Charlie Brown has little to say.**

▶ littleはここでは名詞で「少ししかないもの」という意味。hasの目的語となっている。to sayは不定詞の形容詞的用法。have little to sayは「ほとんど言うべきことがない」という意味。a littleとすると「少しはある」という肯定的な意味になる。

> ✎ 次の英文を日本語に直しなさい。

I arrived late, so there was little to eat at the party.

④ **He just asks Violet to come with him to his father's barbershop.**

▶ 〈ask + O + to 〜〉は「Oに〜するように頼む」という意味。

⑤ **He tells her that no matter how busy his father is, he always has time to give him a big smile because he likes him.**

▶ 〈S + V + O₁ + O₂〉「O₁(人)にO₂(〜)と話す」の形の文。

▶ no matter how busy his father isは「彼の父親がどんなに忙しくても」という意味。〈no matter + 疑問詞〉は〈譲歩〉を表し、「どんなに〜であっても」などの意味を表す。

> ✎ 英文を完成させなさい。

どんなに困難であっても、あなたはそれを仕上げるべきだ。

(　　　)(　　　)(　　　) hard it is, you should finish it.

▶ to give him a big smileはtimeを修飾する不定詞の形容詞的用法。

▶ 文頭のHeと2つのhimはCharlie Brownを指している。he alwaysとhe likesの2つのheはCharlie Brown's fatherを指している。

⑥ **Violet has nothing more to say.**

▶ nothing more to sayは「それ以上何も言う（べき）ことがない」という意味。nothing「何も～ない、少しも～ない」は代名詞。to sayはnothingを修飾する不定詞の形容詞的用法。

⑦ **Her father's money and athletic ability cannot compete with a father's simple love for his son.**

▶ compete with ～は「～と競争する、〔通例否定文で〕～に匹敵する」という意味。

▶ a father's simple love for his sonでa father'sとなっているのは、「（一般に）1人の父親としてのその息子への愛情」という意味を表しているため。

⑧ **Many *Peanuts* episodes would focus on such heart-warming aspects of family life.**

▶ focus on ～は「～に焦点を当てる」という意味。

> 🖋 **英文を完成させなさい。**

その報告書はスマートフォンの悪影響に焦点を当てている。

The report (　　　) (　　　) the negative effects of smartphones.

⑨ **Charles M. Schulz, the cartoonist who created *Peanuts*, would put people and incidents from his childhood into his cartoons.**

▶ Charles M. Schulzと the cartoonist who ～は〈同格〉の関係。

▶ whoは the cartoonistを先行詞とする主格の関係代名詞。

▶ wouldは「（よく）～したものだった」という〈過去の習慣〉を表す。

⇒p.165 G-❷

> 🖋 **次の英文を日本語に直しなさい。**

My parents would take me to the zoo when I was a child.

_____

▶ put ～ into ... は「～を…に含める」という意味。ここでは people and incidents from his childhoodが「～」に当たる。

⑩ **And this may be part of the reason why the *Peanuts* cartoons are so popular among people all over the world.**

▶ thisは文⑧と⑨の内容、つまり「マンガ『ピーナッツ』は家庭生活の心温まる側面に焦点を当てており、作者のシュルツが子ども時代に出会った人々や出来事を題材として描かれている」ということを指す。

▶ be part of ～は「～の一部、～の一端」という意味。この場合、partにはaをつけないのがふつう。

▶ whyは the reasonを先行詞とする関係副詞。〈the reason why + S + V〉で「SがVする理由」という意味。

□ failure [féɪljər]
□ sensitive [sénsətɪv]
□ wealth [wélθ]
□ feel sorry for ~
□ hope for a better day tomorrow
□ keep on V-ing

3

In this cartoon, ①Linus is excited because the home team has won a football game. ②Charlie Brown listens quietly and then asks Linus one simple question: "How did the other team feel?"

③Because Charlie Brown has experienced failure himself, he finds it important to be sensitive to the feelings of other people who fail. ④He makes us think of other people.

⑤In many ways, Charlie Brown is a loser. ⑥He is not a very good student, and he is not good at sports. ⑦The pretty little girl in his class pays no attention to him. ⑧In a world where wealth and power are so important, Charlie Brown is a failure.

But Charlie Brown never really loses. ⑨He never feels sorry for himself. ⑩He always hopes for a better day tomorrow and keeps on trying. ⑪Perhaps that's what makes a real winner.

このセクションの内容

自らが失敗を経験しているチャーリー・ブラウンは、富と権力が重要視される世界では（A.　　　　）かもしれない。しかし、決して自分をあわれまず、いつも（B.　　　　　　）を願い、挑戦し続ける彼の姿勢こそ、真の（C.　　　　）を作る資質である。

① Linus is excited because the home team has won a football game

▶ excited は excite「〜を興奮させる」の過去分詞から派生した形容詞。「(人が) 興奮した」という意味。*cf.* exciting「(人・物・事が) 興奮させる (ような)、わくわくする (ような)」

> ✎ 英文を完成させなさい。

みんながそのわくわくする試合のあとで興奮していた。

Everyone was (　　　) after the (　　　) game.

▶ has won は〈完了〉を表す現在完了。

② Charlie Brown listens quietly and then asks Linus one simple question: "How did the other team feel?"

▶ one simple question の具体的内容をコロン (:) のあとに示している。

③ Because Charlie Brown has experienced failure himself, he finds it important to be sensitive to the feelings of other people who fail.

▶ has experienced は〈経験〉を表す現在完了。

▶ himself は強調語で、「彼自身が失敗を経験してきた」という意味。

▶ he finds it important to be 〜は、〈find + it (形式目的語) + C (形容詞) + to 〜〉の構文で、「〜であることが大切だとわかっている」という意味。

⇒p.165 G-❸

> ✎ 次の英文を日本語に直しなさい。

I think it easy to answer this question.

▶ who は other people を先行詞とする主格の関係代名詞。

④ He makes us think of other people.

▶〈make + O + 原形不定詞〉は「Oに〜させる」という意味。

⑤ In many ways, Charlie Brown is a loser.

▶ in many ways は「多くの面で」という意味。

⑥ He is not a very good student, and he is not good at sports.

▶ not 〜 very ...は「あまり…ではない」という意味。

▶ be good at 〜は「〜が得意である」という意味。*cf.* be poor[bad] at 〜「〜が下手である、不得手である」

> ✎ 英文を完成させなさい。

私は子どものころは泳ぐのが下手だったが、今は得意だ。

I was (　　　) (　　　　) swimming when I was a child, but now I'm
(　　　) (　　　) it.

このセクションの内容 の答え→ A. 敗者　B. よりよい明日　C. 勝者　　155

⑦ **The pretty little girl in his class pays no attention to him.**

▶ pay attention to ～は「～に注意を払う」という意味。no を入れて pay no attention to ～とすれば、「～に注意を払わない」という意味になる。

✑ 英文を完成させなさい。

授業中は先生の話に注意を払うべきだ。

In class, you should (　　　) (　　　) (　　　) what your teacher says.

⑧ **In a world where wealth and power are so important, Charlie Brown is a failure.**

▶ where は a world を先行詞とする関係副詞。where ～ so important は先行詞 a world を後ろから修飾している。the world ではなくて a world とあるのは、いろいろな世界のうちの 1 つという意味。

⑨ **He never feels sorry for himself.**

▶ feel sorry for ～は「～のことをあわれに思う」という意味。

✑ 次の英文を日本語に直しなさい。

He felt sorry for the poor children, but he could do nothing for them.

⑩ **He always hopes for a better day tomorrow and keeps on trying.**

▶ hope for ～は「～を望む、願う」という意味。hope for a better day tomorrow は「明日はもっとよい日になることを望む」（≒ hope that tomorrow will be a better day）という意味。

▶ keep on V-ing は「～し続ける」という意味。keep V-ing とほぼ同じ意味だが、on を用いることによって「継続」の意味合いが強まる。

✑ 次の英文を日本語に直しなさい。

He keeps on trying hard, hoping for a better day tomorrow.

⑪ **Perhaps that's what makes a real winner.**

▶〈S + V（be 動詞）+ C（what 節）〉の形の文。that は文⑨と⑩の内容、つまり「チャーリー・ブラウンが決して自分をあわれまず、いつもよりよい明日を望み挑戦し続けること」を指している。

▶ what は先行詞を含む関係代名詞。what makes a real winner は、〈S（= what）+ V（= makes）+ O（= a real winner）〉という構造で、「真の勝者を作り上げるもの」という意味。

✑ 次の英文を日本語に直しなさい。

This is what surprised the children.

□ be likely to ～
□ burst [bə́ːrst]
□ burst out V-ing
□ fame [féɪm]
□ define [dɪfáɪn]
□ courage [kə́ːrɪdʒ]
□ above all
□ individual [ìndɪvídʒuəl]
□ laugh at ～

4

①The *Peanuts* cartoons are not funny in the ordinary way. ②We are more likely to smile than to burst out laughing. ③But somehow they make us feel good. We want to see Charlie Brown and Linus and Snoopy and all the other *Peanuts* characters again tomorrow in our newspaper. ④If they are not there, we will miss them as we might miss a friend who has gone away. ⑤It is not because our friend always makes us laugh, but because he always makes us feel good about ourselves.

⑥Charles M. Schulz seems to suggest that real success in life is not a matter of money, fame, and power. ⑦Rather, it is defined by hope, courage, respect for others and, above all, by a sense of humor. ⑧He used to say, "⑨If I were given the opportunity to present a gift to young people, it would be the ability for each individual to learn to laugh at himself."

このセクションの内容

『ピーナッツ』というマンガを読むと、私たちはほほえみ、心がなごむ。シュルツは人生における本当の（A.　　　）は金や名声や権力の問題ではなく、希望や勇気、他者を（B.　　　）する心、何より（C.　　　　）によって決まると言っているように思われる。

① **The *Peanuts* cartoons are not funny in the ordinary way.**

▶ in the ordinary way は「ふつうには、ふだんは」という意味。

② **We are more likely to smile than to burst out laughing.**

▶ be likely to ～は「～しそうである」という意味。ここでは比較級で使われている。

> **✍ 英文を完成させなさい。**

赤ちゃんはもうすぐ眠りそうだ。

The baby (　　　) (　　　) (　　　) fall asleep soon.

▶ burst out V-ing は「突然～し始める」(≒ suddenly begin V-ing) という意味。

> **✍ 次の英文を日本語に直しなさい。**

When she read the letter, she burst out crying.

③ **But somehow they make us feel good.**

▶ somehow は「どういうわけか」という意味。

▶ they は文①の The *Peanuts* cartoons を指している。

▶〈make + O + 原形不定詞〉は「Oに～させる」という意味。

④ **If they are not there, we will miss them as we might miss a friend who has gone away.**

▶ they と them は前文の Charlie Brown and Linus and Snoopy and all the other *Peanuts* characters を指している。

▶ as は接続詞で〈様態〉を表し、「～（する）ように、～するのと同様に」という意味。

▶ might は may の過去形だが、ここでは「～かもしれない」という〈現在の控えめな推量〉を表す。

▶ miss は「～がいなくてさびしい」という意味。

▶ who は a friend を先行詞とする主格の関係代名詞。

▶ has gone away は〈結果〉を表す現在完了。go away は「行ってしまう、立ち去る」という意味。現在完了で使うことにより、「（行ってしまって）今ここにいない」という状況が伝わる。

⑤ **It is not because our friend always makes us laugh, but because he always makes us feel good about ourselves.**

▶ It は、前文で「『ピーナッツ』の登場人物たちが明日の新聞に載っていないと、遠くに行ってしまってもういない友だちに感じるのと同じようにさびしく感じる」ことを指している。

▶ not because ～ but because ... は「～だからではなくて、…だからである」という意味。

▶ feel good about *one*selfは、ここでは「自分自身について安心感をおぼえる」という意味。

⑥ Charles M. Schulz seems to suggest that real success in life is not a matter of money, fame, and power.

▶ seem to ～は「～のように思える」という意味。

▶ suggest that ～は「(人に) ～ではないかと提案する、考えを述べる」という意味。

⑦ Rather, it is defined by hope, courage, respect for others and, above all, by a sense of humor.

▶ ratherはあとに続く内容を強調する副詞で、「むしろ、それどころか」という意味。

▶ itは前文のreal success in lifeを指している。

▶ above allは「とりわけ、なかでも」という意味。

> ✐ 次の英文を日本語に直しなさい。

He is good at sports, and above all, soccer.

⑧ He used to say

▶ used to ～は「以前はよく～した」という過去の習慣的な動作を表す。

⇒p.165 G-❷

⑨ If I were given the opportunity to present a gift to young people, it would be the ability for each individual to learn to laugh at himself.

▶ 仮定法過去の文。〈If＋S＋動詞の過去形 ～, S＋助動詞の過去形＋動詞の原形 ...〉で、「もし～なら、…だろう」という意味を表す。

> ✐ 英文を完成させなさい。

もし彼女がここにいたなら、彼女はあなたにどんなことを言うだろうか。

If she (　　　) here, what (　　　) she (　　　) to you?

▶ to present ～はthe opportunityを修飾する不定詞の形容詞的用法。

▶ 後半の主語itは形式主語ではなく、前半にあるa giftを指している。

▶ the ability to ～は「～する能力」という意味。for each individualはto learn ～の意味上の主語。

▶ learn to ～は「～できるようになる」という意味。

▶ laugh at ～は「～を笑う」という意味。

> ✐ 次の英文を日本語に直しなさい。

We should not laugh at other people's failures.

Lesson 10

教科書p.170　Section 5

□ day after day
□ at a time
□ print [print]
□ in print
□ come out
□ woke to learn
□ author [ɔ́ːθər]
□ be no more
□ encouragement
　[ɪnkɔ́ːrɪdʒmənt]
□ carry on
□ for years to come
□ sensitivity [sènsətívəti]
□ difficulty [dífikəlti]

5

①For nearly 50 years, Charles M. Schulz drew *Peanuts*, day after day, one episode at a time. ②However, late in 1999, Schulz learned that he had cancer and could no longer continue. ③To say goodbye to his readers, he drew a farewell cartoon and it appeared some six weeks later. ④If he had lived one day longer, he would have seen it in print. ⑤Sadly, he died the day before the cartoon came out.

⑥On February 13, 2000, *Peanuts* lovers all over the world woke to learn that both the *Peanuts* characters and their author were no more. ⑦We used to think of them as our friends, but they were now gone. ⑧Charles M. Schulz and *Peanuts* helped us face this difficult world with their special type of humor and gentle encouragement to carry on.

⑨Though there will be no new *Peanuts* cartoons, the old ones will be read for years to come. ⑩They will keep reminding us that true success lies in sensitivity to others and in small acts of kindness. ⑪Charles M. Schulz found it important that we never lose hope even in the face of great difficulty.

このセクションの内容

シュルツと『ピーナッツ』の登場人物は、その（A.　　　）と励ましで、私たちがこの（B.　　　）に立ち向かう手助けをしてくれた。シュルツは亡くなったが、今後も本当の（C.　　　）とは何なのかを私たちに思い出させてくれるだろう。

160

① **For nearly 50 years, Charles M. Schulz drew *Peanuts*, day after day, one episode at a time.**

▶ nearly は「ほぼ、ほとんど」(≒ almost、close to) という意味。

▶ day after day は「来る日も来る日も」(≒ every day) という意味。

📝 次の英文を日本語に直しなさい。

They kept on looking for their missing cat day after day.

▶ at a time は「一度に、一回につき」という意味。

📝 次の英文を日本語に直しなさい。

You can send one message to a group of people at a time with this phone.

② **However, late in 1999, Schulz learned that he had cancer and could no longer continue.**

▶ late in ～は「～の終わり近くに」という意味。

▶ learn that ～は「～ということを知る、～ということがわかる」という意味。

▶ that 節の中の動詞は時制の一致により、それぞれ過去形の had、could になっている。

▶ no longer ～は「もはや～でない」という意味。He could no longer continue. は He could not continue any longer. と言いかえ可能。

③ **To say goodbye to his readers, he drew a farewell cartoon and it appeared some six weeks later.**

▶ To say ～は〈目的〉を表す不定詞の副詞的用法。

▶ say goodbye to ～は「～に別れのあいさつをする、～に別れを告げる」という意味。

▶ it は a farewell cartoon を指している。

▶ some はここでは「約～、およそ～」(≒ about) という意味。

④ **If he had lived one day longer, he would have seen it in print.**

▶ 仮定法過去完了の文。〈If + S + had + 過去分詞 ～, S + 助動詞の過去形 + have + 過去分詞 ...〉は、過去の事実に反する仮定を表す。「もし～だったら、…だったのに」という意味。　⇒p.164 G-❶

📝 英文を完成させなさい。

もし私がもっと一生懸命勉強していたら、その試験に合格しただろうに。

If I (　　) (　　) harder, I (　　) (　　) passed the test.

▶ in print は「印刷された状態で」(≒ printed in a newspaper, magazine, etc.) という意味。

⑤ **Sadly, he died the day before the cartoon came out.**

このセクションの内容 の答え→　A. ユーモア　B. 困難な世界　C. 成功

▶ sadly「悲しいことに」は文全体を修飾する副詞。

▶ come out は「出版される」という意味。

⑥ **On February 13, 2000, *Peanuts* lovers all over the world woke to learn that both the *Peanuts* characters and their author were no more.**

▶ woke to learn の to learn は〈結果〉を表す不定詞の副詞的用法。「目を覚ますと～であることがわかった」(≒ woke and learned) という意味。

> 📝 **次の英文を日本語に直しなさい。**
>
> This morning, I woke to find the garden was covered with snow.

▶ both A and B は「A も B も両方とも」という意味。

▶ be no more は「もはやいない」(≒ be gone)、「死んでしまっている」(≒ be dead) という意味。

⑦ **We used to think of them as our friends, but they were now gone.**

▶ used to ～は「～するのが常であった」という過去の習慣的な動作を表す。

⇒p.165 G-❷

▶ think of ～ as ... は「～を…と考える、みなす」という意味。

▶ be gone は「(行ってしまって) もういない」という意味。この gone は完了の意味を表す形容詞。

⑧ **Charles M. Schulz and *Peanuts* helped us face this difficult world with their special type of humor and gentle encouragement to carry on.**

▶〈help + O + (to) ～〉は「O が～するのを助ける、O が～するのに役立つ」という意味。to はしばしば省略されて原形不定詞が使われる。

▶ face は動詞で「～に直面する、立ち向かう」という意味。

▶ with は〈手段・道具など〉を表す前置詞。

▶ to carry on は encouragement を修飾する不定詞の形容詞的用法。

▶ carry on は「(途中であきらめずに) 続ける」(≒ keep trying) という意味。

⑨ **Though there will be no new *Peanuts* cartoons, the old ones will be read for years to come.**

▶ though は〈譲歩〉を表す接続詞で「～だけれども」という意味。

▶ ones は直前に出てきた名詞の繰り返しを避けるために用いられる。ここでは the old ones = the old *Peanuts* cartoons。

▶〈will be + 過去分詞〉は受動態の未来形。will be read で「読まれるだろう」という意味を表す。

▶ for years to come は「(これから)来るべき年月の間」→「将来何年にもわたって」(≒ for many years into the future)という意味。

　　✐ 次の英文を日本語に直しなさい。

　　Their activities will play an important role in society for years to come.

⑩ **They will keep reminding us that true success lies in sensitivity to others and in small acts of kindness.**

▶ They は the *Peanuts* cartoons を指している。

▶ keep V-ing は「～し続ける」という意味。

▶ ⟨remind + O₁ + O₂ (O₂ = that節)⟩は「O₁に～ということを思い出させる」という意味。

　　✐ 英文を完成させなさい。

　　そのメダルを見て、彼は自分があきらめなかったということを思い出した。

　　The medal (　　　) (　　　) (　　　) he hadn't given up.

▶ lie in ～は「～の中にある、存在する」という意味。ここでは in sensitivity to others と in small acts of kindness があとに続いている。

　　例 True happiness lies in contentment.
　　　「真の幸せとは満ち足りることにある」

▶ acts of kindness は an act of kindness「親切な行為」の複数形。

⑪ **Charles M. Schulz found it important that we never lose hope even in the face of great difficulty.**

▶ found it important that ～は、⟨find + it (形式目的語) + C (形容詞) + that節⟩の構文で、「～ということが大切だとわかっている」という意味。⟨S + V + O + C⟩の文で、O (目的語) が that節となる場合は、本来の目的語の位置に形式的な目的語として it が置かれ、真の目的語である that節は C (補語) のあとに置かれる。　　⇒p.165 G-❸

　　✐ 次の英文を日本語に直しなさい。

　　I think it strange that he didn't know the fact.

▶ in the face of ～は「(問題・困難・危険など)に直面して」という意味。動詞の face を使って when we face ～としても、ほぼ同じ意味になる。

　　✐ 次の英文を日本語に直しなさい。

　　He did his best even in the face of great pressure.

▶ even は「～さえ」という⟨強調⟩を表し、ふつう強調したい語 (句) の直前に置かれる。

Grammar for Communication

---

1 仮定法過去完了

過去の事実と反することを仮定したり、願望したりするときに仮定法過去完了を用いる。基本的な表現として次のものを覚えよう。

- 〈If＋S＋過去完了形 (had＋過去分詞) 〜，
  S＋助動詞の過去形＋完了形 (have＋過去分詞) ...〉
  「もし (そのとき) 〜だったら、…だったのに」
- 〈I wish＋S＋過去完了形〉「(そのとき) 〜だったらよかったのに」
- 〈as if [though]＋S＋過去完了形〉「まるで〜だったかのように」
- 〈If it had not been for 〜，S＋助動詞の過去形＋完了形 (have＋過去分詞) ...〉
  「もし (そのとき) 〜がなかったら、…だったのに」

◆ **If** I **had arrived** five minutes earlier, I **could have taken** the train.
 （もし5分早く着いていたならば、電車に乗ることができたのだが）

 ≒ As I didn't arrive five minutes earlier, I couldn't take the train.
  （5分早く着かなかったので、電車に乗ることができなかった）

◆ What **would** she **have done** if she **had been** there yesterday?
 （もし彼女が昨日そこにいたら、どうしただろうか）

◆ **I wish** she **had come** to the concert with us last night.
 （彼女が昨夜私たちといっしょにコンサートに来たらよかったのに）

 ≒ I am sorry [It is a pity] that she didn't come to the concert with us
  last night.
  （彼女が昨夜私たちといっしょにコンサートに来なかったのが残念だ）

◆ You look pale **as if [though]** you **had seen** a ghost.
 （あなたはまるで幽霊でも見たかのように顔が青く見える）

 ★主節の動詞の示すときと同時の事柄を表す場合は、仮定法過去を用いる。
  Jane talked as if [though] she **knew** everything.
  （ジェーンは自分が何でも知っているかのように話した）

◆ **If it had not been for** her advice, I **might have failed**.
 （もし彼女の助言がなかったならば、私は失敗していたかもしれない）

 ≒ As she had advised me, I didn't fail.
  （彼女が私に助言してくれたので、私は失敗しなかった）

2 　used to ～、would ～など

・〈used to ＋動詞の原形〉は助動詞的に用い、現在と対比させた過去の習慣、過去の状態を表す。
・wouldは未来の助動詞willの過去形として用いられるほかに、以下のような特別な意味を表す。

◆ When we were children, we **used to[would]** go skiing every year.
　（子どものころ、私たちは毎年スキーに行ったものだった）〔過去の習慣〕

◆ I **used to**[× would] be afraid of dogs.
　（私はかつては犬が怖かった（今では怖くない））〔過去の状態〕

◆ There **used to**[× would] be a large pond here.
　（かつてはここに大きな池があった（今はない））〔過去の状態〕
　※過去の状態を表す場合、used toの代わりにwouldを使うことはできない。

◆ My daughter **wouldn't** listen to my advice.
　（私の娘は私の忠告を聞こうとしなかった）〔過去の拒絶〕

◆ I **would like to** see your parents next week.
　（来週ご両親にお会いしたいのですが）〔ていねいな表現：現在〕

◆ I **would rather** stay at home than go out in this weather.
　（こんな天気の中を出かけるよりもむしろ家にいたい）〔慣用表現：現在〕

3 　形式目的語it

〈S ＋ V ＋ O ＋ C〉の文で、目的語Oにto不定詞、that節、what節などがくるとき、Oの位置に形式目的語itを置いて、「～が…だとわかる」、「～を…だと思う」などの意味を表す。この構文を作る動詞にはfind、think、believe、makeなどがある。

◆ I found **it** interesting to study a foreign language.
　（私は外国語を学ぶことは興味深いと思った）

◆ I make **it** a rule to get up at five every morning.
　（私は毎朝決まって5時に起きることにしている）

◆ We thought **it** natural that the man should be punished severely.
　（私たちはその男が厳罰に処せられるのは当然だと思った）

確認問題

語彙・表現

1 次の語を（　）内の指示にしたがって書きかえなさい。

(1) fail（名詞に）　　　　　　　　(2) difficult（名詞に）

(3) chance（同意語に）　　　　　　(4) famous（名詞に）

2 第2音節にアクセント（強勢）のある語を2つ選び、記号で答えなさい。

ア　car-toon　　　　　イ　in-di-vid-u-al　　　ウ　en-cour-age-ment

エ　in-ci-dent　　　　オ　as-pect

3 日本語に合うように、（　）内に適切な語を入れなさい。

(1) 彼のおかしな冗談に私たちはどっと笑った。

We (　　　　) (　　　　) laughing at his funny joke.

(2) 彼のチームはそのトーナメントに優勝しそうである。

His team is (　　　　) (　　　　) win the tournament.

(3) 彼の小説の最新作が来月初旬に出版される。

His latest novel will (　　　　) (　　　　) early next month.

(4) 一度に2つの言語をどうやって勉強できるのですか。

How can you learn two languages (　　　　) (　　　　) (　　　　)?

文のパターン・文法

1 次の各組の文がほぼ同じ意味になるように、（　）内に適切な語を入れなさい。

(1) As I didn't wake up early as usual, I couldn't take the train.

If I (　　　　) (　　　　) up early as usual, I (　　　　) (　　　　) (　　　　) the train.

(2) As he helped me, I could finish my work on time.

If he (　　　　) (　　　　) me, I (　　　　) (　　　　) (　　　　) my work on time.

(3) I am sorry that I didn't see that movie star last week.

I wish I (　　　　) (　　　　) that movie star last week.

(4) There were some tall trees on the hill, but now they are gone.

There (　　　　) (　　　　) (　　　　) some tall trees on the hill.

2 （　）内の語句を並べかえて、英文を完成させなさい。

(1) (not / if / been / had / his help / for / it), our project would have failed.

_____, our project would have failed.

(2) (happens / no / what / matter), I won't change my plans.

_____, I won't change my plans.

(3) They (think / that / into / they / it / move / necessary) a bigger house.

They _____ a bigger house.

(4) Andy (if / talked / had / as / traveled / he) into space.

Andy _____ into space.

(5) I (exciting / to / found / Japanese history / study / it).

I _____.

総合

次の文を読んで、あとの問いに答えなさい。

It is Father's Day and Charlie Brown and his friend Violet are talking about their fathers. Violet says that her father is richer than Charlie Brown's dad, and that he is better (　①　) sports. ②Charlie Brown has (　　) (　　) say. He just asks Violet to come with him to his father's barbershop. He tells her that ③(his father / busy / no / how / is / matter), he always has time to give him a big smile because he likes him. ④Violet has nothing more to say. She simply walks away. Her father's money and athletic ability cannot compete (　⑤　) a father's simple love for his son.

Many *Peanuts* episodes would focus (　⑥　) such heart-warming aspects of family life. Charles M. Schulz, the cartoonist who created *Peanuts*, would put people and incidents from his childhood (　⑦　) his cartoons. ⑧And this may be part of the reason why the *Peanuts* cartoons are so popular among people all over the world.

問1　①⑤⑥⑦の（　）内に入る適語を書きなさい。

問2　下線部②が「チャーリー・ブラウンにはほとんど言うべきことがない」という意味になるように、（　）内に入る最も適切な2語を書きなさい。

問3　下線部③の（　）内の語句を並べかえて、英文を完成させなさい。

問4　下線部④についてVioletがとった行動の理由を、日本語で具体的に説明しなさい。

問5　下線部⑧を日本語に直しなさい。

Santa Closet

□ Hilburn [hílbəːrn]
□ undoubtedly [ʌndáutidli]
□ have ~ on *one's* mind
□ move into ~
□ chimney [tʃímni]
□ concerning [kənsə́ːrnɪŋ]
□ Johnny [dʒáni]
□ deliver [dɪlívər]
□ attitude [ǽtətjùːd]
□ critical [krítɪkəl]
□ demand [dɪmǽnd]
□ in a state of ~
□ panic [pǽnɪk]
□ Billy [bíli]

①The following is a paper I recently wrote for my fifth grade English class. ②Mrs. Hilburn gave me an A, undoubtedly for my excellent use of the language.

③Three long years ago, when I was seven, I had a lot on my mind. ④My family had moved into a new house right before Christmas. ⑤A house with no chimney.

⑥No chimney, no Santa Claus.

⑦I asked my parents concerning the problem. "Don't worry, Johnny," they said, "⑧Santa will find a way to deliver your presents."

⑨I was shocked by their attitude. ⑩This was a critical issue. ⑪I demanded an answer.

⑫They laughed and told me I was cute.

But I didn't want to be cute. I wanted my presents.

⑬I found myself in a constant state of panic. ⑭My five-year-old brother, Billy, lived in his own little world. ⑮He was too young to understand the situation.

このセクションの内容

ジョニーの家族はクリスマス直前に新しい家に引っ越したのだが、その家には（A.　　　）がなかった。ジョニーが両親にそのことをたずねると、（B.　　　　　）はきっとプレゼントを届ける方法を見つけるだろうと言う。弟ビリーはまだ5歳で、（C.　　　）が理解できない。

① **The following is a paper I recently wrote for my fifth grade English class.**

▶ a paper のあとに目的格の関係代名詞 that[which] が省略されている。

② **Mrs. Hilburn gave me an A, undoubtedly for my excellent use of the language.**

▶ ⟨S + V + O₁ + O₂⟩「O₁（人）に O₂（もの）を与える」の文。

▶ 成績を表す「A」は可算名詞。1つの「A」には、an が必要。

▶ for my excellent use of the language「私の優れたことばの使い方に対して」は、「A」の成績を与えた理由を表している。

③ **Three long years ago, when I was seven, I had a lot on my mind.**

▶ have ~ on *one's* mind は「気になることがある」（≒ think about ~）という意味。

④ **My family had moved into a new house right before Christmas.**

▶ had moved は過去完了形。ここでは、Christmas が基準となる過去のある時点を表し、その直前には「すでに引っ越していた」こと（完了）を表す。

▶ move into ~ は「~に引っ越す」という意味。

⑤ **A house with no chimney.**

▶ 前文の a new house がどのような家であるかを具体的に述べている。

▶ 前置詞 with は「~を備えた、~を持った」という意味で、人や物の特徴を表す。*cf.* a house with a red roof「赤い屋根を持った家」→「赤い屋根の家」

▶ no chimney は「煙突がない」という意味。⟨no + 名詞⟩は「1つ[1人]の~もない」という全否定を表す。

✎ 次の英文を日本語に直しなさい。

Prehistoric people left no written records.

⑥ **No chimney, no Santa Claus.**

▶「煙突のない家にサンタクロースは来ない」という意味。これは、クリスマスイブの夜、子どもたちにプレゼントを届けるためにサンタクロースが煙突から家に入ってくるという言い伝えによるもの。煙突がなければ家に入れないため、プレゼントを届けられない。

▶ No ~, no ... は「~がなければ、…もない」という意味。*cf.* No pain(s), no gain(s).「苦労がなければ得るものもない、（ことわざ）まかぬ種は生えぬ」

⑦ **I asked my parents concerning the problem.**

▶ concerning は「~に関して」という意味の前置詞。

▶ the problem は、前文⑥の煙突がないのでサンタクロースが来ないという

問題のこと。クリスマス直前に引っ越した家に煙突がないことは、主人公のジョニー（Johnny）と弟のビリー（Billy）にとって重大な問題であった。

⑧ Santa will find a way to deliver your presents.

▶ find a way to ～「～する方法を見つける」という意味。

⑨ I was shocked by their attitude.

▶ be shocked by ～は受動態を使った感情表現で、「～にショック［衝撃］を受ける」という意味。

> ✍ 次の英文を日本語に直しなさい。

We were shocked to hear the news.

▶ their attitude の their はジョニーの両親を指す。ジョニーの真剣な質問を両親が軽く受け流して、前文⑧のように答えたことに、ジョニーはショックを受けている。

⑩ This was a critical issue.

▶ This は、文⑦の the problem と同様、「煙突がない家の子どもたちにサンタクロースはどうやってプレゼントを届けるのか？」という問題を指す。

⑪ I demanded an answer.

▶ demand an answer で「答えを要求する」という意味。ジョニーは文⑧の両親の答え方が不満で、納得のいく答えを要求している。

⑫ They laughed and told me I was cute.

▶⟨tell + O₁（人）+ O₂（that節）⟩で「（人）に～と話す」という意味。ここでは that 節の that が省略されている。

> ✍ 次の英文を日本語に直しなさい。

He told me that he would not accept the invitation.

---

⑬ I found myself in a constant state of panic.

▶ find oneself in a constant state of ～で「気がつくと自分が絶えず～の状態にある」という意味。

⑭ My five-year-old brother, Billy, lived in his own little world.

▶ lived in his own little world「彼自身の小さな世界に住んでいる」とは、幼いためにまだ世間のことがわからないということ。

⑮ He was too young to understand the situation.

▶⟨too ＋形容詞＋ to ～⟩で「あまりにも…で～できない」という意味。

> ✍ 英文を完成させなさい。

マイクはあまりにも疲れていて歩き続けることができなかった。

Mike was (　　　) (　　　) (　　　) continue walking.

□ count down ～

□ carol [kǽrəl]

□ play along

□ sing *one's* heart out

□ fall asleep

□ naive [naɪíːv]

□ get into ～

□ be supposed to ～

□ plumbing [plʌ́mɪŋ]

□ pop *one's* head out of ～

□ exclaim [ekskléɪm]

□ for once

□ shut up

□ a couple of ～

□ be out cold

①I began to count down the days until Christmas. Ten more days. Nine more days. Three more days. Tomorrow is Christmas Eve! ②It was going to be the worst Christmas ever. ③And there was nothing I could do about it.

④On Christmas Eve our house was filled with happiness. My dad read "The Night Before Christmas." Mom led us in singing Christmas carols.

⑤I played along — just to make my parents happy. ⑥Billy laughed and sang his heart out — he didn't understand there would be no Santa that year.

⑦When it was time for bed, my parents gave their usual Christmas Eve speech: "⑧You boys try to fall asleep fast, because Santa won't come until you're asleep."

⑨How could they be so naive? ⑩Did they really think Santa could somehow get into a house without a chimney? ⑪What was he supposed to do — come in through the plumbing? ⑫Pop his head out of the toilet, and exclaim, "Merry Christmas"?

⑬So, for once in my life, I had very little trouble going to sleep on Christmas Eve. ⑭I had to tell Billy to shut up a couple of times. ⑮But after that, we were both out cold.

このセクションの内容

クリスマスイブは（A.　　　　　）に満ちたものだったが、ジョニーは内心では今年のクリスマスは（B.　　　　　）は来ないと思っていた。（C.　　　　　）にサンタがいったいどうやって入れるというのかと彼は思った。

① **I began to count down the days until Christmas.**

▶ count down 〜は「数を逆に数える、秒読みする」という意味。

② **It was going to be the worst Christmas ever.**

▶ was going to 〜と過去形になっているが、実際は主人公のI（＝ジョニー）の〈現在の心境〉を表している。このような過去形の使い方は「描出話法」と呼ばれ、物語文などで登場人物の心の動きを生き生きと伝えるために用いられる。I thought（that）it was going to be the worst Christmas ever. のthat節の中身をそのまま抜き出した形と考えればよい。

▶ the worst Christmas ever で「今までで最悪のクリスマス」という意味。〈the ＋最上級＋ever〉または〈the ＋ ever ＋最上級〉で「今までで最も〜な…」という意味になる。*cf.* the hottest summer ever「（観測）史上最も暑い夏」

③ **And there was nothing I could do about it.**

▶ 描出話法の文。There is nothing I can do about it. で「私にはどうすることもできない」という意味。nothingは「何も〜ない」という全否定を表す。

▶ nothingのあとに目的格の関係代名詞that[which]が省略されている。

> ✍ 次の英文を日本語に直しなさい。

There is nothing we can do to stop him from going.

④ **On Christmas Eve our house was filled with happiness.**

▶ was filled with 〜は、fill 〜 with ...「〜を…で満たす」の受動態で、「〜で満たされていた」という意味。*cf.* be full of 〜「〜でいっぱいである」

⑤ **I played along — just to make my parents happy.**

▶ play alongは「平気なふりをする」（≒ pretend that everything is fine）という意味。

▶ to make 〜は目的を表す不定詞の副詞的用法。

⑥ **Billy laughed and sang his heart out — he didn't understand there would be no Santa that year.**

▶ laugh and sing *one's* heart outで「心ゆくまで[気が済むまで、思い切り]笑って歌う」（≒ laugh and sing as loud as *one* can）という意味。

▶ there would be no Santa that yearは「今年はサンタは来ないだろう」という意味。間接話法で書かれているため、that節の中の動詞は主節の時制に合わせて過去形would、またthis year「今年」がthat yearになっている。

⑦ **When it was time for bed, my parents gave their usual Christmas Eve speech**

▶ it is time for 〜で「〜の時間である」という意味。

▶ gave their usual Christmas Eve speechは「クリスマスイブお決まりの話

をした」という意味。

⑧ **You boys try to fall asleep fast, because Santa won't come until you're asleep.**

▶ fall asleepは「寝入る、眠りに落ちる」(≒ go to sleep)という意味。

▶ until you're asleepは「あなたたちが寝入るまで」という意味。〈until + S + V ...〉で未来の事柄を述べるとき、動詞は現在形を使う。

⑨ **How could they be so naive?**

▶ 文②と同様、この文も描出話法でジョニーの心の動きを伝えている。普通の会話体(直接話法)の文に直せば、"How can they be so naive?" I thought. となる。このあとの文⑩、⑪も描出話法である。

⑩ **Did they really think Santa could somehow get into a house without a chimney?**

▶ get into 〜は「〜に入る」(≒ enter)という意味。

⑪ **What was he supposed to do — come in through the plumbing?**

▶ be supposed to 〜は「〜することになっている、〜しなければならない」(≒ have to 〜)という意味。

▶ ダッシュ (−)のあとに続くcome 〜 plumbing?は、煙突のない家にサンタがどのようにして入るかを想像して述べている。

⑫ **Pop his head out of the toilet, and exclaim, "Merry Christmas"?**

▶ pop *one's* head out of 〜「〜から頭をひょいと出す」(≒ suddenly appear from 〜)という意味。

⑬ **So, for once in my life, I had very little trouble going to sleep on Christmas Eve.**

▶ have very little trouble V-ingで「ほとんど苦労せずに〜する」という意味。

⑭ **I had to tell Billy to shut up a couple of times.**

▶ 〈tell + O (人) + to 〜〉で「(人)に〜するように言う[命じる]」という意味。

▶ shut upは「静かにする」(≒ be quiet)という意味。

▶ a couple of 〜は「2、3の〜、数〜」(≒ a few 〜; several 〜)という意味。

✎ 英文を完成させなさい。

私はその町を2、3回訪れたことがあります。

I have visited the town a (　　　) (　　　) times.

⑮ **But after that, we were both out cold.**

▶ bothは「両方とも、2人とも」という意味の代名詞。

▶ be out coldは「寝入っている」(≒ be asleep)という意味。

Reading

- ☐ except [ɪksépt]
- ☐ wrap [rǽp]
- ☐ thrilled [θríld]
- ☐ package [pǽkɪdʒ]
- ☐ not in the same league as ~
- ☐ league [líːg]
- ☐ punch [pʌ́ntʃ]
- ☐ punched me in the back
- ☐ whisper [(h)wíspər]
- ☐ go back to sleep
- ☐ leave ~ alone
- ☐ get out of ~
- ☐ responsibility [rɪspὰnsəbíləti]
- ☐ guy [gáɪ]
- ☐ appreciate [əpríːʃièɪt]
- ☐ you'd better ~

①There would be no gifts in the morning — except the shirts my mom bought for me at the mall.　②She had wrapped them up beautifully.　③And I would try to look thrilled when I opened the packages.　④But shirts are not in the same league as bicycles.

⑤At 2:13 a.m., Billy punched me in the back and whispered, "Listen."

"⑥I don't hear anything," I said.　"⑦Go back to sleep and leave me alone."　⑧Then I felt Billy get out of the bed.

"Come back here and get in bed," I said.　⑨It was my responsibility to keep the little guy in our room.　⑩My parents did not appreciate night visitors to their bedroom　⑪So, you'd better have a very good reason for waking them up.

このセクションの内容

ジョニーは、今年のクリスマスのプレゼントに（A.　　　）がもらえたらいいと思っていたが、おそらくプレゼントは母親がショッピング・モールで買った（B.　　　）だけだろうと予想していた。夜中の2時過ぎにジョニーは突然弟のビリーにたたき起こされたあと、彼が（C.　　　）から出ていくのがわかった。

① **There would be no gifts in the morning — except the shirts my mom bought for me at the mall.**

▶ 描出話法の文。過去形で書かれているが、現在のジョニーの心の動きを描写している。

▶ There would be no ～ except ... で「…以外は何も～ないだろう」という意味。この文では、クリスマス当日の朝、目を覚ましたジョニーが目にするであろうクリスマスプレゼントを想像している。

▶ the shirts のあとに目的格の関係代名詞 that[which] が省略されている。

② **She had wrapped them up beautifully.**

▶ had wrapped は〈had + 過去分詞〉で〈完了〉を表す過去完了。

③ **And I would try to look thrilled when I opened the packages.**

▶ 描出話法の文。母親からのクリスマスプレゼントの包みを開けるときの気持ちを描写している。

▶ try to ～は「～しようと努める」という意味。

▶ look thrilled は「わくわくした様子である」という意味。〈look + 形容詞〉で「～に見える」という意味。

> ✐ 英文を完成させなさい。

彼女は図書館の中で私を見たとき驚いた様子だった。

She (   ) (   ) when she saw me in the library.

④ **But shirts are not in the same league as bicycles.**

▶ not in the same league as ～は「～ほどよくない」(≒ not as good as ～)という意味。ジョニーがクリスマスに一番ほしいのはシャツではなく自転車。

⑤ **At 2:13 a.m., Billy punched me in the back and whispered, "Listen."**

▶ punched me in the back は「私の背中をこぶしでなぐった」という意味。〈punch +（人）+ in[on] the + 身体の一部〉で「（人）の～をこぶしでなぐる」。同様の表現に次のようなものがある。

・hit him on the head[in the face]「彼の頭[顔]をなぐる」
・pat him on the shoulder[back]「彼の肩[背中]を軽くたたく」
・catch him by the arm[sleeve]「彼の腕[袖]をつかむ」

> ✐ 次の英文を日本語に直しなさい。

He couldn't look her right in the eye.

⑥ **I don't hear anything**

▶ not ～ anything で「何も～ない」という意味。I hear nothing. とほぼ同じ。

⑦ **Go back to sleep and leave me alone.**

> このセクションの内容 の答え→　A. 自転車　B. シャツ　C. ベッド

▶ leave ～ alone で「～を1人にしておく、放っておく」という意味。

📝 **次の英文を日本語に直しなさい。**

Never leave your child alone in your car.

⑧ Then I felt Billy get out of the bed.

▶ I felt Billy get out of ～ は知覚動詞構文。〈feel + O + 原形不定詞〉で「O が ～するのを感じる」という意味。

📝 **次の英文を日本語に直しなさい。**

I felt something cold touch my hand.

⑨ It was my responsibility to keep the little guy in our room.

▶ it が不定詞(to keep ～ our room)の内容を形式的に受ける形式主語構文。動名詞を主語にして、Keeping the little guy in our room was my responsibility. としても、ほぼ同じ意味になる。

📝 **英文を完成させなさい。**

未来の世代のために自然環境を守ることは私たちの義務だ。

(　　　) (　　　) our duty (　　　) protect the natural environment for future generations.

▶〈keep + O + C(状態を表す語句)〉で「O を～な状態に保つ」という意味。O = the little guy は弟の Billy のこと。

📝 **次の英文を日本語に直しなさい。**

He always tries to keep his car in the best condition.

⑩ My parents did not appreciate night visitors to their bedroom.

▶ do not appreciate night visitors to their bedroom とは、「夜子どもたちが寝室に来るのを歓迎しない」という意味。

⑪ So, you'd better have a very good reason for waking them up.

▶ you had better は「～したほうがよい(そうしないとたいへんなことになる)」という非常に強い忠告を表す。you'd better はその短縮形。

📝 **英文を完成させなさい。**

できるだけ早く医者に診てもらったほうがいいですよ。

(　　　) (　　　) see a doctor as soon as possible.

▶ a good reason for V-ing で「V するだけのまともな理由」という意味。

📝 **英文を完成させなさい。**

彼があれほど怒るのにはよほどの理由があるに違いない。

He must have a (　　　) (　　　) (　　　) getting that angry.

教科書 p.180 *l*.14〜p.181 *l*.11　Ⅳ

□ ignore [ɪgnɔ́:r]
□ doorknob [dɔ́:rnὰb]
□ crack [krǽk]
□ just a crack
□ peek [pí:k]
□ peek out
□ rush [rʌ́ʃ]
□ stick 〜 out ...
□ There he was.
□ dress up 〜
□ expect [ɪkspékt]
□ beard [bíərd]
□ in person
□ at the end of 〜
□ hallway [hɔ́:lwèi]
□ load [lóʊd]
□ load *one's* arms with 〜
□ -colored [kʌ́lərd]
□ hidden [hídn]

①He ignored me, turning the doorknob very slowly. He opened the door just a crack and peeked out. ②Then he began to wave wildly for me to join him. I jumped out of bed and rushed over. ③I stuck my head out the door and my heart began to race.

④There he was. ⑤All dressed up in red and white, just as you'd expect. He had a long, white beard and wore a red cap. ⑥I never dreamed I would ever see him in person.

⑦He was standing in the closet at the end of the hallway, loading his arms with bright-colored packages. Then I saw the bicycle. ⑧The one I had asked Santa to bring me.

⑨My parents were right! ⑩Santa had found a way.

⑪I decided there must be a hidden door at the back of the closet! ⑫A door that only Santa could open. ⑬That's how he got into the house.

このセクションの内容

弟のビリーに起こされてジョニーが部屋の（A.　　　）から外をのぞくと、そこに彼はいた。彼は期待したとおりの赤と白の（B.　　　）をして、廊下の突き当たりの（C.　　　）の中に鮮やかな色の包みを抱えて立っていた。

① **He ignored me, turning the doorknob very slowly.**

▶ turning the doorknob very slowly は分詞構文で、「～して…した」という〈連続する動作〉を表す。..., and turned the doorknob very slowly と言いかえ可能。

> ✎ **次の英文を日本語に直しなさい。**
> We left the hotel early in the morning, arriving at the lake before noon.

② **Then he began to wave wildly for me to join him.**

▶〈wave + for +（人）+ to ～〉で「（人）に～するように手を振って合図する」という意味。for me は to join them の意味上の主語。

③ **I stuck my head out the door and my heart began to race.**

▶ stick ～ out ... で「～を…から突き出す」（≒ put ～ out ...）という意味。stick は不規則動詞で、stick − stuck − stuck と変化する。

▶ 動詞の race は「（心臓が）どきどきする、（鼓動が）速まる」という意味。

④ **There he was.**

▶ 場所を表す副詞の there を文頭に置いて強調した文。主語が代名詞の場合、〈主語＋動詞〉の倒置は起きない。

▶ There は、この後の文⑦でわかるように、廊下の一番先にあるクローゼット（衣類用の戸棚）の中を指す。また、he は Santa のこと。

⑤ **All dressed up in red and white, just as you'd expect.**

▶ ビリーとジョニーが目撃したサンタの服装を説明している。All dressed up ～の前に He was を補って考える。

▶ all dressed up in red and white は「赤と白の服でめかしこんでいる」という意味。

▶ just as you'd expect は「まさに期待[予想]どおりに」という意味。you'd は you would の短縮形。

⑥ **I never dreamed I would ever see him in person.**

▶ never dreamed (that) ～で「～とは夢にも思わなかった」という意味。

▶ 否定文の中での ever は「決して～ない、今後～ない」という意味を表す。

▶ in person は「じかに、実物で」（≒ face to face）という意味。

⑦ **He was standing in the closet at the end of the hallway, loading his arms with bright-colored packages.**

▶ at the end of ～は「～の終わりに、～の端に」という意味。ここでは at the end of the hallway が直前の the closet を修飾しているので、「廊下の突き当たりに」クローゼットがあるとわかる。

▶ loading his arms ～は分詞構文で、「腕に～を抱えて」という〈付帯状況〉

このセクションの内容 の答え→　A. ドア　B. 服装　C. クローゼット

を表している。

⑧ **The one I had asked Santa to bring me.**

▶the one が関係詞節や不定詞などの修飾語句の前に置かれると、「特定の物〔人〕」を表す。ここでは The one ＝ The bicycle。

> 🖉 次の英文を日本語に直しなさい。

That's the one I've been looking for.

_____

▶The one のあとに目的格の関係代名詞 that〔which〕が省略されている。この文では、The one は〈bring ＋ O₁（人）＋ O₂（物）〉「（人）に物を持ってくる」の O₂ を兼ねている。

▶〈ask ＋ O（人）＋ to ～〉で「（人）に～するように頼む」という意味。

⑨ **My parents were right!**

▶「両親の言ったことは正しかった」という意味。これは、教科書 p.179 の 1 ～ 2 行目で、「煙突がない家にサンタクロースはどうやってプレゼントを届けるのか」をたずねたジョニーに、両親が Santa will find a way to deliver your presents. と答えたときのことを指している。

⑩ **Santa had found a way.**

▶had found は〈完了・結果〉を表す過去完了。

▶a way のあとに to deliver our presents を補って考える。

⑪ **I decided there must be a hidden door at the back of the closet!**

▶I decided ～ は「（結論として）～と考えた」という意味。

▶〈there must be ～ ＋場所を表す語句〉で「…に～があるにちがいない」という意味。助動詞の must には過去形がないため、「～にちがいない」という推量を表す場合は、must をそのまま用いる。

▶at the back of ～ で「～の後ろに、～の裏手に、～の奥に」という意味。_cf._ at the back of a drawer「引き出しの奥に」

⑫ **A door that only Santa could open.**

▶文⑪の a hidden door について説明している。that は A door を先行詞とする目的格の関係代名詞。

⑬ **That's how he got into the house.**

▶〈That's how ＋ S ＋ V〉で「このようにして S は V する」という意味。関係副詞の how は「～する方法」という意味を表す名詞節を作る。

> 🖉 次の英文を日本語に直しなさい。

The book will tell you how a dam works.

_____

Reading

□ feel a chill run down *one's* spine
□ chill [tʃíl]
□ spine [spáin]
□ hold *one's* breath
□ breath [bréθ]
□ slip [slíp]
□ ruin [rúːin]
□ plummet [plʌ́mət]
□ plummet into 〜
□ reserve [rizə́ːrv]
□ naughty [nɔ́ːti]
□ naught [nɔ́ːt]
□ for naught
□ wise [wáiz]
□ especially [ispéʃəli]
□ search [sə́ːrtʃ]
□ search for 〜

①I felt a chill run down my spine. ②Billy and I had already seen too much. ③I closed the door, and we held our breath as we slipped back into bed. ④I prayed we hadn't ruined everything. ⑤I pictured our Christmas hopes plummeting into some black hole reserved for the lost dreams of naughty children.

⑥But my fears were for naught. ⑦Christmas morning turned out to be the best ever. ⑧I realized my parents were wiser than I had imagined.

⑨Billy and I loved our presents — especially the ones from Santa. ⑩But it wasn't just about the gifts. ⑪It was about the magic.

⑫And now I know the truth. ⑬You don't need a chimney. ⑭Santa will find a way

⑮As you might imagine, I've searched for that hidden door at the back of the closet. ⑯But I've never found it. ⑰I figure it's just part of the magic of Christmas. ⑱That closet is like any other closet — until Christmas, when it becomes ...

⑲The Santa Closet.

このセクションの内容

多くを見すぎてしまったジョニーは、これですべてが （A.　　　　）になるのではないかと恐れたが、翌朝は今までで最高の （B.　　　　）だった。クローゼットの後ろには、クリスマスになるとサンタだけが入れる （C.　　　　）ができるのだとジョニーは思った。

① **I felt a chill run down my spine.**

▶〈feel＋O＋原形不定詞〉で「Oが〜するのを感じる」という知覚動詞構文。feel a chill run down *one's* spine で「背筋に寒気が走る、ゾクゾクしたものが背筋を走り抜ける」という意味。

② **Billy and I had already seen too much.**

▶ had already seen は過去完了で、「すでに〜してしまっていた」という過去のある時点までに完了していた動作を表す。

✐ （　）内の語を適切な形に変えなさい。

私がサラに電話したとき、彼女はもう夕食を食べ終えていた。

Sarah (has) already (finish) dinner when I called her.

▶ see too much は「（見てはいけないものを）見すぎる」という意味。

③ **I closed the door, and we held our breath as we slipped back into bed.**

▶ hold *one's* breath は「息を殺す、息をひそめる」（≒ stop breathing）という意味。

④ **I prayed we hadn't ruined everything.**

▶ pray（that）〜は「〜と祈る」という意味。

▶ hadn't ruined は過去完了で、過去のある時点までに〈完了〉していた動作を表す。

⑤ **I pictured our Christmas hopes plummeting into some black hole reserved for the lost dreams of naughty children.**

▶ この picture は動詞で、imagine「〜を想像する」とほぼ同じ意味。どちらも〈V＋O＋C（現在分詞）〉の構文を作る。

例 He pictured his daughter singing on the stage.
「彼は自分の娘がステージで歌っている姿を想像した」

▶ plummet into 〜は「〜へと真っ逆さまに落ちる」（≒ go down quickly into 〜）という意味。

▶ reserved 〜は some black hole を修飾する過去分詞の形容詞的用法。

⑥ **But my fears were for naught.**

▶ for naught で「むだに」（≒ for nothing）という意味。この文では、「私が恐れていたことは結局取り越し苦労だった」というよい意味で用いられているが、悪い結果にも用いる。

✐ 次の英文を日本語に直しなさい。

All their efforts were for naught.

⑦ **Christmas morning turned out to be the best ever.**

▶ turn out to be 〜で「（結局）〜とわかる」という意味。

このセクションの内容 の答え→　A. 台なし　B. クリスマスの朝　C. 魔法のドア

⟫ 英文を完成させなさい。

彼の話は本当だとわかった。

His story (　　　) (　　　) to be true.

▶ the best ever は「これまでで最高のもの」という意味。〈the + 最上級 + ever〉で「これまでで最も~な」という意味になる。

⟫ 次の英文を日本語に直しなさい。

The concert last night was the best ever.

---

⑧ **I realized my parents were wiser than I had imagined.**

▶ realize (that) ~で「~とわかる」という意味。

▶〈比較級 + than + S + V〉で「SがVするよりも~」という意味。

⟫ 次の英文を日本語に直しなさい。

The movie was more exciting than I had expected.

---

⑨ **Billy and I loved our presents — especially the ones from Santa.**

▶ the ones は the presents のこと。

⑩ **But it wasn't just about the gifts.**

⑪ **It was about the magic.**

▶ 文⑩と⑪は、it wasn't just about ~. It was about ...「それ (= 私たちが気に入ったこと) は~についてだけではなかった。それは…についてもであった」という意味。〈not just ~ but ...〉「~だけではなく…も」の変形。

⑫ **And now I know the truth.**

▶ the truth「真実」とは、具体的には、この物語で繰り返し出てきた、「煙突のない家にサンタクロースはどうやってプレゼントを届けるのか」というジョニーの疑問に対する答えのこと。

⑬ **You don't need a chimney.**

⑭ **Santa will find a way.**

▶ 文⑫の the truth の具体的な内容。ジョニーがクリスマスイブの晩に目撃した光景から、ジョニーは「サンタクロースは煙突がない家にもプレゼントを届けることができる」と信じている。

⑮ **As you might imagine, I've searched for that hidden door at the back of the closet.**

▶ As you might imagine は「ご想像のとおり」という意味。might は控えめな推量。

▶ I've (= I have) searched ~は現在完了の〈完了〉用法。search for ~で「~

を探す」（≒ look for ～）という意味。

▶ that hidden door at the back of the closetとは、教科書p.181の9～10行目で、ジョニーがI decided there must be a hidden door at the back of the closet!と言っていた「秘密のドア」のこと。

⑯ But I've never found it.

▶ 現在完了のI've never found ～は「（今までのところ）～は見つかっていない」という意味。

▶ itは前文のthat hidden door at the back of the closetを指す。

⑰ I figure it's just part of the magic of Christmas.

▶ I figure (that) ～は「（状況から）～と思う」という意味。

▶ itはthat hidden door at the back of the closetを指している。

▶ part of ～は「～の一部」という意味。

　✍ 英文を完成させなさい。

これらの絵はその美術館の所蔵品のほんの一部です。

These paintings are just (　　　) (　　　) the museum's collection.

⑱ That closet is like any other closet — until Christmas, when it becomes ...

⑲ The Santa Closet.

▶ is like any other closetは「ほかのクローゼットと何ら変わらない」という意味。このlikeは前置詞で「～と同じような」という意味。

　✍ 次の英文を日本語に直しなさい。

Ellen is not like any other woman I've ever met.

▶ until ～は「～までずっと」という〈時間の継続〉を表す前置詞。

　✍ 次の英文を日本語に直しなさい。

The exhibition will be open until November 30.

▶〈, when〉は非制限用法の関係副詞。〈先行詞＋コンマ (,) ＋関係副詞〉の形で、先行詞に補足的に説明を加える。ここではwhen it becomes ... The Santa Closetが先行詞のChristmasに補足的に説明を加えている。

　✍ 次の英文を日本語に直しなさい。

My father was born in 1964, when Tokyo hosted the Olympics for the first time.

▶ 文⑲のThe Santa Closetは、前文⑱のbecomesの補語。この物語の中心であることを強調するために、あえて改行して大文字で始めている。

確認問題

語彙・表現

1 次の各組で下線部の発音がほかと異なる語を１つずつ選び、記号で答えなさい。
(1) ア critical イ chill ウ hidden エ spine
(2) ア league イ breath ウ peek エ appreciate
(3) ア naughty イ hallway ウ load エ bought

2 日本語に合うように、（ ）内に適切な語を入れなさい。
(1) 私はその男性にお会いして、助けてくれたお礼をご本人に直接言いたいのです。

I'd like to meet the man and thank him (　　　) (　　　) for helping me.
(2) アリスはすっかりおめかししてパーティーにやって来た。

Alice came to the party all (　　　) (　　　).
(3) 若いころ私はいろいろ気になることがあった。

I had a lot (　　　) (　　　) (　　　) when I was young.
(4) 絵美の家族は数か月前に新しい家に引っ越した。

Emi's family moved into a new house (　　　) (　　　) (　　　) months ago.

文のパターン・文法

1 （ ）内に適切な関係代名詞または関係副詞を入れなさい。
(1) This is a special room (　　　) only club members can access.
(2) They're waiting for the day (　　　) peace returns to their country.
(3) That's (　　　) he got interested in cooking.

2 次の各組の文がほぼ同じ意味になるように、（ ）内に適切な語を入れなさい。
(1) Keeping the garden clean is my responsibility.

(　　　) is my responsibility (　　　) (　　　) the garden clean.
(2) The girl put on her new dress and looked very happy.

The girl looked very happy (　　　) her new dress.
(3) I said to Makoto, "Please lend me the book."

I (　　　) Makoto (　　　) (　　　) me the book.
(4) We looked out the window, and waved to our uncle.

(　　　) (　　　) the window, we waved to our uncle.

3 （　）内の語句を並べかえて、英文を完成させなさい。

(1) (recently / a short story / this / wrote / Mai / is) for children.

_____ for children.

(2) (winter / have / we're / to / ever / the coldest / going) this year.

_____ this year.

(3) (do / I / there / nothing / could / was) about it.

_____ about it.

(4) (busy / Jane / to / was / go out / too) for lunch.

_____ for lunch.

> 総合

次のジョニーの文を読んで、あとの問いに答えなさい。

---

　①I felt a chill (　　　　) (　　　　) my spine. Billy and I had already seen too much. I closed the door, and we held our breath as we slipped back into bed. ②I prayed we hadn't ruined everything. I pictured our Christmas hopes plummeting into some black hole reserved for the lost dreams of naughty children.

　But my fears were for naught. ③Christmas morning turned out to be the best ever. I realized my parents were ④(I / wiser / imagined / than / had).

　Billy and I loved our presents — especially the ⑤ones from Santa. But it wasn't just about the gifts. It was about the magic.

　And now I know the truth. You don't need a (　⑥　). Santa will find a way.

問1　下線部①が「私は背筋に寒気が走るのを感じた」という意味になるように、（　）内に入る最も適切な2語を書きなさい。

問2　下線部②についてジョニーはなぜこのように思ったのですか。その理由を日本語で答えなさい。

問3　下線部③を日本語に直しなさい。

問4　下線部④の（　）内の語を並べかえて、英文を完成させなさい。

問5　下線部⑤が表す具体的内容を本文中の英語1語で答えなさい。

問6　⑥の（　）内に入る適切な1語を答えなさい。ただしcで始まる語とします。

Find Your Own Donut

□ donut [dóunʌt]

□ CEO [síːíːóu]

□ emeritus [ɪmérətəs]

□ Sorenson [sɔ́ːrensn]

□ Babson [bǽbsn]

□ Healey [híːli]

□ Capozzi [kəpóuzi]

□ provost [próuvoust]

□ Rice [ráɪs]

□ dean [díːn]

□ Rolleg [róuleg]

□ governing [gʌ́vərnɪŋ]

□ governing board

□ spouse [spáus]

□ fellow [félou]

□ extreme [ɪkstríːm]

□ honor [ɑnər]

□ anniversary [æ̀nɪvə́ːrsəri]

□ congratulate [kəngrǽtʃəlèit]

□ get to the point

□ stressed [strést]

□ stressed out 〜

□ take 〜 off the table

□ each and every 〜

□ HR [éɪtʃ áːr]

①Toyoda Akio, CEO of Toyota, gave the graduation speech at Babson College in May 2019. ②The speech asks us not to be boring and to find our own donuts.

Thank you, President Emeritus Sorenson, for that kind introduction, and thank you to Babson for inviting me here today.

President Healey, Chair Capozzi, Provost Rice, Dean Rolleg, members of the governing boards, parents, spouses, friends, babies, and my fellow graduates. ③It is my extreme honor to speak to you today as Babson College celebrates its 100th anniversary.

④And may I be among the first to congratulate this very special class of 2019!

⑤So, let me get right to the point. ⑥I know that some of you may be sitting there, stressed out about where you will work after graduation. ⑦You may be wondering what company will offer you a job. ⑧Well, let me take that worry off the table for you right now and offer each and every one of you a job at Toyota!

⑨I haven't actually cleared that with my HR department yet, but I'm sure it will be OK.

このセクションの内容

豊田章男氏は、2019年5月に（A.　　　　　　）の（B.　　　　　　）で行った演説の冒頭で、（C.　　　　　）がまだ決まらず不安でいる卒業生たち全員に、トヨタ自動車への仕事の口を提供すると語った。

① **Toyoda Akio, CEO of Toyota, gave the graduation speech at Babson College in May 2019.**

▶ CEOはchief executive officer（最高経営責任者）の略。

▶ give a speech at ～で「～でスピーチ［講演］を行う」という意味。

▶ 本課で取り上げられているのは、トヨタ自動車株式会社の代表取締役社長兼CEO（2021年9月現在）である豊田章男氏（1956年5月生まれ）が、2019年5月18日に米国マサチューセッツ州ボストン郊外のバブソン大学（Babson College）の卒業式で行った講演である。豊田氏は1982年にバブソン大学で経営学修士（MBA）を取得している。

② **The speech asks us not to be boring and to find our own donuts.**

▶ ⟨ask + O（人）+ not to ～⟩で「（人）に～しないように求める」という意味。

🖎 次の英文を日本語に直しなさい。

My mother always tells me not to skip breakfast.

▶ and to find our own donutsは「そして私たち自身のドーナツを見つける」という意味の比喩的な表現。具体的な内容は本文で述べられる。この不定詞には前半のnotはかからない。

③ **It is my extreme honor to speak to you today as Babson College celebrates its 100th anniversary.**

▶ It is my honor to ～で「～するのは私にとって光栄なことです」という意味。講演などの冒頭で使われる決まった表現。

▶ asは「～するとき、～するに際して」という意味を表す接続詞。

④ **And may I be among the first to congratulate this very special class of 2019!**

▶ ⟨may + S + be ～!⟩で「Sが～であらんことを祈ります」という意味。

▶ 前置詞のamongは、ここでは「～の1人で」という意味。

▶ the first to ～は、「最初に～する者」という意味。*cf.* the last to ～「最後に～する者、最も～しなさそうな人」

🖎 次の英文を日本語に直しなさい。

Who was the first to get to the scene?

▶ this very special class of 2019のclassは、米国では「同期生」を表す。class of 2019は「2019年卒業生」という意味。

⑤ **So, let me get right to the point.**

▶ ⟨let + O（人）+ 原形不定詞⟩は「（人）に～させる」という意味。

▶ get right to the pointは「単刀直入に言う、（前置きは省いて）早速要点に入る」という意味。

⑥ **I know that some of you may be sitting there, stressed out about where you will work after graduation.**

　▶ may be sitting ～は「座っているかもしれない」という控えめな推量。

　▶ stressed out about ～は過去分詞で始まる分詞構文で、「～のことでストレスがたまった状態で」という付帯状況を表す。

　▶ about where you will work ～は、前置詞の目的語の位置に名詞節（疑問詞節）が来た形。

　　　✍ 次の英文を日本語に直しなさい。

　　　He told his teacher about how the fight started.

⑦ **You may be wondering what company will offer you a job.**

　▶ You may be wondering what company will ～は「どの会社が～だろうかと（不安に）思っているかもしれない」という控えめな推量。

　▶ what company will ～ a jobは名詞節（疑問詞節）で、wonderの目的語。

　▶〈offer + O₁ + O₂〉で「O₁（人）にO₂（物・機会など）を提供する」という意味。

⑧ **Well, let me take that worry off the table for you right now and offer each and every one of you a job at Toyota!**

　▶ let me take ～は、〈let + O（人）+ 原形不定詞〉で「（人）に～させる」という意味の使役動詞構文。

　▶ take that worry off the tableは「その心配事をテーブルから取り下げる」→「その心配事を解消する」という意味。cf. lie on the table「（提案などが）棚上げされる」

　▶ that worryは、前文⑥⑦で触れている「就職先がまだ決まらない」という悩みを指す。

　▶ offer each ～ at Toyotaは、前文⑦のoffer you a jobをより具体的に述べている。

⑨ **I haven't actually cleared that with my HR department yet, but I'm sure it will be OK.**

　▶ haven't actually clearedは〈完了〉を表す現在完了。〈haven't［have not］+ 過去分詞 ～ yet〉で「まだ～していない」という意味を表す。

　▶ actuallyは「実は、実を言うと」という意味。

　▶ I'm sure (that) ～は「きっと～だと思う、～だと確信している」という意味。

　▶ itは前文⑦⑧で述べている豊田氏の申し出、つまり「就職先が決まっていない卒業生にトヨタ自動車が仕事を提供する」ことを指す。

□ now that ～
□ enployment [ɪmplɔ́ɪmənt]
□ momentous [moʊméntəs]
□ occasion [əkéɪʒən]
□ stay out
□ finale [fɪnǽli]
□ Game of Thrones
□ challenge [tʃǽlɪndʒ]
□ hockey [hɑ́ki]
□ dorm [dɔ́ːrm]
□ in a word
□ make up for ～

①So now that the employment issue has been solved, let's talk about more important things, like how you plan to celebrate this momentous occasion.　②I mean, how wild is tonight's party going to get?　③And more importantly, can I come?

④But I can't stay out too late because tomorrow is the finale of "Game of Thrones"!

⑤I have to tell you, when I was at Babson, I had no social life.　⑥For me, taking classes in English was a real challenge.　⑦It took all of my focus and free time.　⑧I never went to parties.　I never went to a hockey game.　I just went from my dorm to class, to the library, to my dorm, to class, to the library.

⑨So when I attended Babson, I was, in a word, boring.　⑩But once I graduated, I went to work in New York, where I immediately made up for lost time and became "the King of the Night"!

⑪Now I'm not suggesting you do the same.　⑫I can tell, just by looking at you, that none of you are boring.　⑬I'm sure you have enjoyed a very active social life while you were here.　⑭But since I'm here to offer you words of advice, let the first be this: *Don't be boring.*　Have fun!

⑮Really figure out what makes you happy in life, what brings you joy.

このセクションの内容

豊田氏は、バブソン大学在学中は、英語で授業を受けることが大きな課題で、（A.　　　　）を楽しむ余裕などなかったと語った。豊田氏の卒業生への最初のアドバイスは、生活の中で（B.　　　　）を感じさせてくれるもの、（C.　　　　）をもたらしてくれるものを見つけるように、というものだった。

① **So now that the employment issue has been solved, let's talk about more important things, like how you plan to celebrate this momentous occasion.**

▶ now that ～は「～した今では、～したから」という意味で、この2語で接続詞と同じ働きをする。

　　✎ **英文を完成させなさい。**

　　試験が終わった今は、気分をリフレッシュしたい。

　　(　　　　) (　　　　) the exam is over, I want to refresh myself.

▶ has been solvedは〈have[has] + been + 過去分詞〉で受動態の現在完了形。

▶ likeは「～のような」という意味を表す前置詞。ここでは目的語の位置に、howで始まる疑問詞節(間接疑問)が置かれている。

② **I mean, how wild is tonight's party going to get?**

▶ how wild is ～ going to get?で「～はどれくらい羽目を外したものとなるだろうか」という意味。

▶ 形容詞のwildは、口語では「熱狂的な、狂った、羽目を外した」などの意味で用いられる。*cf.* go wild「熱狂する」

③ **And more importantly, can I come?**

▶ more importantlyは「これはもっと重要なことであるが」という意味で、文全体を修飾する副詞。

▶ can I come?は、前文で話した今夜の卒業生たちのパーティーに「自分も行っていいかな？」という意味。

④ **But I can't stay out too late because tomorrow is the finale of "Game of Thrones"!**

▶ stay out lateは「夜遅くまで外出している、夜遊びする」という意味。

▶ "Game of Thrones"『ゲーム・オブ・スローンズ』(略称GOT)は、ジョージ・R・R・マーティン(George Raymond Richard Martin)原作のファンタジー小説シリーズ『氷と炎の歌』に基づいたテレビドラマシリーズである。制作はアメリカのHBO。2011年春から全8シーズン全73話が放送され、最終話は豊田氏が講演を行った翌日、2019年5月19日に放送された。

⑤ **I have to tell you, when I was at Babson, I had no social life.**

▶ I have to tell youは、話し手にとって恥ずかしいこと、または話すのに躊躇するようなことを敢えて話すときの決まり文句。

▶ have no ～は「～は全くない」という全否定。

⑥ **For me, taking classes in English was a real challenge.**

▶ 動名詞句のtaking classes in Englishが文の主語。

▶ challengeは「難しいこと、難問、難題」という意味。

⑦ **It took all of my focus and free time.**
  ▶ it takes 〜は「〜を必要とする」という意味。

⑧ **I never went to parties.**
  ▶ neverは「（どんな場合でも）決して〜ない」という強い否定を表す。

⑨ **So when I attended Babson, I was, in a word, boring.**
  ▶ in a wordは「一言で言えば」という意味。

⑩ **But once I graduated, I went to work in New York, where I immediately made up for lost time and became "the King of the Night"!**
  ▶ onceは接続詞で、ここでは「〜するとすぐに」（≒ as soon as）という意味。
  ▶〈, where〉はNew Yorkを先行詞とする関係副詞の非制限用法。where以下で、ニューヨークで就職したあとで起きたことを述べている。固有名詞を先行詞とする関係詞はすべて非制限用法となる。

  > ✎ 次の英文を日本語に直しなさい。

  Mike stayed in London for two weeks, where he met a famous artist.

  ▶ make up for 〜は「〜の埋め合わせをする、〜の穴埋めをする」という意味。

⑪ **Now I'm not suggesting you do the same.**
  ▶ suggest (that) 〜は「〜と提案する」という意味。
  ▶ do the sameは、前文のmade up for lost time and became "the King of the Night"を指す。

⑫ **I can tell, just by looking at you, that none of you are boring.**
  ▶ none of 〜で「〜のうちのだれも〜ない」という全否定。

⑬ **I'm sure you have enjoyed a very active social life while you were here.**
  ▶ have enjoyedは〈完了〉を表す現在完了。

⑭ **But since I'm here to offer you words of advice, let the first be this**
  ▶ to offer 〜は〈目的〉を表す不定詞の副詞的用法。
  ▶ let the first be thisは「皆さんへのまず最初のアドバイスはこれにさせてください」という意味。the first = the first words of advice

⑮ **Really figure out what makes you happy in life, what brings you joy.**
  ▶ figure outは「（答えなど）を見つけ出す」という意味。
  ▶ what makes you happy in lifeとwhat brings you joyは、どちらも疑問詞節（間接疑問）で、figure outの目的語。

- □ joyful [dʒɔ́ɪfəl]
- □ astonishing [əstánɪʃɪŋ]
- □ discovery [dɪskʌ́vəri]
- □ go ahead
- □ assume [əsjúːm]
- □ work out
- □ tricky [tríki]
- □ ladder [lǽdər]
- □ talented [tǽləntɪd]
- □ golden [góʊldən]
- □ handcuff [hǽndkʌf]
- □ golden handcuffs
- □ mortgage [mɔ́ːrgɪdʒ]
- □ put ~ through ...

①When I was a student here, I found joy in donuts. ②American donuts were a joyful, astonishing discovery. ③I want to encourage all of you to find your own donut. ④Find what makes you happy, and don't let go.

⑤You should know I didn't come here to tell you the usual stories about the mountains you may have to climb, or the challenges you'll have to meet. No! ⑥Because I think we should just go ahead and assume everything is going to work out great!

⑦I think all of you are going to be a big success! ⑧I really do. ⑨And that's where it gets tricky, because you are going to be successful. ⑩You are going to climb that ladder and make that money.

⑪But will it be doing something that is fun? ⑫Something that you really love? ⑬Because when you are as talented as I know all of you are, it is so easy to wake up one day and find yourself in golden handcuffs, with a mortgage and three kids that you need to put through Babson.

⑭So, whether you're entering a family business or not, now's the time to figure out what speaks to your heart the most.

このセクションの内容

豊田氏は、卒業生たちが将来、（A.　　　）を収めていると仮定して、そのとき自分がおもしろいと感じること、本当に（B.　　　）をしているかどうかが重要だと語っている。豊田氏は、そのためにも、今こそ自分がいちばん（C.　　　）を感じることを見つけておくべきだ、と勧めている。

① **When I was a student here, I found joy in donuts.**
　▶ find joy in ～で「～に楽しみを見いだす」という意味。

② **American donuts were a joyful, astonishing discovery.**
　▶バブソン大学在学中、社交を楽しむ余裕もなかった豊田氏が好きになった
　ものとして、American donutsを挙げている。

③ **I want to encourage all of you to find your own donut.**
　▶〈encourage ＋ O（人）＋ to ～〉で「（人）に～するように勧める」という意味。

④ **Find what makes you happy, and don't let go.**
　▶ what makes you happyで「あなたを幸せにしてくれるもの」という意味。
　whatは先行詞を含む関係代名詞で、名詞節を作る。ここではFindの目的語。
　▶ let goは「（手にしているもの）を放す」という意味。

⑤ **You should know I didn't come here to tell you the usual**
　stories about the mountains you may have to climb, or the
　challenges you'll have to meet.
　▶ the mountains、およびthe challengesのあとに、それぞれ関係代名詞
　that[which]が省略されている。

⑥ **Because I think we should just go ahead and assume**
　everything is going to work out great!
　▶ assume（that）～は「～と仮定する」という意味。that以下では、これか
　ら起こると予想されることを仮定して述べている。
　▶ work out greatで「（物事が）すばらしくうまくいく」という意味。口語の
　greatは、副詞のwell「うまく」とほぼ同じ意味で用いられる。

⑦ **I think all of you are going to be a big success!**
　▶ a big successは「大成功（した人、もの）」という意味。

⑧ **I really do.**
　▶ doは直前に出てきた動詞の繰り返しを避ける代動詞。ここではdo ＝ think。

⑨ **And that's where it gets tricky, because you are going to be**
　successful.
　▶〈that's where ＋ S ＋ V〉で「そこがSがVするところだ」という意味。この
　whereは先行詞を含む関係副詞で、名詞節を作る。

　　✎ 次の英文を日本語に直しなさい。
　　This is where I took this picture.

　　────────────────────────────
　▶ get trickyは「難しい[厄介な、扱いにくい]状況になる」という意味。

⑩ **You are going to climb that ladder and make that money.**
　▶ climb that ladderとmake that moneyは、どちらも前文のyou are going

to be successfulを踏まえた言い方で、それぞれ「(成功へと導く)階段を昇る」、「(成功した結果)お金をもうける」という意味。

⑪ **But will it be doing something that is fun?**

▶ 主語のitはclimb that ladder and make that moneyを指す。

▶ will it be doingは未来進行形it will be doingの疑問文で、未来のあるときに進行中の行為を予想して述べるときに用いる。

✎ 次の英文を日本語に直しなさい。

I'll be flying to Paris about this time tomorrow.

▶ thatは代名詞somethingを先行詞とする主格の関係代名詞。

⑫ **Something that you really love?**

▶ 前文⑪と共通する語句が省略されている。(Will it be doing) something that you really love?と補って考える。

⑬ **Because when you are as talented as I know all of you are, it is so easy to wake up one day and find yourself in golden handcuffs, with a mortgage and three kids that you need to put through Babson.**

▶ when you are as talented as I know all of you areは「皆さんのように有能な場合は」という意味。

▶ 主節のit is so easy to wake up one day and find yourself ～は「ある日目を覚ますと～な自分を発見する」という意味。itは不定詞to wake up以下の内容を受ける形式主語。

▶ find *one*self ～は「自分が～な状態にあると気づく」という意味。

▶ golden handcuffs「黄金の手錠」とは、住宅や家族など、大切なものであるが自由を制限するもののたとえ。

▶ thatはthree kidsを先行詞とする目的格の関係代名詞。

⑭ **So, whether you're entering a family business or not, now's the time to figure out what speaks to your heart the most.**

▶ whether ～ or notは「～であろうとなかろうと」という〈譲歩〉を表す副詞節。

✎ 次の英文を日本語に直しなさい。

Many people believe rumors whether they are true or not.

▶ now's the time to ～で「今こそが～すべきときだ」という意味。to以下はthe timeを修飾する不定詞の形容詞的用法。

▶ what speaks to your heart the mostで「あなたがいちばん興味を感じること[もの]」という意味。

194

Find Your Own Donut

教科書p.186 *l.*19〜p.187 *l.*11　Ⅳ

- ☐ inevitable [ɪnévɪtəbl]
- ☐ pile up
- ☐ youth [júːθ]
- ☐ in some respects
- ☐ at a very early age
- ☐ for sure
- ☐ completely [kəmplíːtli]
- ☐ all the time
- ☐ weave [wíːv]
- ☐ loom [lúːm]
- ☐ automatic [ɔ̀ːtəmǽtɪk]
- ☐ fabric [fǽbrɪk]
- ☐ generation [dʒènəréɪʃən]
- ☐ hardship [hɑ́ːrdʃip]
- ☐ hopefully [hóupfəli]

①The beginning of your career is really the best part, because you have the freedom to try different things before the inevitable responsibilities of life pile up. ②So, use this time, this freedom that your youth provides, to find your happy world. ③And don't be afraid if it's not what's "expected."

④I'm lucky in some respects, because I knew what I wanted to do at a very early age. ⑤When I was a little boy, I knew for sure that I wanted to be a taxi driver. ⑥It didn't completely work out, but it's pretty close. ⑦I get to drive cars and be around cars all the time. ⑧And if there's one thing I love more than donuts, it's cars.

⑨Toyota has been building cars for over 80 years now, but we actually started out in the weaving loom business. My great-grandfather invented the automatic weaving loom. ⑩But it was my grandfather, Kiichiro, who took us from making fabric to making cars and created the company we have today.

⑪I'm actually the third generation Toyoda to run our company, and perhaps you have heard the saying: ⑫The third generation knows no hardship, or the third generation ruins everything.

⑬Well, hopefully, that will not be the case. ⑭I mean, I did graduate from Babson after all!

このセクションの内容

豊田氏は卒業生たちに、「（A.　　　　）の出発点にいる皆さんには、人生の責任が積み上がる前に、いろいろなことを試す（B.　　　　）がある。（C.　　　　）どおりに行かなくても恐れずに、今のこのときを活用してほしい」と勧めている。

195

① **The beginning of your career is really the best part, because you have the freedom to try different things before the inevitable responsibilities of life pile up.**

▶ the best part は「いちばんよいところ」という意味。

▶ have the freedom to ～で「～する自由がある」という意味。to try ～は the freedom を修飾する不定詞の形容詞的用法。

▶ pile up で「積み重なる、蓄積する」という意味。

② **So, use this time, this freedom that your youth provides, to find your happy world.**

▶ this time と this freedom は同格の関係。

▶ that は this freedom を先行詞とする目的格の関係代名詞。

▶ to find ～は〈目的〉を表す不定詞の副詞的用法。

③ **And don't be afraid if it's not what's "expected."**

▶ don't be afraid で「恐れてはいけない」という意味。

▶ 接続詞の if は、ここでは「たとえ～でも」（≒ even if ～）の意味。

▶ if 節の主語 it は前文②の your happy world を指す。

▶ what は関係代名詞で、what's（= what is）"expected" は「『予想されて』いること」という意味。

④ **I'm lucky in some respects, because I knew what I wanted to do at a very early age.**

▶ in some respects は「いくつかの点で」という意味。

▶ what は先行詞を含む関係代名詞で、名詞節を作る。この文では、what I wanted to do ～が動詞 knew の目的語。

▶ at a very early age は「まだ非常に幼いときに」という意味で、このあとの文⑤の When I was a little boy とほぼ同じ意味。

⑤ **When I was a little boy, I knew for sure that I wanted to be a taxi driver.**

▶ for sure は「確かに、確実に」という意味。

⑥ **It didn't completely work out, but it's pretty close.**

▶ not completely で「完全には～ない」という部分否定を表す。

▶ work out は「（物事が）うまくいく」という意味。

▶ pretty close は「非常に近い」という意味。豊田氏が今している仕事が子どものころに思い描いていた将来の夢と「非常に近い」ことを述べている。

⑦ **I get to drive cars and be around cars all the time.**

▶ get to ～は「～する機会を得る」（≒ get a chance to ～）という意味。

▶ be around cars は「車の周りにいる」という意味。

▶ all the time は「年がら年中、四六時中」という意味。

⑧ **And if there's one thing I love more than donuts, it's cars.**

▶ one thing のあとに目的格の関係代名詞 that[which]が省略されている。

⑨ **Toyota has been building cars for over 80 years now, but we actually started out in the weaving loom business.**

▶ has been building は〈動作の継続〉を表す現在完了進行形。ここでは for over 80 years「80年以上の間」が〈継続〉の期間を表している。

> ✍ ( )内の語を適切な形に変えなさい。

亜紀はその本を今朝からずっと読んでいます。

Aki (is reading) the book since this morning.

▶ start out は「出発する、（活動などを）開始する」という意味。

⑩ **But it was my grandfather, Kiichiro, who took us from making fabric to making cars and created the company we have today.**

▶ it was 〜 who ... で「…したのは〜だった」という強調構文。ふつうの文に直せば、my grandfather, Kiichiro, took us from 〜となる。強調構文で最も多いのは、以下のような It is[was] 〜 that ... の形である。

> ✍ 次の英文を日本語に直しなさい。

It was curry that Mike cooked for his family last night.

▶ from 〜 to ... で「〜から…へと」という意味。

⑪ **I'm actually the third generation Toyoda to run our company, and perhaps you have heard the saying**

▶ to run 〜は the third generation Toyoda を修飾する不定詞の形容詞的用法。

⑫ **The third generation knows no hardship, or the third generation ruins everything.**

▶ この文は、前文⑪の the saying の具体的内容。

▶ knows no 〜は「〜を何も知らない」という全否定。

⑬ **Well, hopefully, that will not be the case.**

▶ hopefully は「願わくは〜だといいのだが」という意味で、文全体を修飾する副詞。I hope that will not be the case. と言いかえ可能。

▶ that is not the case で「それは事実ではない」という意味。that は前文⑫に引用されている格言の内容を指している。

⑭ **I mean, I did graduate from Babson after all!**

▶ I did graduate の did は強調を表す助動詞で、強く発音される。主語の人称・時制に応じて do ／ does ／ did のあとに強調したい動詞の原形を置く。

▶ after all は、前文に続けて「何と言っても〜なのだから」と理由を付け加える表現。

Optional Lesson

□ as luck would have it
□ as soon as ~
□ recession [riséʃən]
□ recall [rikɔ́:l]
□ testify [téstɪfàɪ]
□ Congress [káŋgrəs]
□ Washington D.C.
　[wáʃɪŋtən di: si:]
□ at that moment
□ entrepreneurship
　[à:ntrəprə́nə:rʃɪp]
□ instill [ɪnstíl]
□ start-up [stɑ́:rtʌ̀p]
□ willing [wílɪŋ]
□ be willing to ~
□ dramatic [drəmǽtɪk]
□ objectively [əbdʒéktɪvli]
□ hang on to ~
□ sentimental [sèntəméntəl]
□ take the risk of V-ing

①As luck would have it, though, as soon as I became CEO, we had the great recession, an earthquake and tsunami and a recall that meant I had to testify to Congress in Washington D.C. ②At that moment, I really did want to take a job as a taxi driver! ③But I'm happy to say, we're doing fine now, partly because I use what I learned here at Babson every day at Toyota. ④Perhaps the greatest lesson of all was the sense of entrepreneurship that was instilled in me here. ⑤Even with a company as big as Toyota, I still try to think of it as a start-up company.

⑥In fact, one of the challenges of running a business that's been in your family for decades is: "⑦How willing are you to make dramatic change when it's called for?" ⑧How do you look at things objectively and not hang on to something for sentimental reasons? ⑨How do you take the risk of making fabric one day and cars the next?

このセクションの内容

豊田氏は自分がCEOになった直後に直面した多くの困難を振り返り、バブソン大学で学んだ（A.　　　　　）の感覚が現在のトヨタの経営に生きていると語った。豊田氏は、トヨタほどの（B.　　　　　）であっても、設立したばかりの（C.　　　　）企業であると考えるようにしているという。

① **As luck would have it, though, as soon as I became CEO, we had the great recession, an earthquake and tsunami and a recall that meant I had to testify to Congress in Washington D.C.**

▶ as luck would have it は「幸運にも、運よく」と「不運にも、運悪く」のどちらの意味でも用いられる慣用句。ここでは、we had 以下の内容から考えて、「不運にも」の意味に解釈できる。

▶ the great recession はここでは「リーマン・ショック」と呼ばれている世界的な金融危機のこと。recession は「景気後退」という意味。

▶ a recall that meant 〜の that は、a recall を先行詞とする主格の関係代名詞。

▶ testify to Congress は「アメリカ連邦議会で証言する」という意味。

② **At that moment, I really did want to take a job as a taxi driver!**

▶ at that moment は「そのとき」という意味。

▶ I really did want の did は強調を表す助動詞。この文では、さらに really が did を強調している。

③ **But I'm happy to say, we're doing fine now, partly because I use what I learned here at Babson every day at Toyota.**

▶ do fine は「うまくやる」という意味であるが、ここでは「会社の経営が順調である」ことを表している。

▶ partly because 〜は「1つには〜の理由で」という意味。

▶ what I 〜 every day は関係代名詞 what が導く名詞節で、use の目的語。

④ **Perhaps the greatest lesson of all was the sense of entrepreneurship that was instilled in me here.**

▶ the greatest lesson of all は「すべての中で最も大きな教訓」という意味。

▶ that は the sense of entrepreneurship「起業家精神」を先行詞とする主格の関係代名詞。

▶ here は at Babson を指す。

⑤ **Even with a company as big as Toyota, I still try to think of it as a start-up company.**

▶ Even with a company as big as 〜は「〜ほどの大きな企業であっても」という意味。

▶ think of 〜 as ... で「〜を…と考える」という意味。it = Toyota

　✐ 次の英文を日本語に直しなさい。

　Many people think of him as a great scientist.

⑥ **In fact, one of the challenges of running a business that's been in your family for decades is**

▶ in factは「実際のところ」という意味。前文で述べた内容を強調している。

▶ a challenge of V-ingで「Vすることという大きな課題」という意味。この ofは〈同格〉を表し、V-ingがchallengeの具体的内容を述べている。〈the ＋名詞＋of V-ing〉で〈同格〉を表す名詞には、ほかにidea「考え」、dream 「夢」、possibility「可能性」などがある。

　✐次の英文を日本語に直しなさい。

He never gave up the dream of playing in the Majors.

▶ that's been (＝that has been) のthatはa businessを先行詞とする主格の 関係代名詞。has beenは〈継続〉を表す現在完了。

⑦ **How willing are you to make dramatic change when it's called for?**

▶ be willing to ～で「進んで[喜んで]～する、～するのをいとわない」とい う意味。How willing are you to ～?は「どれほど積極的に～する意欲が あるか?」という自分への問いかけ。

　✐次の英文を日本語に直しなさい。

She was willing to help me with my homework.

▶ when it's called for「それが必要とされるときに」という意味。itは直前 のto make dramatic changeを指す。

▶ call for ～で「～を要求する、必要とする」という意味。

⑧ **How do you look at things objectively and not hang on to something for sentimental reasons?**

▶前文⑦に続いて、この文も自分への問いかけとなっている。How do you ... and not hang on to ～?で「～にしがみつかずに、いかに…できるか?」 という意味。hang on to ～「(既成概念や古い考え方など)にしがみつく」 はstick to ～とほぼ同じ意味。

⑨ **How do you take the risk of making fabric one day and cars the next?**

▶前文⑦⑧に続いて、この文も自らへの問いかけである。

▶ take the risk of V-ingで「Vするリスクを冒す」という意味。このofも〈同 格〉を表す。

▶ making fabric one day and cars the nextは、「ある日は織物を作り翌日に は自動車を作る」→「それまで織物を作っていたのに突然自動車を作り始め る」という意味。教科書p.186の30行目、p.187の4行目で豊田氏が述べて いる、当初の自動織機生産から自動車生産へという方向転換に言及している。

□ industry [índəstri]
□ undergo [ʌndərgóu]
□ revolutionary [rèvəlúːʃənèri]
□ as are many others
□ predict [prɪdíkt]
□ embrace [ɪmbréɪs]
□ ～ rather than …
□ burdened [bə́ːrdnd]
□ I might have said yes.
□ be proud of ～
□ hundreds of thousands of ～
□ fast forward
□ screw [skrúː]
□ screw up ～
□ grant [grǽnt]
□ take ～ for granted

①Our industry is undergoing revolutionary change today, as are many others. ②Even I can't predict what kind of cars we will be driving 20 years from now, but my time at Babson taught me to embrace change rather than run from it. ③And I urge all of you to do the same.

④I am often asked whether I am burdened by having the name Toyoda, and ⑤when I was your age, I might have said yes. ⑥But today, I'm very proud of what the name represents and the hundreds of thousands of people it supports around the world.

⑦So, let's fast forward and assume you have become successful doing what you really love. ⑧Now let me give you some advice from one CEO to another:

⑨Don't screw it up.

⑩Don't take it for granted.

Do the right thing. Because if you do the right thing, the money will follow.

⑪Try new things, even if you're old.

このセクションの内容

豊田氏はバブソン大学で学んだ経験から、（A.　　　）から逃げるのではなく、それを（B.　　　）ようにと卒業生にアドバイスしている。さらに、たとえ年をとっても常に（C.　　　）を試すようにと勧めている。

① **Our industry is undergoing revolutionary change today, as are many others.**

▶ undergoは「〜を経験する」(≒ go through 〜)という意味。

▶ as are many othersは「ほかの多くの産業がそうであるように」という意味。as many others (= other industries) are <u>undergoing revolutionary change today</u>から、主節と共通するundergoing 〜 todayが省略され、残ったas many others areの〈S + be動詞〉が倒置されてas are many othersとなったもの。

② **Even I can't predict what kind of cars we will be driving 20 years from now, but my time at Babson taught me to embrace change rather than run from it.**

▶ 〈predict + O (疑問詞節)〉の文。what kind of 〜 from nowが目的語となる疑問詞節。

▶ will be drivingは未来進行形で、未来のある時点に進行中の出来事を予想して述べている。この文では、20 years from nowが未来のある時点を表す。

▶ 〈teach + O (人) + to 〜〉で「(人)に〜するように教える」という意味。

▶ 〈〜 rather than ...〉で「…するよりもむしろ〜」という意味。

　　✍ 次の英文を日本語に直しなさい。

　　I feel like doing some exercise outdoors rather than staying home.

③ **And I urge all of you to do the same.**

▶ 〈urge + O (人) + to 〜〉で「(人)に〜するように強く促す[勧める]」という意味。

▶ do the sameとは、前文②のembrace change rather than run from itの言いかえ表現。

④ **I am often asked whether I am burdened by having the name Toyoda**

▶ 〈ask + O (人) + whether 〜〉で「(人)に〜かどうかたずねる」という意味。ここでは受動態am asked whether 〜の形で用いられている。

　　✍ 英文を完成させなさい。

　　警察は私に以前にその男性に会ったことがあるかとたずねた。

　　The police (　　　) (　　　) (　　　) I had met the man before.

⑤ **when I was your age, I might have said yes**

▶ might have said yesで「はいと言っていたかもしれない」という意味。〈might[could] + have + 過去分詞〉が過去の事実とは異なる現在の想像を表すことがある。

⑥ **But today, I'm very proud of what the name represents and the hundreds of thousands of people it supports around the world.**

　このセクションの内容 の答え→　A. 変化　B. 受け入れる　C. 新しいこと

▶ be proud of ～は「～を誇りに思う」という意味。この文ではofのあとに目的語が2つ並んでいる。

▶ what the name represents は、関係代名詞whatが導く名詞節で、「その名前が表すもの」という意味。これがofの1つ目の目的語。

▶ the hundreds ～ around the world がofの2つ目の目的語。it（= the name Toyoda）の前に the hundreds of thousands of people を先行詞とする目的格の関係代名詞that［which］が省略されている。hundreds of thousands of ～は「何十万もの～」という意味。

⑦ **So, let's fast forward and assume you have become successful doing what you really love.**

▶ fast(-)forward は「（テープ・ビデオ）を早送りする」という意味。現在では「先を急ぐ」という意味でも用いられる。

▶ become successful (in) V-ingで「Vすることに成功する」という意味。

▶ what you really love は関係代名詞whatが導く名詞節で、「あなたがたが本当に大好きなこと」という意味。豊田氏は講演の中で、what makes you happy in life（教科書 p.185の28行目）、something that you really love（教科書 p.186の11～12行目）など、同様の表現を繰り返し使っているが、これらはすべて your own donut を言いかえたものである。

⑧ **Now let me give you some advice from one CEO to another**

▶ let me give you some advice は〈let + O（人）+ 原形不定詞〉の形で、「みなさんにアドバイスをさせてください」という決まった言い方。

▶ from one ～ to another は「1人の～から別の…に対して」という意味。前文⑦で述べたとおりに「時間を早送りして」、目の前にいる卒業生が成功を収めてCEOになったと仮定して、話をしている。

⑨ **Don't screw it up.**

▶ Don't screw it up. で「へまをするな」という決まった表現。screw up は「～を台なしにする、しくじる」（≒ ruin）という意味で使われる。

⑩ **Don't take it for granted.**

▶ take ～ for granted は「～を当然のことと考える」という意味。take it for granted that ～「～を当然のことと考える、てっきり～だと思う」の形でもよく使われる。it は that 節を受ける形式目的語。

　✍ 次の英文を日本語に直しなさい。

　We took it for granted that she would accept our offer.

⑪ **Try new things, even if you're old.**

▶ even if ～は「たとえ～でも」という意味。even if you're old は「たとえあなたがたが（これから先）年齢を重ねても」という意味。

Optional Lesson

- ☐ mentor [méntɔːr]
- ☐ take ～ seriously
- ☐ unless [ənlés]
- ☐ at the age of ～
- ☐ take on ～
- ☐ master driver
- ☐ dismay [dɪsméi]
- ☐ much to *one's* dismay
- ☐ you've always got to ～
- ☐ Oprah [óuprə]
- ☐ Yoda [jóudə]
- ☐ Tom Brady [tám bréidi]
- ☐ feed off ～
- ☐ global [glóubəl]
- ☐ citizen [sítəzən]
- ☐ stand for ～

①When I became CEO of Toyota 10 years ago, I was told by one of my mentors that I couldn't expect to be taken seriously by our engineers unless I really knew how to drive at the highest level. ②So, at the age of 52, I took on the challenge of training to become a master driver. ③Not just so I could drive our race cars, which I do, much to my father's dismay, but so I could communicate how I think our cars should drive with our engineers.

④The point is, you've always got to be learning something new, no matter how old you are. ⑤Never give up being a student, because being a student is the best job you will ever have.

⑥Find people that inspire you: Oprah. Yoda. Tom Brady. Your parents. Your friends. Feed off their energy!

⑦Be a person that inspires others.

Be a good global citizen.

⑧Care about the environment, the planet ... about what's happening in other parts of the world.

Don't worry about being cool ... be *warm*.

⑨Decide what you stand for.

このセクションの内容

豊田氏は自分がトヨタのCEOになったあと、52歳のときに、マスター・ドライバーになるための（A.　　　）を受け始めたことを明かした。要するに、何歳になっても常に（B.　　　）を学び続けることが必要なのであり、（C.　　　）であることをやめてはいけないのだと豊田氏は語る。

① **When I became CEO of Toyota 10 years ago, I was told by one of my mentors that I couldn't expect to be taken seriously by our engineers unless I really knew how to drive at the highest level.**

▶ expect to ～は「～することを期待[予想]する」という意味。

▶ to be taken seriouslyは「（発言などが）真摯に受け止められること」という意味。〈to be＋過去分詞〉は受動態の不定詞。

▶ unlessは「もし～でなければ」という意味の接続詞。

> ✐ 次の英文を日本語に直しなさい。
>
> You'll cause an accident unless you drive more carefully.

▶ how to ～は「～する方法、～のし方」という意味で、ここでは動詞knewの目的語。

② **So, at the age of 52, I took on the challenge of training to become a master driver.**

▶ at the age of 52 ≒ when I was 52 years old

▶ take on ～は「～を引き受ける」という意味。take on the challenge of V-ingで「～するという困難な課題に挑戦する」という意味。

▶ to become ～は目的を表す不定詞の副詞的用法。

③ **Not just so I could drive our race cars, which I do, much to my father's dismay, but so I could communicate how I think our cars should drive with our engineers.**

▶ 豊田氏が前文②のような課題に挑戦した2つの目的がnot just ～ but（also）...「～だけでなく…もまた」の形で述べられている。

▶ so I could drive ～、およびso I could communicate ～は、どちらも〈so（that）＋S＋can＋V〉のthatが省略された形で、「SがVできるように」という〈目的〉を表す。説明語句や挿入句を除くと、以下のように整理できる。

> Not just | so (that) | I | could drive | our race cars
>   S   V   O
>
> but | so (that) | I | could communicate
>   S   V
>
> how our cars should drive with our engineers
>   O（疑問詞節）

▶ which I doのdoは直前のdrive our race carsの代わり。豊田氏が今では実際にレーシングカーを運転することを挿入句で付け加えている。

▶ much to one's dismayは「～が大いに動揺したことには」という意味。

④ **The point is, you've always got to be learning something new, no matter how old you are.**

▶ The point is, 〈that〉 ～ は「要するに～ということだ」という意味。you've always から文末の you are まで全体が that 節の中身である。

✎ 英文を完成させなさい。

要するに手を洗うことで病気から身を守ることができるということだ。

( ) ( ) ( ) washing your hands can save you from illness.

▶ have got to ～ は「～しなければならない」(≒ have to ～) という意味。

▶ to be learning は〈to be ＋現在分詞〉で進行形の不定詞。

▶〈no matter how ＋形容詞 ＋ S ＋ be 動詞〉で「S がいかに～であろうと」という意味。

✎ 次の英文を日本語に直しなさい。

They could not solve the mystery no matter how hard they tried.

⑤ **Never give up being a student, because being a student is the best job you will ever have.**

▶ Never give up V-ing. で「(どんな場合でも) 決して～することをやめてはいけない」という命令文。前文④の you've always ～ you are という勧めを別の表現で言い表している。

▶ being a student is ～ は、動名詞句が主語の文。

▶ the best job のあとに目的格の関係代名詞 that[which] が省略されている。〈the ＋形容詞の最上級 ＋名詞〉と ever を組み合わせて、「今後あなたが手に入れるであろう中で最良の仕事」という意味を表している。

⑥ **Find people that inspire you**

▶ that は people を先行詞とする主格の関係代名詞。

⑦ **Be a person that inspires others.**

▶ that は a person を先行詞とする主格の関係代名詞。

⑧ **Care about the environment, the planet ... about what's happening in other parts of the world.**

▶ care about ～ は「～を大切にする、～を気にかける」という意味。

▶ what's happening in ～ は「～で起きていること」という意味。what は関係代名詞で、名詞節を作る。

⑨ **Decide what you stand for.**

▶ stand for ～ で「～を支持する、～に賛成する」という意味。

▶ what you stand for は疑問詞節 (間接疑問) で、Decide の目的語。

□ a set of ～
□ integrity [ɪntégrəti]
□ humility [hjumíləti]
□ North Star [nɔ̀ːrθ stáːr]
□ inform [ɪnfɔ́ːrm]
□ today is where ～
□ every time ～
□ emperor [émpərər]
□ ascend [əsénd]
□ era [íərə]
□ start over
□ harmony [háːrməni]
□ ～ of one's own
□ set back ～
□ possibility [pàsəbíləti]
□ endless [éndləs]

①At Toyota we have a set of values that include integrity, humility, and respect for others. ②We call it the "Toyota Way." ③And it gives our company a North Star, a guiding light.

④Find your own guiding light, and let it inform every decision you make. ⑤Let it help you make the world a better place.

Ladies and gentlemen, fellow students, ⑥today is where it ends, and today is where it all begins.

⑦In Japan, every time a new emperor ascends to the throne, a new era begins. ⑧And the calendar starts over at year one. ⑨We just had a new era begin in Japan on May 1st. ⑩Every era has its own name, and this one is called Reiwa, which means "beautiful harmony."

⑪In many respects, all of you are beginning a new era of your own, where the clock is set back to one ... and the possibilities are endless.

⑫I hope your era is one filled with beautiful harmony, much success ... and many, many donuts.

Thank you very much.

このセクションの内容

豊田氏が講演の最後に卒業生たちに語ったのは、「（A.　　　）のように、進むべき道を教えてくれる道しるべを見つけて、それを（B.　　　）の助けとしなさい。あなた自身の新しい時代を生き始めた皆さんに、その時代が美しい調和、多くの成功、そしてたくさんの（C.　　　）で満たされていることを願います」ということだった。

① **At Toyota we have a set of values that include integrity, humility, and respect for others.**

> ▶ a set of ～は「１組の～、一連の～」、a set of valuesは「価値観」という意味。thatはvaluesを先行詞とする主格の関係代名詞。

② **We call it the "Toyota Way."**

> ▶〈call + O + C〉で「O（人・もの）をC（名前）と呼ぶ」という意味。itは前文のa set of valuesを指す。

③ **And it gives our company a North Star, a guiding light.**

> ▶〈give + O_1 + O_2〉で「O_1にO_2を与える」の文。itは、前文のthe "Toyota Way"を指す。

> ▶ North Starは「北極星」という意味で、ここでは「方角を指し示すもの、道しるべ」という比喩的な意味で用いている。実際の北極星には定冠詞を付けて the North Star と表す。

> ▶ a guiding lightは「（進むべき道を教える）誘導灯」という意味。直前のa North Star とは〈同格〉の関係。

④ **Find your own guiding light, and let it inform every decision you make.**

> ▶ let it informは〈let + O + 原形不定詞〉の使役構文で、「それに～を教えてもらいなさい」という意味。itはyour own guiding lightを指す。

> ▶ you makeの前に目的格の関係代名詞that[which]が省略されている。

⑤ **Let it help you make the world a better place.**

> ▶ Let it help you makeは、〈let + O + 原形不定詞〉「Oに～させる」の使役構文に、〈help + O（人）+ 原形不定詞〉「（人）が～するのを助ける」が組み込まれた形。itは前文④のyour own guiding lightを指している。

> ▶ make the world a better placeは、〈make + O + C（名詞）〉「OをCにする」の形。

⑥ **today is where it ends, and today is where it all begins**

> ▶ where it ends「終着点」、およびwhere it all begins「すべてが始まる出発点」は、先行詞を含む関係副詞whereが導く名詞節。この文ではbe動詞の補語として使われている。

⑦ **In Japan, every time a new emperor ascends to the throne, a new era begins.**

> ▶ every timeは「～するたびに」という意味を表し、この２語で接続詞と同じ働きをする。

> **✍ 次の英文を日本語に直しなさい。**
>
> Every time she listens to the song, she feels happy.

このセクションの内容 の答え→　A. 北極星　B. 決断　C. ドーナツ

▶ ascend to the throne は「即位する」という意味。

▶ era は「(歴史上の)時代」を表す名詞。*cf.* at the beginning of the Reiwa era「令和時代の始まりに」

⑧ **And the calendar starts over at year one.**

▶ start over at year one は「元年から新たに始まる」という意味。

⑨ **We just had a new era begin in Japan on May 1ˢᵗ.**

▶ had a new era begin は「新たな時代の始まりを体験した」という意味。〈have + O + 原形不定詞〉で「Oが〜するのを体験する[目の当たりにする]」という意味を表す。

⑩ **Every era has its own name, and this one is called Reiwa, which means "beautiful harmony."**

▶ *one's* own は「〜自身の、〜固有の」という意味。

▶ this one = this era

▶〈, which〉は非制限用法の関係代名詞(主格)で、先行詞は Reiwa。

⑪ **In many respects, all of you are beginning a new era of your own, where the clock is set back to one ... and the possibilities are endless.**

▶ in many respects で「多くの点で」という意味。

▶ are beginning 〜は「〜を始めようとしている」という意味。この現在進行形は、今まさに起ころうとしている行為を表す。

▶〈名詞 + of *one's* own〉で「その人自身の〜」という意味。

　　✍ 次の英文を日本語に直しなさい。

　　Ryan wants a car of his own.

▶〈, where〉は a new era of your own を先行詞とする関係副詞の非制限用法。

▶ set a clock back to 〜で「時計の針を〜に戻す」という意味。

⑫ **I hope your era is one filled with beautiful harmony, much success ... and many, many donuts.**

▶ 過去分詞の filled 〜は直前の one (= era) を修飾している。filled with 〜は「〜に満ちた、〜で満たされた」という意味。fill 〜 with ...「〜を…で満たす」の受動態である。

▶ donuts とは、本講演で繰り返し出てきたように、「その人の人生において幸せを感じさせるもの」(what makes you happy in life 教科書 p.185 の 28 行目)、または「あなたが真に愛するもの」(something that you really love 教科書 p.186 の 11〜12 行目)のことである。

確認問題

語彙・表現

1 次の語を（　）内の指示にしたがって書きかえなさい。

(1) graduate（名詞に）　　　　　(2) young（名詞に）

(3) information（動詞に）　　　　(4) possible（名詞に）

2 第1音節にアクセント（強勢）のある語を2つ選び、記号で答えなさい。

ア　dis-may　　　　イ　as-cend　　　ウ　cit-i-zen

エ　chal-lenge　　　オ　ex-treme　　　カ　em-brace

3 日本語に合うように、（　）内に適切な語を入れなさい。

(1) 彼は絵画のコレクションを誇りに思っている。

He is (　　　) (　　　) his collection of paintings.

(2) 一言で言えば、その島は楽園なのです。

(　　　) (　　　) (　　　), the island is a paradise.

(3) 彼女は失われた時間を取り戻そうと必死だった。

She tried hard to (　　　) (　　　) (　　　) lost time.

(4) 何が起きたのか私にははっきりとはわからない。

I don't know (　　　) (　　　) what happened.

(5) あなたのアイディアはいくつかの点で興味深いと思います。

I've found your idea interesting (　　　) (　　　) (　　　).

(6) 彼らは危険を冒して国境を越えた。

They (　　　) the (　　　) (　　　) crossing the border.

文のパターン・文法

1 日本語に合うように、（　）内に適切な語を入れなさい。

(1) 誠は祖父母を訪ねるたびに家事を手伝う。

(　　　) (　　　) Makoto visits his grandparents, he helps them with housework.

(2) 明日の今ごろ、私たちは東京で観光を楽しんでいることでしょう。

We (　　　) (　　　) (　　　) sightseeing in Tokyo about this time tomorrow.

(3) その会社はもう20年以上もの間、船を作っている。

The company (　　　) (　　　) (　　　) ships for over 20 years now.

(4) 彼女はそれが本物のダイヤモンドだとすっかり信じていたのだ。

She (　　　) (　　　) it was a real diamond.

2　(　)内の語句を並べかえて、英文を完成させなさい。

(1) (might / he / the wrong train / have / gotten).

_____.

(2) She hung on to the rail of the stairs (she / that / fall off / not / so / might).

She hung on to the rail of the stairs _____.

(3) (the purse / this / I / where / is / found).

_____.

総合

次の文を読んで、あとの問いに答えなさい。

> 　　When I became CEO of Toyota 10 years ago, I was told by one of my mentors that I couldn't expect ①(take) seriously by our engineers unless I really knew how to drive at the highest level. So, at the age of 52, I took on the challenge of training to become a master driver. Not just so I could drive our race cars, which I do, ②(　　　) (　　　) my father's (　　　), but so I could communicate how I think our cars should drive with our engineers.
>
> 　　The point is, you've always got to be learning something new, ③(old / matter / are / how / no / you). Never give up ④being a student, because being a student is the best job you will ever have.

問1　①の(　)内の語を適切な形(3語)に変えなさい。

問2　下線部②が「私の父が大いに動揺したことには」という意味になるように、(　)内に入る最も適切な3語を書きなさい。

問3　下線部③の(　)内の語を並べかえて、英文を完成させなさい。

問4　下線部④とほぼ同じ意味で使われているひと続きの英語3語を、本文中から探して答えなさい。

問5　豊田氏が52歳のとき、マスター・ドライバーになる訓練を始めた目的は何でしたか。日本語で2つ挙げなさい。

解答

Lesson 1

▶Section 1

① カナは8歳です。／カナは8歳の少女です。

⑥ It is, for

⑦ Doing, is

▶Section 2

① to go

⑤ 私は夕食のための食料品［食材］を買いにスーパーマーケットへ行った。

▶Section 3

① 私の家族は大阪に10年住んでいます。／私の家族は全員サッカーファンです。

⑥ did the same

⑧ これまでに5万人以上の人々がその美術館を訪れた。

⑫ making

確認問題

《語彙・表現》

1 (1) confusion　(2) met
(3) waiter　　(4) brought

2 (1) ウ　(2) エ

3 (1) Would, like　(2) over here
(3) went for
(4) in learning[studying]

《文のパターン・文法》

1 (1) エ　(2) ウ　(3) イ
(4) ア　(5) オ

2 (1) collecting stamps
(2) It is, to be
(3) leaving

3 (1) Listening to music always makes me
(2) need to wear special glasses to watch

《総合》

問1 （スティーブの）ホストファミリーの朝食がいつも和食のスタイル［和風］であること。

問2 彼らは私に洋食を楽しむ機会を与えたいと思ったのです。

問3 イ

問4 pancakes、French fries、coffee（順不同）

問5 和製英語

Lesson 2

▶Section 1

① 田中先生は生徒たちに英語で短い物語を書くように言った。

⑥ 運動のしすぎは健康によくないこともある。

⑦ has lost

⑧ どちらの登山路を行きましょうか[行くべきでしょうか]。

▶Section 2

③ has been playing

⑫ ニューヨーク滞在中、私はその劇場を訪れることがなかった。／私はニューヨークにあるその劇場を訪れたことが一度もない。

⑮ That's how

▶Section 3

⑧ sad to hear

⑫ ジェーンは明日、ロンドンに向けて出発します。

▶Section 4

① 何時間もサッカーを練習したあとでは、きみが疲れているように見えるのも無理はない。

② 悪天候のため、私たちは計画を変更した。

④⑤ ブラウン先生は数学の教師であるだけではない。彼は一流のアスリートでもある。

⑥⑦ learned to

確認問題

《語彙・表現》

1 (1) decision　(2) solution
(3) fashionable　(4) uncertain

2 ウ、オ

3 (1) threw away
(2) give it, try
(3) was filled

(4) not only[just], but

《文のパターン・文法》

1 (1) d　(2) c　(3) a
(4) c　(5) b

2 (1) must　(2) may　(3) will
(4) should

3 (1) I was surprised to see Mina
(2) How long have you been studying
(3) it has not arrived yet

《総合》

問1　エ

問2　which

問3　unread books

問4　doesn't spark joy

問5　手にとったときに喜びを感じさせる本。

Lesson 3

▶ Section 1

① マイクは弟[兄]と部屋を共有している。

③ has always wanted

⑤ spent, repairing

⑥ 私には日本のアニメが大好きなアメリカ人の友人がいます。

⑩ dancing

▶ Section 2

① 私が電話したとき、ビルはたまたま出かけていた。

③ was able to

④ were fascinated

⑦ 私はあなたに公園を案内していただきたいです。

⑫ ユカは看護師になろうと決心した。

▶ Section 3

② cheer her up

⑫ その国で何が起きているのか私にはわかりません。

⑬ built

▶ Section 4

② To our surprise

⑥ 私たちは列車が川に架かった橋を渡っているのを見た。

⑦ 通りは色とりどりのライトで飾られていた。

確認問題

《語彙・表現》

1 (1) anger　(2) refuse
(3) creation　(4) destroy

2 エ、オ

3 (1) based on
(2) lived[led][had], life
(3) in collaboration
(4) decorated with

《文のパターン・文法》

1 (1) which[that]　(2) whose
(3) which[that]　(4) that[which]

2 (1) spoken　(2) swimming
(3) talking　(4) written

3 (1) The first country we visited on our tour was
(2) Look at the students working
(3) I've never seen any pictures taken by
(4) the paintings that were collected by the gallery
(5) Alice was wearing a yukata made in Japan

《総合》

問1 店全体を鮮やかな色で塗ったこと。

問2 in the face

問3 人々が寄付するお金や(援助)物資は大いに役に立ちます。

問4 イ

問5 (最初) People can　(最後) worst conditions

Lesson 4

▶Section 1

④ その曲を聴くといつも私は高校時代を思い出す。

⑤ drawn

⑦ what you saw

⑩ 彼女はボランティア活動を通して学んだことについてスピーチをした。

▶Section 2

① 私は昨晩からずっとジョンと連絡を取ろうとしている。

④ エマは日本に来るまでに3年間日本語を勉強していた。

⑤ how to use

⑦ 彼は仙台に引っ越すまで東京に20年間住んでいた。

▶Section 3

③ あそこで遊んでいる少女はだれですか。

④ why she looks

⑦ 私はこの問題をどのように解決したらよいかわかりません。

▶Section 4

③ had lived, came

⑤ マイクとビルは互いに理解し合うようになってきている。／インターネットは私たちが短時間で情報を集めることを可能にした。〔インターネットのおかげで、私たちは短時間で情報を集めることができるようになった。〕

⑨ その動物園ではたくさんの動物を間近で見ることができる。

確認問題

《語彙・表現》

1 (1) introduction　(2) mysterious
(3) prehistoric　(4) earthen

2 (1) ウ　(2) ア

3 (1) take a look
(2) made a guess

(3) up close

(4) due to[because of]

《文のパターン・文法》

1 (1) a　(2) d　(3) c　(4) e

2 (1) what you can do today
(2) what you asked me to buy
(3) tell when an accident will happen
(4) know if David will come to the party

3 (1) where Anne is going to spend her vacation
(2) how Emma got to know the man
(3) had been listening to the radio for two hours when I visited him

《総合》

問1 みなさんはなぜ縄文時代の人々が土偶を作り出したのだろうかと不思議に思うかもしれません。

問2 日本の各地で1万8千体以上の土偶が見つかっているから。

問3 the true reason behind the creation of *dogu*

問4 know what the real purpose of *dogu* was

問5 ウ

Lesson 5

▶ Section 1

① そのピアニストは日本国内だけでなく外国でも人気がある。

② Thank you for coming

③ spent, finishing

⑧ 留学するためには英語を一生懸命に勉強すべきだ。

⑨ 私たちのチームがその試合に勝ったのは驚くべきことだ。

▶ Section 2

① メアリーは友人たちと話しながら、私たちのところにやってきた。

⑤ one another[each other]

⑦ 親切は時として残酷になり得る。

▶ Section 3

⑥ 水は私たちの体の半分以上を構成している。

⑪ このレストランでは、私たちは食べたいだけピザを食べることができる。

▶ Section 4

② That's why

確認問題

《語彙・表現》

1 (1) loving　(2) conserve
(3) friendly　(4) billion

2 (1) イ　(2) ウ

3 (1) advantage of　(2) in common
(3) in danger of　(4) as much, as

《文のパターン・文法》

1 (1) waving to us
(2) Feeling very sleepy
(3) Taking a rest

2 (1) It is clear that she did this work
(2) Living in a village far away from the city
(3) the fact that the child population is decreasing

3 (1) in number
(2) what to
(3) It, that we
(4) of worrying

《総合》

問1 あなたは自然保護についての講演をしながら、世界中を旅しています。

問2 wild animals have the right to live

問3 エ

問4 ガンなどの治療薬を破壊してしまう。

問5 plants and insects

Lesson 6

▶ **Section 1**

① 新聞が常に私たちに真実を伝えてくれるとは限らない。

② It's time
彼の話が本当かどうか私にはわからない。

③ 私は1人の男性が川で釣りをしているのを見ました。

⑨ それらの人々は十分な水を手に入れられない状況にある。

▶ **Section 2**

② 彼女の愛らしい笑顔はいつも私たちを幸せな気持ちにしてくれる。〔彼女の愛らしい笑顔を見ると、私たちはいつも幸せな気持ちになる。〕

③ 多くの犬の飼い主がその公園で犬を遊ばせる。
たとえ雨が降っても、彼は毎朝散歩に行く。

▶ **Section 3**

⑧ ジョンはつまらないことでくよくよしてばかりいる。

⑩ was asked to

▶ **Section 4**

③ on, for

⑬ 新しい車を買うことを検討するのもいいかもしれません。

▶ 確認問題

《**語彙・表現**》

1 (1) ability　(2) mentally
(3) pleasant　(4) negative

2 (1) ウ　(2) イ

3 (1) not always
(2) even if
(3) matters worse
(4) on average

《**文のパターン・文法**》

1 (1) why　　(2) where
(3) when　　(4) how

2 (1) standing　(2) left
(3) sung　　(4) know

3 (1) who were on the beach saw the sun rise
(2) He had his secretary copy the document
(3) know why this store has remained closed
(4) This is how I solved the problem

《**総合**》

問1　とても幼い子どもたちを楽しませるためにスマートフォンを使うことは、彼らの成長に悪影響を及ぼすかもしれません。

問2　イ

問3　make us pay attention to them

問4　distract

問5　他者や現実の世界との接触。

Lesson 7

▶**Section 1**

① その国は1980年代から多くの観光客を引き寄せてきた。

④ ジェーンは最初は日本食があまり好きではなかった。

⑩ It seems that

▶**Section 2**

② 彼は20分かそこらで戻るでしょう。

⑦ problem is that

⑩ seemed to be

▶**Section 3**

④ ついに出発の日がやってきた。

⑤ 値段が高いものがいつもよいとは限らない。

⑥ came singing

⑦ 私はドアに鍵をかけたのを覚えている。
忘れずにドアに鍵をかけてね。
私は1頭のクマが森から出てくるのを見た。

⑨ 彼女は説明書の指示に従って、新しいパソコンをセットアップした。

▶**Section 4**

⑦ 明日何が起こるか、だれにわかるでしょうか[だれにもわかりません]。

⑫ 彼女はかごの中の鳥を自由にした。

確認問題

《語彙・表現》

1 (1) movement   (2) imagination
   (3) seasonal   (4) successful

2 ウ、オ

3 (1) or so
   (2) At first
   (3) home to
   (4) came, his mind

《文のパターン・文法》

1 (1) running   (2) laughing
   (3) seated   (4) skiing

2 (1) It, that, wants
   (2) It seemed, was
   (3) The trouble, that

3 (1) The problem was that we had little time
   (2) The truth is that nobody saw
   (3) The party seemed to be a success
   (4) It seemed that the man had nothing to eat
   (5) She got caught in a shower

《総合》

問1 （遠い自然の中で生きる）カリブーやほかの野生動物がいなくなること。

問2 distant nature in your imagination

問3 all sorts of

問4 ア

問5 私の考えでは、遠い自然は身近な自然と同じくらい大切なのです。

Lesson 8

▶ Section 1

⑦ Tens of millions of

⑧ この写真は私たちに当時の人々がどのように生活していたかを見せてくれる。

⑩ もし私たちがこの知らせを彼に伝えたら、彼は何と言うだろうか。

▶ Section 2

③ 彼は両手にその重いかばんを持って走り出した。

⑥ as if, were

⑦ 祖父はメガネを外し、別のメガネをかけた。

▶ Section 3

① この指輪を（ちょっと）見てもよろしいですか。

④ with, closed[shut]

⑫ 彼女のことばは私たち全員に環境問題について考えさせた[彼女のことばによって私たち全員が環境問題について考えさせられた]。

▶ Section 4

② 過去の自然災害は私たちに多くのことを教えてくれる。

⑫ 今私たちに必要なのは行動です。

確認問題

《語彙・表現》

1 ア、オ

2 (1) a great many

(2) is[was] when

(3) turned around

(4) held, by

(5) fast asleep

(6) went through

《文のパターン・文法》

1 (1) If I had enough money, I could buy this CD.

(2) If he knew your phone number, he would call you.

(3) I wish I could speak English as well as you.

(4) She talks as if[though] she were[was] a journalist.

2 (1) walking with a heavy bag on his back

(2) with her hair blowing in the wind

(3) tell us how the people in the village live[live in the village]

(4) is what we will do for him

(5) could play baseball if it were sunny now

(6) I wish he were kinder to others

《総合》

問1 freedom

問2 living

問3 tens of millions

問4 もしこれらがあなた自身の家族や友人の写真だったら、あなたはどのように感じるでしょうか。

問5 あなたや私のような人々が20世紀にどのような体験をしたかということ。

Lesson 9

▶ Section 1

④ その患者は深刻な容態にある。

⑦ 私の妹［姉］はピアノがとても上手で、そのコンクールで1位になった［優勝した］。

▶ Section 2

⑥ 彼女はいったん何かを始めたら、決してあきらめない。

⑦ 今日の新聞によれば、アラスカで大きな地震があったらしい。

⑨ そろそろ決断すべきときだ。
子どもに火遊びをさせてはいけない。

⑩ to him

▶ Section 3

④ had been, damaged

⑤ 問題を違う観点から見ることは大切だ。

▶ Section 4

⑩ その辞書をもとあった場所に戻しなさい。

確認問題

《語彙・表現》

1 (1) stolen　　(2) attraction
　　(3) height　　(4) deny

2 ア、カ

3 (1) came, life
　　(2) in, condition
　　(3) large number
　　(4) bring back

《文のパターン・文法》

1 (1) which　　(2) whose
　　(3) who　　(4) which

2 (1) must be cleaned
　　(2) have, been baked
　　(3) should be kept

3 (1) Can the mountain be seen from your room
　　(2) The old city has been visited by many tourists

(3) The problem has not been solved

(4) might be shocked to know the fact

《総合》

問1　point of view

問2　ア

問3　像は現在、離島にいるよりもずっと多くの人々によって見られることができる。

問4　reasons

問5　ホアハカナナイア［モアイ像］は無断で（島から）持ち出されたもので、島民の人々の意に反して保持されているから。

Lesson 10

▶ Section 1

① to be read

③ 世界中の何億という人々がその映画を見た。

④ 運動場にいる子どもたちは走り回るのをやめようとしなかった。

⑪ 会議を開くのに十分ないすがあるかどうか確かめよう。

▶ Section 2

② 彼は明日早くここに来る、そして1人で来ると言った。

③ 私は遅く着いたので、パーティーに食べ物はほとんど（残ってい）なかった。

⑤ No matter how

⑧ focuses on

⑨ 私が子どものころ、両親はよく私を動物園に連れて行ってくれたものだ。

▶ Section 3

① excited, exciting

③ 私はこの質問に答えるのは簡単だと
思う。

⑥ poor[bad] at, good at

⑦ pay attention to

⑨ 彼はその貧しい子どもたちをあわれ
に思ったが、彼にはどうすることも
できなかった。

⑩ 彼は明日がもっとよい日になること
を願いながら、懸命に努力し続けて
いる。

⑪ これが子どもたちを驚かせたものだ。

▶Section 4

② is likely to
その手紙を読むと、彼女は突然泣き
出した。

⑦ 彼はスポーツ、とりわけサッカーが
得意だ。

⑨ were, would, say
私たちはほかの人の失敗を笑うべき
ではない。

▶Section 5

① 彼らは来る日も来る日も、行方不明
になった彼らの猫を探し続けた。
この電話を使えば、一度にグループ
全員にメッセージを送ることができる。

④ had studied, would have

⑥ 私は今朝起きて、庭が雪でおおわれ
ていることに気づいた。[私が今朝起
きると、庭は雪でおおわれていた。]

⑨ 彼らの活動は、将来何年にもわたっ
て社会で重要な役割を果たすだろう。

⑩ reminded him that

⑪ 彼がその事実を知らなかったのはお
かしいと思う。
彼は大きなプレッシャーに直面して
も全力を尽くした。

確認問題

《語彙・表現》

1 (1) failure　　(2) difficulty
(3) opportunity　(4) fame

2 ア、ウ

3 (1) burst out
(2) likely to
(3) come out[be published]
(4) at a time

《文のパターン・文法》

1 (1) had woken, could have taken
(2) hadn't helped, couldn't have
finished
(3) had seen　(4) used to be

2 (1) If it had not been for his help
(2) No matter what happens
(3) think it necessary that they
move into
(4) talked as if he had traveled
(5) found it exciting to study
Japanese history

《総合》

問1 ①　at　　⑤　with　　⑥　on
⑦　into

問2 little to

問3 no matter how busy his father is

問4 彼女の父親が持っているお金やス
ポーツの能力は、チャーリー・ブラ
ウンの父親の息子に対する愛情には
かなわないことがわかったから。

問5 そして、これがマンガ『ピーナッツ』
が世界中の人々の間でこれほど人気
がある理由の1つかもしれない。

Reading

▶Scene I

⑤ 先史時代の人々は書かれた形での記
録を何も残さなかった。

⑨ 私たちはその知らせを聞いてショッ
クを受けた。

⑫ 彼は私にその招待を受けるつもりは
ないと言った。

⑮ too tired to

▶ Scene Ⅱ

③ 彼が行くのを止めるために私たちにできることは何もない。

⑭ couple of

▶ Scene Ⅲ

③ looked surprised

⑤ 彼は彼女の目をまともに見ることができなかった。

⑦ 決して子どもを車の中に1人にしてはいけない。

⑧ 私は何か冷たいものが手に触れるのを感じた。

⑨ It is, to

彼はいつも自分の車を最良の状態にしておこうと努める。

⑪ You'd better

good reason for

▶ Scene Ⅳ

① 私たちは早朝にホテルを出発し、昼前に湖に着いた。

⑧ それこそ私が探していたものだ。

⑬ その本はあなたにダムの仕組み[ダムがどのように働くか]を教えてくれる。

▶ Scene Ⅴ

② had, finished

⑥ 彼らの努力はすべてむだだった。

⑦ turned out

昨晩のコンサートは今までで最高だった。

⑧ その映画は私が思っていたよりもおもしろかった。

⑰ part of

⑲ エレンは私が今までに会ったどの女性とも違うのです。

その展覧会は11月30日まで開催される予定です。

私の父は1964年に生まれたが、この年は東京で初めてオリンピックが開催された年だった。

《語彙・表現》

1 (1) エ (2) イ (3) ウ

2 (1) in person
(2) dressed up
(3) on my mind
(4) a couple of

《文のパターン・文法》

1 (1) which[that] (2) when
(3) how[why]

2 (1) It, to keep
(2) in
(3) asked, to lend
(4) Looking out

3 (1) This is a short story Mai recently wrote[wrote recently]
(2) We're going to have the coldest winter ever
(3) There was nothing I could do
(4) Jane was too busy to go out

《総合》

問1 run down

問2 ビリーと自分はすでに多く(のもの)を見すぎてしまったから。

問3 (結局)クリスマスの朝はこれまでで最高のものだった。

問4 wiser than I had imagined

問5 presents[gifts]

問6 chimney

Optional Lesson

▶ Scene Ⅰ

② 母はいつも私に朝食を抜かないようにと言う。

④ 現場に最初に着いたのはだれでしたか。

⑥ 彼は先生にそのけんかがどのようにして始まったかを話した。

▶ Scene Ⅱ

① Now that

⑩ マイクはロンドンに2週間滞在した
　が、そこで有名な画家と会った。

▶**Scene Ⅲ**

⑨ 私がこの写真を撮ったのはここです。

⑪ 明日の今ごろ、私は飛行機でパリに
　向かっていることだろう。

⑭ それらが本当であろうとなかろうと、
　多くの人々はうわさを信じてしまう。

▶**Scene Ⅳ**

⑨ has been reading

⑩ 昨晩マイクが家族のために作ったの
　はカレーだった。

▶**Scene Ⅴ**

⑤ 多くの人々が彼を偉大な科学者だと
　考えている。

⑥ 彼はメジャーリーグでプレイすると
　いう夢を決して捨てなかった。

⑦ 彼女は喜んで私の宿題を手伝ってく
　れた。

▶**Scene Ⅵ**

② 家にいるより外で運動したい気分だ。

④ asked me whether

⑩ 私たちは彼女が私たちの申し出を受
　けるものとばかり思っていた。

▶**Scene Ⅶ**

① もっと慎重に運転しないと事故を起
　こしますよ。

④ The point is
　彼らはどんなに懸命に試しても、そ
　の謎を解くことができなかった。

▶**Scene Ⅷ**

⑦ 彼女はその歌を聞くたびに幸せな気
　分になる。

⑪ ライアンは自分の車を欲しがっている。

■ 確認問題

《**語彙・表現**》

1 (1) graduation　(2) youth
　　(3) inform　(4) possibility

2 ウ、エ

3 (1) proud of

(2) In a word

(3) make up for

(4) for sure

(5) in some respects

(6) took, risk of

《**文のパターン・文法**》

1 (1) Every time

(2) will be enjoying

(3) has been building

(4) did believe

2 (1) He might have gotten the
　　wrong train

(2) so that she might not fall off

(3) This is where I found the purse

《**総合**》

問1　to be taken

問2　much to, dismay

問3　no matter how old you are

問4　learning something new

問5　レーシングカーを運転できるように
　　なること。／自動車の走りがどうあ
　　るべきかについて技術者たちと意見
　　を交換するため。(順不同)

Acknowledgments

Lesson 8 Section 2: Based on an interview by Seiko Uyeda

Section 3: Adapted from *The Face of War*, The Daily Yomiuri, October 13, 1999

Kim Phuc, *The Long Road To Forgiveness*, NPR

Reading Copyright © 2009 by Robert Burton Robinson,

Arranged through Japan UNI Agency, Inc., Tokyo

http://www.robertburtonrobinson.com/

Optional Lesson

Quoted from Babson College, *Remarks by Akio Toyoda*

https://www.babson.edu/about/news-events/babson-events/

commencement/2019-ceremony-recap/graduate-ceremony/remarks-by-akio-

toyoda/